8/24/93

WORLD OF WASTE

Dilemmas of
Industrial Development

K.A. Gourlay

Poisoners of the Seas

What the critics said

'A plain-language, often blunt presentation of pollution problems, a subject that needs more public awareness ... Gourlay's book can be used as a handy reference for college and university courses that deal with environmental problems.' **Choice**

'this terrifying, deeply stimulating book' **The Times Educational Supplement**

'A lively book drawing on journalistic as well as official records which seeks to promote understanding of the realities behind current media discussion and political manoeuvring.' **Geography**

'Action has to be at a global level . . . *Poisoners of the Seas* provides much of the ammunition.' **New Scientist**

'A very comprehensive and well-written demonstration that humanity is now extending destruction to the furthest reaches of the seas.' **Econews**

'A superb, timely persuasion that our complacency is as out of place on the sea-bed and around our coasts, as it is in our rivers or up in the ozone layer ... This is a key text.' **Partizans**

WORLD OF WASTE

Dilemmas of
Industrial Development

K. A. GOURLAY

World of Waste: Dilemmas of Industrial Development was first published by Zed Books Ltd, 57 Caledonian Road, London N1 9BU, U.K. and 165 First Avenue, Atlantic Highlands, New Jersey 07716, U.S.A. in 1992.

Copyright © K.A. Gourlay, 1992

Cover designed by Andrew Corbett
Cover picture by David Modell
Typeset by Action Typesetting, Gloucester
Printed and bound in the United Kingdom by
Billing & Sons Ltd, Worcester

British Library Cataloguing and Publication Data

A catalogue record for this book is available from the British Library.

US CIP is available from the Library of Congress.

ISBN 0 86232 988 4 hb
ISBN 0 86232 989 2 pb

Contents

Author's note and acknowledgements

This book is not a sequel to *Poisoners of the Seas*, though waste and its dumping in water occur in both books and, in consequence, it is impossible to avoid overlapping. To eliminate repetition I have 1) omitted some detailed technical descriptions, e.g. on hydrocarbons or radiation, and referred the interested reader to the earlier work; 2) concentrated on incidents that have occurred, or information that has become available, since research for *Poisoners* was completed at the beginning of 1987. Inevitably this has meant relying on current publications, articles and press reports, a procedure that will lead some reviewers to approach the evidence with scepticism, and one must admit that the spate of environmental books and articles marking the end of the eighties has had its share of dubious publications. There were, however, a number of outstanding productions for the use of which I would like to express my indebtedness – the two Goldsmith and Hildyard *Earth Reports*, the annual Worldwatch Institute's *State of the World* surveys and (with reservations) the annual statistical summaries of the *World Resources Institute* and its collaborators. Of the weekly publications the *New Scientist* has a remarkable group of consultants and contributors, my indebtedness to whom appears from the frequency with which they are listed in the Bibliography, while the *Observer's* Geoffrey Lean has gained an international reputation for combining reliability with readability. I would also like to thank and acknowledge my indebtedness to S. M. Mohd Idris and the Penang-based Third World Network, whose *Toxic Terror* and *Newsletters* were a stimulant in the early days of research; to Roger Moody for supplying lesser known data on mining and introducing me to the US-based National Coalition Against Mass Burn; and to Jeremy Leggett, whose report of the Pugwash Conference supplied me with the most dire dilemma of them all.

The evidence presented here is of necessity selective. No single author can hope to cover the whole globe and do justice to all human iniquity and folly. My personal contribution is that of assemblage and structuring around a central theme – a task that any reasonably intelligent person armed with a mass of source books and press cuttings should be capable of accomplishing, yet one that turned out to be more difficult than anticipated. I am, therefore, especially grateful to Robert Molteno of Zed Books for his continued enthusiasm and support, and to Meg Howarth for her meticulous copy-editing.

No topical book can hope to be up-to-date by the time it reaches the shops. In view of the changes that have recently taken place in the map of Europe, I have used the terms 'West Germany' and 'East Germany' throughout and trust that the context will make clear whether the reference is to a geographical area or to the former FRG and GDR.

Prologue: The Waste Merchants

In the late 1980s few events aroused greater consternation and anger among the general public, in both the industrialized West and the Third World, than the spectacle of a series of dilapidated ships, laden with hazardous waste, making their way from one country to another in search of a port that would accept their rapidly deteriorating cargo. The full story, and even the numbers of this shadowy fleet and the extent of the trade in which they were involved will doubtless never be known. Sufficient has now emerged, however, through the work of investigative journalists, environmental organizations and concerned Members of the European Parliament (MEP), to reveal the motives behind this trade, the proposed schemes for offloading some of the West's most hazardous waste onto Third World countries, the companies, countries and individuals who planned to profit from them and the voyages of the ill-fated vessels chosen for this enterprise.

The mystery voyage of the *Khian Sea*

On 31 August 1986 the Liberian-registered *Khian Sea*, under charter to Amalgamated Shipping of the Bahamas, left Philadelphia in the United States with 13,476 tons of toxic ash from the municipal incinerators, which it had received from the waste haulage firm, Paolino and Sons. The ship itself belonged to Lily Navigation of Liberia, of which Amalgamated Shipping was an offshore branch.

Originally destined for the Bahamas, the cargo's reputation must have preceded it, for the Government of the Bahamas refused the *Khian Sea* permission to offload and the ship set out on what was to become an apparently endless search for a dumping place. Rejected in turn by Bermuda, Honduras, Guinea-Bissau and the Dominican Republic, it passed through the Panama Canal to Colombia in mid-1987 but its business there remains unclear.

On 26 October 1987 the Department of Commerce in Haiti issued an import permit for what was described as 'fertiliser'. The deal was arranged by a group calling itself the Cultivators of the West, which in practice consisted of two brothers of Haitian Colonel Jean-Claude Paul, whose reputation includes control of right-wing military groups and who, with one of the brothers, was indicted in the United States in March 1988 for alleged involvement in cocaine smuggling. On the last day of 1987 the *Khian Sea* reached Gonaives, Haiti, and three weeks later some hundred labourers began offloading. On 29 January 1988 the Haitian Government ordered the ash out of the country on the grounds that the constitution included a provision against importing foreign waste, the Minister of Commerce, Mario Celestin, declaring that all quantities dumped would be reloaded and the ship dealt with according to law. The *Khian Sea*'s response was to sail in the middle of the night of 4 February, leaving an estimated 3,000 tons on a remote peninsula outside Gonaives, from which it is likely that some of the ash may enter the Bay of Gonaives, an area of beach and mangrove swamps, and strong sea breezes carry it towards the city.[1]

How dangerous was this ash, that Philadelphia was so anxious to dispose of and which had been rejected in so many places? At the moment when the *Khian Sea* received permission to offload its 'fertiliser', the Inspector General of the US Environmental Protection Agency (EPA) reported: 'the ash presents a significant potential danger to human health and the environment due to concentrations of dioxins higher than those identified at Times Beach, Missouri'.[2] Dioxins are 'a family of 75 closely related compounds, the most notorious of which is tetrachlorodibenzo-paradioxin (or TCDD for short). It first achieved notoriety as the chemical released during the Seveso accident and as a contaminant of Agent Orange'.[3] Times Beach was the small town evacuated and later abandoned as the result of dioxin contamination. In 1984 the EPA's Carcinogen Assessment Group concluded that TCDD was the 'most potent animal carcinogen' it had ever evaluated, being fifty times more carcinogenic than vinyl chloride. While admitting its effects on animals, industry maintains that its worst effect on human beings is a severe skin disease. The EPA has concluded that TCDD should be regarded as 'probably carcinogenic in humans'.[4] The ash also included heavy metals such as barium, cadmium, lead and mercury.

By 1 March 1988 the *Khian Sea* had returned to Delaware Bay and anchored 100 miles south of Philadelphia. With nowhere to dispose of the ash, Amalgamated Shipping proposed to return it to Paolino and Sons. A fire at their pier in Philadelphia and a financial dispute between the two companies delayed action, and on 22 May the *Khian Sea* disobeyed the orders of the US Coast Guard to remain anchored and headed for the open ocean. Fifty miles offshore a pursuing Coast Guard vessel lost track of the ship, which Lloyds of London reported as heading for an undisclosed destination in the Caribbean. Still with 10,000—11,000 tonnes of ash on board, the *Khian Sea* was declared a renegade and stripped of its Liberian flag.[5]

What happened next is unclear. For four months it disappeared, then, according to one report, at the beginning of August 1988 it was sighted in Yugoslav waters and by September, still flying the Liberian flag, had entered the small port of Bijela on the Adriatic coast, south of the tourist area of

Dubrovnik. Although not permitted to unload, the vessel was allowed time for repairs before leaving. By then, however, the publicity given to another waste ship, the *Karen B*, made it almost impossible to discharge its cargo in Europe.[6]

Alternatively, an editorial in the Philippine *Daily Inquirer* of 25 October 1988 refers to the *Khian Sea*, now renamed the *Felicia*, as heading in their direction. In consequence, the Department of Environment and Natural Resources (DENR) had alerted the military and Coast Guard to be on the watch. Conversely, an article by Moinuddin Nasser in the Bangladesh weekly *Holiday* of 31 March 1989, in which the ship is stated to have begun its voyage in August 1986 'under the false name of *Felicia*' with 15,000 tons of toxic waste on board, 4,000 of which it dumped in Haiti in February 1988, maintains that the vessel then went to 'New Guinea' (sic) in Africa, where it attempted to negotiate dumping the waste in exchange for money. When this failed, it anchored in deep water in the Bay of Bengal and began negotiations, first with the Bangladeshi authorities over the possibility of dumping the waste in the bay and, when this also failed, with businessmen who were told the waste could be used as raw material for producing energy. By the time the government had made inquiries and turned down this proposal, it was reported that the ship, renamed *Khian Sea*, had secretly begun dumping its wastes in the bay. The most readily credible item in this account is the government's refusal to confirm this as Bangladesh had no monitoring unit to record the movement and activities of ships in its territorial waters.[7] We can deduce what happened to the waste from a report in the British 'Fragile Earth' television programme of 28 April 1991 that when, after 18 months at sea, the vessel was sighted off Singapore, its holds were empty.

'Sick to the Stomach'

While the *Khian Sea* was still searching the Caribbean for a potential landfall, another cargo of toxic waste left Europe on a journey that would last 14 months, take it to four continents and cover 17,400 nautical miles.[8] In February 1987 the Maltese-registered vessel *Lynx* left the Italian port of Marina di Carrara loaded with 2,200 tons of waste collected from various European producers by the north Italian firm of Jelly Wax.[9] The waste was delivered to Intercontract, headed by Gian-Franco Ambrosini, which, with its official office at Belfaux near Fribourg, has been implicated in numerous, if at times abortive, schemes for shipments to Guinea-Bissau, Senegal, Benin, Mauritania and South Africa.[10] On this occasion the cargo's destination was Djibouti. Ambrosini declared that disposal permits were in hand, even if the documents failed to identify the producers or give a detailed inventory of the sources and composition of the wastes. The authorities apparently gave him permission to load and depart, though there were protests, and the *Lynx* left Italy more quickly than intended with only

2,200 tons on board and not the 3,000 originally planned. Nor was the enterprise without its anticipated financial reward. With Jelly Wax receiving US$500 a ton from the producers but paying Ambrosini US$225, while in turn he proposed to pay his Djibouti correspondent US$36, it is not difficult to calculate their respective gains on over 2,000 tons.[11]

When the *Lynx* reached Djibouti, it was found that there was no contractual agreement with the local authorities for disposal and the ship was forbidden to unload. Following legal action against Ambrosini, Jelly Wax assumed responsibility for finding another destination and reached agreement with a Panamanian firm, Mercantil Lemport SA, which claimed that it had permission to dispose of the wastes in Venezuela. In March the *Lynx* sailed directly to Venezuela and in April unloaded its cargo at Puerto Cabella, where 10,876 barrels, dumped above ground without protection, remained for six months. After leaks of waste and (according to Reuter) toxic gases had caused sores on nearby inhabitants (a further report claimed the death of a boy who unwittingly played on the waste) the Venezuelan Government ordered Jelly Wax to take the waste out of the country.

In October 1987 Jelly Wax chartered the Cypriot-registered *Makiri*, which reached Puerto Cabella, retrieved the waste (and also possibly some other wastes dumped by French and German firms) and on 17 November sailed with the intention, at Venezuela's request, of returning the waste to Italy. After stopping at Cagliari on Sardinia, however, the *Makiri* changed destination and headed for Tartous in Syria. Sometime between 10 and 23 December it arrived, unloaded its cargo and, on 27 December, left. For these transactions, Jelly Wax paid the Greek shipping agency Alsa Shipping US$102,000 and the Syrian company of Mohamed Samin US$200,000.

Thirteen months after it had first left Italy, the waste was again at sea on the final, and most notorious, stage of its travels. Given that it had been loaded onto three different ships, offloaded from two, spent six months in the open in Venezuelan heat and humidity and a further two in Syria, the only surprise was that some of the barrels were not in a worse state than they were. In February 1988 the wastes were loaded on to the *Zanoobia*, which flew the Syrian flag and was reputedly owned by Tabalo Shipping, Ahmed Tabalo being the vessel's captain. The only *Zanoobia* listed in shipping registers, however, is owned by the Government of Iraq, while an Italian source claimed that Tabalo himself may have been involved in the illegal export of weapons from Italy to the Middle East. Tabalo himself stated that the Syrian Government had ordered Samin to remove the waste from the country.

The *Zanoobia* left Tartous on 10 March, called at Salonika, Greece (where the vessel may have been denied permission to offload) and reached Marina di Carrara, original starting point of the waste's travels, on 26 April. Here the Port Authorities refused to allow offloading on the grounds that the ship lacked a permit to dispose of the wastes in Italy and the major parties concerned indulged in arguments and recriminations. Tabalo declared that Jelly Wax was the owner of the cargo, while Jelly Wax refused to accept responsibility, maintaining that it now belonged to Samin.

The main concern, however, was the state of the cargo. Throughout May the *Zanoobia* remained at Marina di Carrara, the waste barrels corroded, and the crew suffered from skin inflammation and shortness of breath, so that several had to be treated in hospital. Tabalo achieved worldwide, if not entirely wanted, publicity for the seagoing traffic in toxic wastes when he declared, 'The condition of my crew is very bad. For three months we have not entered a port. Now we are all nauseous and sick to the stomach.' Lawyers for Tabalo Shipping also maintained that a member of the crew had died on the way to Italy, though whether this was the result of exposure to the cargo remained unclear.

Late in May the Italian Government agreed to take the waste. A strike of port workers in protest at the prospect of fumes from the 'ship of poison' delayed unloading at Genova and not until 8 August did waste disposal experts being preliminary work. The Italian authorities earmarked 1.7 billion (bn) lira (£740,000) for the task, including eventual destruction of the waste by incineration.[12]

Arousing Nigerian wrath

As the *Makiri* and *Zanoobia* were returning their consignments to Europe other vessels were travelling in the opposite direction. Between August 1987 and May 1988 some 3,884 tonnes of chemical waste in 10,000 drums from five separate shiploads were deposited near the port of Koko in Bendel State, Nigeria. The waste, allegedly from Italy, the Netherlands, Norway, the USA and the UK, was again collected by Jelly Wax and imported by an Italian businessman in Nigeria, Gianfranco Raffaelli. The latter used false import permits and offered a local Nigerian, Sunday Nana, a sum of 500 Nigerian naira (ör, in another report, US$500 a month) for the hire of his land as a store. According to one report, the story broke when, at the beginning of June, Nigerian students in Italy alerted their government.

Nigeria's military ruler, President Babangida, reacted angrily and swiftly. He recalled his ambassador to Rome, summoned the Italian Chargé d'Affaires in Lagos to demand that Italy remove the waste, evacuated the village of Koko when it was suspected that the dump contained radioactive waste, arrested 15 Nigerians involved and announced that any suspect found guilty by a special tribunal would risk execution by firing squad. Nor would foreigners involved in what the Information Minister, Tony Momoh, called 'this inhuman conspiracy' be spared or the Federal Government 'deterred by appeals from international communities'. Their threats came too late for the major foreigner involved. Raffaelli reportedly escaped without a passport by bribing officials; his associate, Desiderio Perazzi, was less fortunate and saw the inside of a Lagos gaol.[13]

To ensure that the Italian Government acted swiftly the Nigerians seized an Italian ship, the *MV Piave*, and ordered the captain to remove the waste, an impossible task as the *Piave* was too large to negotiate the creeks leading to the dump. They also arrested a Danish coaster, the *Danix*, accusing it of being involved in toxic dumping.

In mid-June the UK and the USA sent scientific teams to test for radioactivity. They failed to find any but reported that the dump comprised some 10,000 drums, each containing about 225 litres of waste. Highly inflammable solvents in sealed containers lay unshaded in temperatures that at times exceeded 40°C. The dump itself was in very poor condition. A list of proposed imports totalling nearly 100,000 tonnes included 2,500 tonnes of polychlorinated biphenyls, 20,000 tonnes of exhausted earth, 5,000 tonnes of asbestos fibre and 12,000 tonnes of assorted pharmaceutical and industrial residues. How much of this actually reached Nigeria is not clear; the worst discovery was the presence of PCBs, which it would have been impossible to destroy without high temperature incineration, unavailable in Nigeria.

Italy announced that it would take back the waste if the Nigerians released the crew of the *Piave*, and authorized the state-owned firm ENI to take charge of the operation. ENI chartered the *MV Karin B*, owned by the West German company Werner Böksiegel, and a second ship, the *Deep Sea Carrier*, to remove the waste.[14]

As the scene changed to follow the voyages of these 'leper ships', there were further revelations of the dumping of waste in West Africa. Nigeria's neighbour, Benin, was one of the countries (see pp.10–11) that had agreed to accept waste and had used its own marine vessel, the *Ganvié*, to import it. Local dockers, however, now informed the head of state, General Mathieu Kérékou, that they would refuse to unload further consignments. African reaction against importing waste had reached the length of stopping ships from Italy or Denmark at sea to ensure that no waste was on board, while, off Togo, a cargo ship was reported as seen in the act of dumping its contents into the Bay of Benin. For Kérékou, concerned about the effects of waste dumping on tourism, the immediate problem was to dispose of waste already received. A proposed plan to bury it on Benin's border with Nigeria near the Ouémé river that feeds Lagos harbour so provoked the wrath of President Babangida that he threatened that, if dumping took place, the Nigerian army would 'descend on Cotonou'.[15]

Meanwhile, the *Karin B* had reached Cadiz, which it left on 24 August at the request of the authorities, with the waste allegedly in a highly dangerous condition. Ostensibly making for Ravenna in Italy (where there were already protests against its landing), five days later it was reported 25 miles south of Plymouth, England, seeking to berth. Leigh Interests plc of Walsall, one of the UK's largest waste treatment companies, had apparently stated that it was prepared to analyse the waste and hoped to 'deal with it' in Britain. Leigh, which had contracted to build treatment plant in Italy, further maintained that it had been approached by Ambiente, a subsidiary of ENI, and was negotiating with harbour boards for berthing rights. While the port authorities at Neath in south Wales, through which Leigh import much of their normal waste, refused to allow the *Karin B* to enter the harbour with the cargo in the present hazardous state, the Department of the Environment (DoE), alerted by Friends of the Earth, maintained that, under present legislation, it could not prevent the ship from landing. With its ideological commitment to free trade and aware that the British hazardous waste disposal industry was highly profitable, the British Government had refused to implement a European Community (EC) directive on the Transfrontier Shipment of Hazardous Waste. The publicity given to the arrival of the *Karin B* in British waters now combined with the NIMBY (Not-In-My-Back-Yard) syndrome (which had already forced the government to have second thoughts on nuclear waste disposal) to arouse public opinion. To most people's surprise, on 30 August the responsible minister of the DoE, Virginia Bottomley, announced that the *Karin B* would be refused entry under a little known clause of the Control of Pollution (Special Wastes) Regulations 1980, namely failure to comply with the rule that 'operators must specify what they wish to import',[16] which obliging civil servants had unearthed.

This decision left little option. On 2 September the Italian Council of Ministers decided that the waste would be returned to Italy for repacking and disposal. It also announced plans to build 20 public plants to handle toxic waste, one in each administrative region, and banned the export of chemical wastes to the Third World, a decision greeted with approval by British hazardous waste companies as good for business. On 31 August the *Karin B* left its anchorage off Plymouth for Rotterdam to take on fuel and food. Meanwhile the *Deep Sea Carrier*, which had left Nigeria on 15 August, had reached Gibraltar and was heading east towards Italy. A Dutch company, Tankcleaning, offered to repack and label the *Karin B*'s waste but the Environment Minister banned it from offloading in Netherlands' harbours, and the Hague District Court upheld his right to do so. It sailed for Italy, its cargo in an even more dangerous state than before.[17]

The Government had, however, reckoned without the Italian people. When the Environment Minister, Giorgio Ruffolo, announced that the *Karin B* would dock in Livorno and the *Deep Sea Carrier* in Ravenna, he aroused a storm of opposition. The ports were chosen because Ravenna had had previous experience and possessed one of the three disposal plants with furnaces able to destroy the waste, while at Livorno the unloading zone was distant from the city centre. The disadvantage was that the Livorno waste would then have to travel 200 miles overland across the peninsula to Ravenna on a road or rail route by which it was difficult to avoid the cities of Florence and Bologna. In Livorno, with a communist administration, dockers prepared for a general strike, while residents planned road blocks and demonstrations. In Ravenna, the mayor declared that the city 'is not and never will be on the Government's list of possibilities'. The Rome Government overrode all opposition; towards the end of September, while the *Deep Sea Carrier* was still off Sicily, the *Karin B* docked at Livorno. After nearly three months in the port, offloading began on 20 December. The waste was back where it had started.[18]

How not to get rid of ash

Despite the fiasco of the *Khian Sea* and even before that ship had returned to Philadelphia, the US authorities made a further attempt to rid themselves of their 'ash mountain'. This time the agents were Bulkhandling Inc., a consortium of shipping companies based in Oslo, 48 per cent of the shares in which were held by Klaveness Chartering, a company with extensive Third World connections, especially in Guyana, China and Guinea, from which it exports bauxite to Europe; it also owns the vessel *Bark*.[19]

Bulkhandling's first plan was to ship 250,000 tons of the ash to Panama for use as roadfill through wetlands. The deal involved a development project, including a hotel, and the road was needed for tourist access across the wetlands and mangrove swamps. These are important breeding grounds of Panama's chief food export, the white shrimp. A report from the Inspector-General of the EPA suggested that there were dangers both from leaching and from the road being washed away, so the dioxins would be discharged into the waters, and recommended against the project. When the EPA refused to take action, a media leak alerted the Panamanian Government, which promptly cancelled the contract and threatened to intercept any ship bringing ash into its territorial waters.[20]

Bulkhandling found themselves left holding 30,000 tons of the ash. Half of this they sent for landfill in Ohio, the remainder they loaded on board the *Bark* with no clear destination in mind. Faced with a court order to remove the ash from the pier or pay a fine of $10,000 a day, the consortium calculated it would be cheaper to have the vessel at sea. Accordingly on 7 February 1988 the *Bark* left Philadelphia, its destination listed as Haiti, despite the fact that, less than ten days previously, the Haitian Government had ordered the *Khian Sea*'s consignment of ash out of the country.

At this point the company's Norwegian connections came to the rescue. The next news of the *Bark* was that it had reached Guinea and, after assuring the Government that the ash was harmless and could be used for making a type of concrete-like building material, the company was allowed to dump the 15,000 tonnes on Kassa Island, opposite Conakry. Inaccurate, if reassuring, reports that the ash was not hazardous according to US regulations prompted the logical question from African cynics, 'In that case, why not keep it?'[21]

Two events led to a crisis. On 7 March the Agency for Toxic Substances and Disease Registry (ATSDR), an arm of the US Center for Disease Control, released a 'health consultation' document which stated that the ash posed a risk to anyone coming into contact with it. In consequence Philadelphia should 'restrict all public and unprotected worker access to the ash pile'. The second was a report that the ash had killed off vegetation and affected trees on Kassa Island itself.

Investigations now revealed that the joint Norwegian – Guinean company organizing the dumping, Guinomar, had as a director the Norwegian Consul-General Sigmund Stromme, who, on being arrested, reportedly confessed to forging documents to cover the transaction. He had worked with two associates, named as Diallo Seydou and Richard Millimono, both heads of departments at the Ministry of Trade, who were also arrested, while a third employee of the ministry, Diallo Mamado, was also wanted. Fortunately for him he was out of the country 'on official business in Italy'. The Government of Guinea ordered the waste to be removed.

Later Strømme was released, but on 22 July the ash sailed again on board the *Banja*, its destination Philadelphia.[22]

Uncompleted missions

The voyages of the *Zanoobia* and the *Karin B* and the anger of the Nigerians on discovering the dump at Koko had a major impact on the trade in toxic waste — they made public what had hitherto been largely unknown, both in Europe and the United States, and in Africa. One result was that, at its 48th Ordinary Session in Addis Ababa from 19 to 23 May 1988, the Organization of African Unity (OAU) passed a resolution branding the dumping of nuclear and industrial waste in that continent as a 'crime against Africa', condemning all societies and transnational enterprises involved, and calling on African states that had already entered into contracts to renounce them and those that had not to abstain from such arrangements.[23] The outcome was a hurried backtracking by a number of African governments, which found it impossible to deny accusations of complicity when the European Parliament voiced its outrage at the trade and a Green member (MEP), François Roelant de Vivier, produced copies of contracts naming the parties concerned. The countries affected included Guinea-Bissau, the Congo Republic, Benin, Senegal, Namibia and Angola.

Guinea-Bissau
On 16 October 1987 Gianfranco Ambrosini of Intercontract (and the *Lynx*) signed a contract with Filinto Barros, Minister of Natural Resources and Industry of Guinea-Bissau, for the import of at least 50,000 tonnes of toxic waste a year for five years. Intercontract was responsible for obtaining, collecting and shipping the waste and for the construction, over 10 years, of a depository capable of holding 50,000—100,000 tonnes. In return Guinea-Bissau would receive US$40 a tonne, a meagre contribution towards resolving its external debt of US$400,000,000.

Asked about the suitability of the site at Farim, Ambrosini maintained that the geology was extremely favourable. Ecologists disagreed, calling it a sponge with marshy waters that would quickly corrode metal containers. Moreover, the area was earmarked for a fishing project to be financed by the European Economic Community (EEC), which would become impossible should the plans go ahead. When the news of the deal broke in May 1988, Barros denied involvement but, faced with a copy of the contract, he was forced to admit it. Under pressure from both the European

Parliament and the OAU, on 30 May he announced that Guinea-Bissau had renounced the project.

Intercontract was not the only firm seeking, or sought by, Guinea-Bissau. Bis-Import Ltd. of London and Lindaco Ltd. of Detroit, acting through Hobday Ltd. of the Isle of Man, actually obtained a much larger contract. For the same price of US$40 a tonne they proposed to offer not 50,000 tonnes but three million! A copy of the contract, signed on 9 February 1988, also found its way to the European Parliament. By this time Lindaco had contacted the (US)EPA for clearance and Barros had given the EP the go-ahead. The scheme collapsed, like that of Intercontract.[24]

The Congo Republic
The Republic of the Congo was also much sought after, but with similar results. A deal was organized by Luciana Spada, director of Bauwerk, Liechtenstein, operating on behalf of Waste Management Inc. (or Waste Export Management), New Jersey, in collaboration with the Dutch transport company, Van Staten. At the Congolese end the initiative was taken by Jean Passi of the Congolaise Récuperation de Déchets Industrielle (CRDI) at Pointe-Noire, who signed the contract with Spada. The proposal was for up to six million tonnes of chemical waste at the rate of 15,000 tonnes a week, with a million tonnes of oil, acids, solvents and wastes containing barium and mercury, which would go to the gorges at Diosso. In May 1988 Van Staten were ill-advised to announce that they had received a licence from the Congolese Government authorising shipments, while Waste Management's application to the EPA had given it knowledge of the terms of the contract. After the OAU Declaration, Congo at first denied that it was involved in such activities; unfortunately, documents showed that Gamissamy Issanga, Director of Environment in the research ministry, had approved the dumping. As a ship waited in Richmond, California, ready to leave, the Congolese Government announced the arrest of five people. Both the Interior Minister, Christophe Bouraove, and the Information Minister, Christian Bembet, were dismissed.[25]

Benin
Benin's European contact was the British company, Sesco, with a convenience address in Gibraltar, which, like the Isle of Man, is not subject to EEC regulations on the shipment of hazardous waste. Sesco offered Benin a contract, which was signed on 12 January 1988 by Lamta Catche, Sesco's executive vice-president, and two ministers of the Benin Government, to store five million tonnes of waste at the ridiculously low sum of US$2.5 per tonne. But Benin had an external debt of US$700 million and was regarded as an easy touch, especially if there was any truth in the rumours that the 26 March 1988 attempted coup against General Kérékou arose because he had secretly agreed to accept radioactive waste from France. The Sesco contract offered investment of US$0.5 a tonne in agriculture and tourism, a three-year storage package, the setting up of processing factories and

10-years exclusive rights. It said nothing about toxicity or possible dangers to the environment. Publicity and the OAU resolution caused a change of heart. Kérékou revoked the deal, but there was evidence that he had intended going ahead. In January 1989, while filming at Akisa in the Abomey region, a British Channel 4 TV team came across a large hole about a kilometre square and seven metres deep. Workers had been told that they were digging the foundations of a new factory.[26]

Senegal

At the end of 1986, Gianfranco Ambrosini (again) contacted René Lehmann, sole director (and member) of Overseas Commercial Supply, a Swiss company based in Geneva. Lehmann, who knew Africa well, was given the task of finding a country willing to accept toxic waste and decided on Senegal. His contact was a local businessman, Mansou Bouna Ndiaye, who not only enjoyed prestige in his own right but had the advantage of being a cousin of President Abdou Diouf.

Lehmann went into partnership with a Hubert Lefèbvre-Despeaux, a Frenchman living in Geneva, who was also active in the import – export business. Together they sent a brochure to four French firms and two Swiss laboratories, offering assistance in the disposal of toxic waste and announcing the availability of 30 hectares of African land near to port facilities able to receive consignments of 10,000 tonnes and to take 200,000 cubic metres in its first phase. At the Senegalese end, Ndiaye became director of Project Sodilo and was congratulated on his initiative by the Frenchman, Jean Collin, the President's powerful grey eminence. On 15 December 1987 Collin wrote to Cheikh Abdoul Khadre Cissokho, Minister for the Protection of Nature, that Sodilo existed to treat industrial and commercial waste and would produce electricity as well as create 250 new jobs and boost transport from Dakar. The minister's assistance was 'requested' in enabling the project to proceed as rapidly as possible.

On 12 January 1988 Ndiaye signed a contract with Ambrosini on behalf of Intercontract to receive a minimum of 100,000 tonnes a year of European or North American industrial waste. The contract was for five years (renewable), named Dakar as the port of entry for each 10,000 – 20,000 tonne consignment, excluded nuclear material, stated the laws applicable to the shipment, listed the types of containers and placed the onus of undertaking local construction on both parties.

On 15 January 1988 Abdoul Aziz Ndaw, mayor of Mekhe, who three months previously had become president of the National Assembly, agreed to a request from Ndiaye and placed four hectares of land at his disposal in his commune as a site for treating 'household refuse and industrial waste'. By the end of January the promoters had obtained land space in the port of Dakar and customs exemption from the Ministry of Finance.

All was apparently proceeding to plan when, in March, news of the project reached the young director of the Senegalese Environment Ministry, Bakary Kante. Despite pressure from his superiors to expedite the necessary permission, Kante demanded an impact study from Ambrosini. He received an assessment which was so obviously amateurish that he requested the French Bureau of Geological and Mining Research (BRGM) to carry out a proper one, for which Ambrosini paid.

On 29 March Ambrosini requested authorization from the Environment Ministry to import and store a first shipment of 50,000 tonnes of waste. Under intense pressure, citing that the risks involved were technologically manageable, Kante conceded. Later he defended himself by stressing his demand for the impact assessment. But it was the outcry against the *Lynx* and the *Zanoobia* that helped him. At the moment when public opinion was incensed by the dumping of waste in Africa, BRGM reported that the site was 'unsuitable'. Without even a dumping ground, the deal collapsed, as ministers, officials and businessmen attempted to extricate themselves from a project over which they now preferred to draw a veil.[27]

Namibia and Angola

The Namibia and Angola affair was even more of a soap opera, its 'hero' the former geologist, member of the British forces in 1960s Kenya, mercenary in Katanga, arms dealer and associate of Idi Amin Dada, the flamboyant Arnold Andreas Künzler, now promotor of trade in toxic waste to 'benefit' both Europe and Africa. Regarded by his friends as a philanthropist and by his enemies as a swindler, no one disputes the ability of this colourful character as a promoter of visionary schemes, and it was hardly his fault that, so far as Namibia and Angola were concerned, they failed.

The Namibian proposal was grandiose in scope. As 'representative of a group of international investors and end-users of waste disposal licences for the importation and permanent storage of waste materials', Künzler proposed to capitalize a Namibian company for the construction, over a ten-year period, of a deep-water port and facilities, two 100,000-ton waste-burning plants capable of producing electricity, one 60,000-ton waste-burning plant, a double railway track from the plants to underground storage depots and the necessary equipment, and a new township for employees, together with airport, up to a maximum expenditure of US$300 million. The company would be licensed to import up to five million tons of waste a year, including chemical waste, for storage in a 50,000 sq.km. site in the Skeleton Coast region; the licences would last for 50 years with the possibility of renewal. For this Künzler would pay in all some US$2 billion at stated times in the contractual process. His partners in this visionary enterprise — the 'Namibian Government in Exile', that is, the South-West Africa People's Organisation (SWAPO).

There were two snags: SWAPO was not yet the Namibian Government in power; and the contract, which eventually remained unsigned, specified the need for a satisfactory feasibility study before the scheme could go ahead. Accordingly, in the summer of 1988 Künzler requested the highly respected Swiss engineering firm of Suter and Suter to undertake a study of the geological suitability for two incineration projects (Namibia and Angola); the projects were to be on the same standard as those of CIBA-GEIGY at Basel. In August Suter and Suter agreed; the studies would take six months and cost two million dollars. The Namibian proposal quickly ended when Suter and Suter announced its suspension pending political negotiations on the future of Namibia, while Künzler now accepted that there was no guarantee that SWAPO would gain power.

Turning to Angola, Künzler announced that he intended to use the same type of incineration plant that CIBA-GEIGY were constructing in Basel, a statement designed to give the impression that CIBA-GEIGY were involved and which evoked the response from CIBA that it was not interested. On 17 November 1988 Künzler reported that Angola had agreed to import five million tons of toxic waste for incineration and that there would be three incinerators at Namibe in the extreme south, 200 km from the Namibian frontier, where the ash could be buried in the nearby desert. The project would employ 15,000 Angolan workers, under European supervision, while Künzler and his associates offered the government US$2 billion towards a development programme, including hospitals. Künzler himself anticipated making between five and ten million dollars from the project.

His immediate problem was to raise the two billion dollars. To this end he approached, and secured the co-operation of, Roland Straub of the influential Swiss makers of telecommunications equipment. In December, however, both Suter and Suter and Straub withdrew their support, ostensibly on the grounds that conditions were not yet ripe for the project's realization. Undeterred, Künzler announced that he had American backers from Texas, who were resented by his other partners, and, for full measure, that the Sultan of Brunei was 100 per cent behind him! The situation was, however, more complex. As a condition of his support, and possibly urged on by South African pressure, Straub had demanded the inclusion in the Angolan Government of Jonas Savimbi, leader of the National Union for the Total Independence of Angola (UNITA), while Suter and Suter had their own plans. On 14 December their director wrote to Künzler's Angolan contact, Daniel Chipenda, who was passing through Basel at the time, arguing that a 'feasibility study should remain neutral in it's [sic] context' — which could not always be guaranteed when a 'private' party', i.e. Künzler, was involved — and offering to act as the government's 'independent consultants'. Nor was Straub idle, attempting to involve CIBA-GEIGY in a project and suggesting that they meet the Angolan mission then in Basel. The most that CIBA eventually admitted was that its contacts with Straub were 'for information'; it claims that its representatives would have refused to meet the Angolans.

On 17 December Chipenda and his associates met Künzler in a Basel hotel. Künzler now claimed that one of his backers, the US Casualty Agency Inc., a Miami insurance company, would put up an initial US$8 million, that a financial group including the Texas Halley Bank and the Millen Bank at Houston would support him, that the Texan engineering firm, Forster and

Wheeler, would carry out an impact study, and, of course, there was also the Sultan of Brunei. The euphoric impact of this announcement was somewhat reduced when the Brussels daily *Le Soir* reported that both the banks and the insurance company were unknown in American banking circles.

Stressing that nothing had been finally agreed and that President Dos Santos had not been informed, Chipenda nevertheless affirmed the Angolan Government's interest in the project by which Luanda would receive US$2 billion for accepting the waste and a further US$7 – 8 billion in supplementary aid. Chipenda feared that the USSR would shortly decrease its economic aid, but maintained that Angola was not prepared to risk the lives of its people for money and that he demanded complete security for installations and storage.

On 19 December the European Entente for the Environment organized a press conference in Brussels at which it made the whole affair public. The Angolan Government denounced Künzler and affirmed its support for the OAU resolution on the import of toxic waste. Whether, under economic pressure, Angola would ever have agreed to become a dustbin for European waste must remain matter for speculation; but when, at the end of January 1989, President Dos Santos reshuffled his government, two ministers were dropped, Henrique de Carvallo dos Santos Onambwe and de Galvao Branco, Minister and Vice-Minister of Industry respectively, whose image had been tarnished by the toxic waste affair. As for Daniel Chipenda, he became Ambassador to Cairo![28]

These episodes show clearly the three essentials of the toxic waste trade: 1) an industrialized country, usually Western, with firms anxious to dispose of their waste at the lowest possible prices; 2) a recipient country, usually Third World and so indebted that it is prepared to risk the health of its inhabitants to obtain dollars; and 3) a group of middlemen, the entrepreneurs, adventurers or corruptible politicians who are prepared to organize the collection, shipping, importation and ultimate disposal of the waste. Two other groups are involved: first, the victims, the crews, again mainly from the Third World, of ships carrying waste, deterioration of which throughout long voyages and torrid climates makes their very existence at the least unpleasant, at most a hazard, or the impoverished inhabitants of Third World countries, who, for a pittance or because the local Big Man gives them orders, have dangerous substances dumped on their land; second, there are what may loosely be called 'opponents of the trade', a mixed group ranging from environmentalists to investigative journalists and from MEPs to President Babangida of Nigeria.

The activities of the waste merchants pose one central question: why is the industrialized West so keen to offload its superfluous waste on to Third World countries? Answering this question involves asking others. What happened to the waste previously? Why is this method of disposal no longer available? Is this the only material that the West is trying to dispose of

elsewhere? What about nuclear waste? And what of the Third
World itself? Will it not, as industrialisation proceeds, have its own disposal
problems? Is not the fundamental issue not merely hazardous waste, or even
nuclear waste, but waste in general? Above all, why is there so much of it?
Is it an inevitable product of industrialised society or does the technology
exist to dispose of it by other means than simply transferring it elsewhere?
What are the potential dangers to both humanity and the environment if the
present situation continues? Ultimately, these questions boil down to two
words: Why Waste? In attempting to find answers the logical starting point
is to ask: What is Waste?

Notes

1. Greenpeace International 1988 pp. 46–7
2. Quoted Ibid. p. 48
3. Goldsmith and Hildyard 1988 p. 134
4. Ibid.
5. Greenpeace International 1988 p. 47
6. *Guardian* 2 September 1988
7. All date from TWN *Newsletter* of 29 June 1989
8. Greenpeace International 1988 p. 44
9. Ibid.
10. BRRI 1989 p. 83
11. Ibid. pp. 42, 44
12. Greenpeace International 1988 pp. 45–6
13. BRRI 1989 p. 60; TWN 1989 pp. 68–70 press reports
14. *Guardian* 12, 16 June 1988, 21 August 1988; *New Scientist* 8 September 1988
15. *New African* (nd or place of publication) August 1988
16. *Observer* 28 August 1988; *Guardian* 30, 31 August 1988
17. *Guardian* 1, 3, 6 September 1988
18. *Guardian* 15, 17 September 1988, 20 December 1988; *Observer* 18 September 1988
19. Greenpeace International 1988 pp. 47–8
20. Weir and Porterfield 1987 p. 32
21. *Daily Nation*, Kenya 17 June 1988
22. Greenpeace International 1988 pp. 49, 52; BRRI 1989 p. 60
23. CM/Res. 1153 XLVIII reproduced BRRI 1989 pp. 51–2
24. BRRI 1989 p. 53
25. Ibid. p. 57; *Guardian* 21 August 1988; *New Scientist* 23 June 1988
26. Greenpeace International 1988 p. 42; BRRI 1989 pp. 49–51; *Observer* 29 May 1988
27. BRRI 1989 pp. 71–82
28. Ibid. pp. 61–70

Part I:
Waste and its Makers

1. In search of waste

Waste is more easily recognised than defined. To individuals in Western society, the leftover blob of mustard on the rim of a dinner plate, like chicken bones or unchewable bits of gristle, is regarded as 'waste' and disposed of in the 'waste bin', while, on completing the digestive process, our bodies emit waste matter that is flushed into the local sanitary system. On our journeys to work our cars, buses and lorries emit waste fumes into the dust-laden air of our cities, and in our offices the daily consignment of junk mail, 40 per cent of which, in the USA at least, is never opened, ends up in the 'waste paper' basket. Throughout the day our industries, and the power stations on which they depend for energy, discharge waste effluent into streams, rivers or the sea and waste emissions into the air, while our farmers, using intensive methods of cultivation to maximise produce and profits, dowse their vast fields with chemical fertilizers that are 'wasted' when they leach beyond the intended soil, or spray their crops with synthetic pesticides in such quanitities that some are invariably carried away by the wind and wasted. As the first generation of Magnox nuclear reactors reaches the end of its working life, we can no longer escape the problem of the radioactive waste that will remain a hazard into the next century; and, having seen how discharges of waste gases into the atmosphere have caused acid rain, with subsequent death of trees and blight of buildings, we now contemplate, with feelings that range from outright disbelief to permanent unease, the prospect that the continued discharge of Greenhouse gases will bring about climatic change, cause the polar icewaps to melt and Pacific islands to disappear beneath the waters, and affect the lives of our children and grandchildren in ways yet unknown.

The more we consider the industrialised world of today, and the Third World of tomorrow, the more we realise that we live in a world dominated by waste, a World of Waste, most of it undesirable, and that, unless we do something about it, humanity may disappear under its own detritus, and the world we know with it.

Defining waste

What, then, is waste? Is there such a thing, or are there only different *wastes*? Is the difference in degree between a blob of mustard on a dinner plate and a worn-out nuclear reactor so great (in terms of size or hazard) that it becomes a difference in kind? Or are there features common to all wastes that not only justify one designation but also suggest a common solution to the problems they pose?

The world's lexicographers and lawyers offer little help. Under the heading 'waste matter, refuse', the Oxford English Dictionary (OED) defines 'refuse matter' as 'unserviceable material remaining over from any process of manufacture; the useless by-products of any industrial process; material or manufactured articles so damaged as to be useless or unsaleable', a concept of waste, which, in its limitation to industry and omission of domestic or agricultural forms of waste, fails to reflect common usage. The first two definitions, however, view waste as part of a process, while all three direct attention to its uselessness or unserviceability.

Webster's *New International Dictionary* (3rd Edition) echoes the OED in considering waste as 'damaged, defective or superfluous material produced during or left over from a manufacturing process or industrial operation' and, having used the word 'superfluous', proceeds to add, 'material not usable for the ordinary or main purpose of manufacture'. Webster, however, is broader in examples, which include not only 'material rejected during a textile manufacturing process' but 'fluid (or steam) allowed to escape without being utilised' and 'worthless material removed in mining or digging operations'. Finally, we reach 'refuse from places of human or animal habitation', on the one hand GARBAGE, RUBBISH, on the other, EXCREMENT, ORDURE, and so eventually to SEWAGE. But, like the OED, nowhere does Webster actually define the essence of waste.

Legislative sources, concerned with precise and unambiguous instructions for particular types of waste, often avoid the issue by assigning parameters to the limiting adjective, such as toxic, nuclear, domestic, without defining 'waste', or fall back on reduplication. The UK 1974 Control of Pollution Act (COPA), for example, defines 'controlled wastes' as 'those wastes subject to its control,'[1] and to the South African 1982 Environmental Conservation Act (ECA) waste 'in terms of this Act is defined as any waste originating from any residential, commercial or industrial area'.[2] The definitions are not of waste *per se* but explanations of how that term is used in a particular piece of legislation. Within these definitions, waste remains 'waste' without elucidation. If its scope becomes clearer as the Act proceeds, for example, COPA's provisions exclude 'explosives, wastes from mines and quarries, and agricultural wastes',[3] while the ECA's include 'any solid, liquid or gaseous substance contained therein'[4], there are no further insights into the nature of waste itself.

In contrast, the World Health Organisation (WHO) experts' discussion of 'hazardous waste' defines waste as 'something which the owner no longer wants at a given place and time and which has no current or perceived market value'.[5] This has the merit of recognising that waste exists in context, that it has an owner and occupies a given place and time, the essence of the definition being that the owner does not want it. To maintain, however, that the owner 'no longer' wants it, with the implication that there was a time when s/he may have done so, is both too restrictive and unnecessary within the terms of the definition itself, in which the waste exists only when and where it is *not* wanted. And while the 'no longer' may apply to the worn-out cars or refrigerators of the OED's third definition, it is not appropriate for many hazardous chemical wastes the WHO then goes on to consider, the 'useless by-products' which the owner never wants.

The final criterion of waste as having 'no current or perceived market value' is its weakest. It eliminates all personal or domestic waste, and even in its own terms, is not true. Toxic chemical waste may have no market value to the owner but its disposal provides a lucrative income to the Ambrosinis and Künzlers of this world. Even the blob of mustard may be construed as having a market value. I recall as a boy being told, with what truth I have never discovered, though the motive behind the information was transparent, that Mr. Colman made his money, not by selling mustard, but because millions of people left blobs on their plates!

If waste is something an owner possesses but does not want, the obvious question is why does s/he not want it? The OED's concepts of uselessness or unserviceability offer an equally obvious answer. The owner does not want a worn-out car, aerosol or video because they are useless; their properties have changed so that they no longer fulfil the functions for which they were made, To conclude, however, that 'waste is useless matter' omits the blob of mustard which, retaining its original properties, remains useful, if not to the owner. It becomes waste, not because it is useless but because the owner has *failed to use it*. Even this concept needs further clarification. In agricultural or fishery activities, those pesticides or fertilizers that fail to reach their target or go beyond it, for example, nitrates that leach into the soil, or the poisonous chemicals used in fish farming that end at the bottom of the sea, are wasted, not becuase they have changed their properties or the owner has failed to use them — paradoxically the waste arises because he has used them to excess — but because s/he has *failed to use them for the purpose for which they were intended*.

Our working definition of waste thus becomes *Waste is what we do not want or what we fail to use*, with the proviso that 'failure to use' includes 'failure to use for its proper purpose'. Waste can be produced as the unwanted by-product of a process, or something can become waste when it is no longer useful to the owner, or it is so used that it fails to fulfil its purpose.

Waste in context occupies both space and time, In terms of space its first and most obvious characteristic in Western society is its ubiquitousness. Encouraged by increased consumption, the mountains of unwanted matter pile up daily, sick symbols of an affluent throwaway culture, to satisfy which industry discharges additional wastes into air, sea and land, and mounds of battered, rusting cars, rejected as the owner goes for a newer and bigger model, replace the slagheaps of a defunct mining industry, now greened over.

In terms of time, waste *as we know it* is essentially a modern problem. The first use of the word in the OED (excluding a dubious fifteenth-century reference) is from the VIth Report of the Deputy Keeper of Public Records in 1764; The Refuse or Waste used in the making of Allom called Allom Slam, though if the 'waste' was used it was hardly 'waste'. The earliest reference to disposal is in Michael Faraday's *Chemical Manipulation* of 1827: 'The object of the preceding directions is to enable the economical experimenter to cut up into useful forms, old glass, which would otherwise be thrown away as waste'. The Victorians objected to throwing away things that might still be used. The 'waste-collector' of Mayhew's 1852 – 62 *London Labour* who complained, 'I don't know how it is sir, . . . but paper gets scarcer or else I am out of luck', would be much heartened by contemporary London's litter-ridden streets. The dates are significant. Humanity has always produced waste, if only the discarded bones of animals slaughtered for food, the hundreds of stone axes found at Olorgesaile or Olduvai, or the stinking cesspits and midden heaps of medieval Europe, but the momentous increase in waste that characterises contemporary society dates only from the Industrial Revolution. As time passes, the only certainty is that accumulation will outstrip disposal. Throughout the Western world there are no longer enough convenient holes in the ground into which to tip unwanted matter, while the Third World, having refused to become the dustbin of the First, will, in its struggles to industrialise, exacerbate the problem by producing its own volumes of waste.

Errors of incompleteness and division

In their discussions of waste in context, the most eminent specialists have compounded the problem rather than solved it. Their writings suggest that this arises from two characteristics of waste itself: first, that it is produced as part of a process; second, that, despite its common features, waste is distinguished by a variety of forms. These factors have affected not only the treatment of the problem and the solutions advocated but, because of the respect accorded to specialists, the subsequent attitude of the public.

The 'waste process', its 'pathway', is usually framed in terms of generation, storage, treatment, and disposal, with transportation inserted between stages as required. It is thus possible to stress one aspect at the expense of others and, given the vast quantities of undesirable waste already in existence, it is not surprising that writers have concentrated on how to get rid of it. However valid this approach, it causes problems when the disposal aspect is incorporated into the original definition. Thus WHO distinguishes 'hazardous waste' as having 'physical, chemical or biological characteristics which *require special handling and disposal procedures* to avoid risk to health and/or other adverse environmental effects'[6] (my stress). The UK House of Commons Environment Committee describes 'Special Wastes' as 'those which may be *difficult or dangerous to dispose of* because of their physical or chemical characteristics'[7] (my stress); and in the more comprehensive definition formulated by the Organisation for Economic Co-operation and Development (OECD) and the Commission of the European Community (EC), the term 'hazardous waste' excludes domestic and radioactive wastes but 'because of its quantity, physical, chemical and infectious characteristics can cause significant hazards to human health or the environment when improperly *treated, stored, transported or disposed of*[8] (my stress).

All three definitions are factually correct, but fail to include all the facts and thus fall into the logical fallacy of *suppressio veri, suggestio falsi*, that is, suppression of the (whole) truth so that what they suggest is false. The OECD definition is particularly outrageous; it includes all aspects of the waste process except one, its production, and the aspects mentioned are tagged on, irrelevantly, to what is otherwise an admirable definition! Nor is there a logical reason why WHO should not have placed its emphasis elsewhere and defined hazardous waste as 'that form of waste which, because its physical, chemical or biological characteristics pose a risk to health and/or the environment, *should not be produced*! (except, of course, that this falls into the same trap of illogical selection). Under present circumstances such a definition is an absurdity; the waste is there and the problem is to dispose of it.

But this is to fudge the issue by including the potential and the existing within the same category. Granted that we must get rid of the millions of tons of waste now in existence, does this imply that future production of similar types of waste is (a) desirable, (b) necessary? By omitting this aspect all three bodies are guilty of distorting the emphasis and turning readers' attention in one direction rather than another. Far from offering a solution to the problem, they have become part of it.

Similar objections of incompleteness apply to the 'cradle to grave' concept, which the British Royal Commission on Environmental Pollution (RCEP) advocated as a 'duty of care'. At first sight this includes all aspects of the waste pathway, from the cradle of production to the grave of final disposal into earth, water or, through incineration, air. But are these the true beginning and end of the waste process? Is there not, in terms of the metaphor, 'life after death'? Or even questions to be asked about the possibility of monstrous birth? As later chapters reveal, when hazardous chemicals are buried in landfill, sewage discharged into the sea, or even PCBs 'destroyed' by fire, this consignment to the grave is unfortunately by no means always the final act. Our concern at the moment is not, however, with possibilities of resurrection so much as with the logic of postulating a 'cradle to grave' syndrome. By framing their answer to the problem of hazardous waste in metaphorical terms that apparently cover *all* stages of the process, writers convey the impression that everything is under control and that, in the end, all will be well, when the syndrome itself fails to allow for other options so that, in a less than perfect world, the reality is far from well.

Variety and quantity have further exacerbated the problem through compartmentalisation, that is, the extraction of identifiable parts of a phenomenon for treatment in isolation, a practice inevitably justified by the need to specialise. Hence, along a never clearly defined scale, there are *separate* studies of domestic or municipal waste at one end, radioactive waste at the other and, somewhere in between, the various hazardous, dangerous or toxic wastes of agro-industry. Rarely is the problem of waste considered *as a whole* and the public comes to think of waste as a series of disparate problems — how to dispose of radioactive waste, or the best method of handling sewage — that have nothing in common beyond the fact that both substances are undesirable.

The process is facilitated by linguistic sleight of hand in which wastes are 'disguised'. Either the word 'waste' is omitted or the reference is to its effects rather than to waste as the cause. Waste gases become 'emissions', waste liquids 'discharges'; the term 'radioactive waste' is applied only to the high, medium and low level material left over from the nuclear process and attention diverted from the fact that continuous 'emissions' into the air or 'discharges' of 'effluent' into rivers or directly into the sea are both waste and radioactive. Waste gases from cars, lorries or coal-fired power stations are disguised as causes by transferring attention to results, for example, acid rain, or the Greenhouse Effect, while the most enduring and natural form of waste, that from human bodies, is rarely conceived of as 'what the owner does not want', but appears under the guise of 'sewage'.

So waste gets lost, and the problem with it. By isolating toxic wastes and concentrating on the toxicity we lose sight of the fact that they are basically a form of waste; by concentrating on the 'receiving end' and investigating the potential effects of acid rain and the greenhouse gases, we direct attention away from the waste that is our real problem.

The way out of this dilemma is to restore the parts to the whole. If we must, for the purpose of exposition, divide them, then each must be considered in relation to their common base. They are all things we do not want or which we have failed to use.

Dilemmas of description

There is no satisfactory way of *writing* about waste because there is no method of treating the subject that avoids all objections. Attempts to produce a taxonomy by applying the same criteria throughout inevitably lead to overlapping or omissions and end in compromise.

In theory there are numerous ways of classifying waste; by source (domestic, industrial, agricultural), form (solid, liquid, gas), inherent properties (biodegradable, non-biodegradable) or its effects (harmless/

harmful to human beings/animals/the environment). One could even use the method of disposal — into the earth (landfill), the water (discharges/dumping) or the air (emissions /incineration). In practice, as soon as one opts for a particular approach, there are problems that necessitate a change of course or combining two methods.

The *World Resources 1988–89* study contains a carefully constructed table of 'Waste Generation in Selected Countries'[9] which, at first sight, appears to use 'source' as its basis since it separates 'Municipal' from 'Industrial'. There is, however, a third category, 'Hazardous or Special Waste Generation' which, while appearing to be of immaculate conception, is presumably also a product of industry. Doubts about the usefulness of the data arise as we read: 'Waste data were collected by various means, and are not strictly comparable among countries'.[10] Municipal Waste is defined as 'the trash collected from households, commercial establishments and small industries', that is, it includes a proportion of industrial waste, the importance of which will increase as urban-based high-technology industries replace traditional large-scale production. The amounts of industrial waste *per se* 'depend on the definition of waste used in a country', while Hazardous Waste is 'waste known to contain potentially harmful substances'. For some countries, for example, Australia and Austria, industrial waste includes hazardous or special waste, or both, while France's annual 18 million tons of special waste are for some (unspecified) reason not included, and the Netherlands industrial waste comes only from 'enterprises employing ten or more people' but includes 'office and canteen wastes'. Finally, while New Zealand's industrial waste 'is non-chemical waste only', Norway's 'includes chemical waste only'.[11] Nuclear waste is not included, though data on spent fuel appear elsewhere, nor is waste from agriculture, and there is no information on spoils from extractive industries. Also omitted are 'personal wastes', e.g. sewage or the discharge of chlorofluorocarbons (CFCs) from aerosols, industrial emissions into the atmosphere and similar waste emissions from cars (which may be either 'domestic' or 'commercial' and lorries, which, one assumes, are 'industrial'. These comments are not made to detract from appreciation of the industry of the compilers, but to illustrate the impossibility of their task.

The British House of Commons Environment Committee's attempt to quantify wastes arising in England and Wales further illustrates the problem. Of their 12 categories of waste, 'domestic and trade' refers to 'municipal' sources, to which 'medical' waste may be added as a special category; agriculture, mines and quarries, and sewage sludge appear in their own right (though the last is a product, not a source) but the remaining seven (liquid effluent, industrial (general), industrial (hazardous and special), industrial (special), power station ash, blast furnace slag and building[12] all have industry as their source. Waste emissions into the air, whether from industry, transport or human beings, are omitted. Quantitatively, as the DoE put it in its evidence, 'There are no reliable statistics on wastes produced or disposed of in the UK with the exception of special wastes which are...quantified to some extent.... Even statistics for special wastes cannot be said to be wholly accurate.'[13] One admires the department's honesty but prefers not to think of its effectiveness.

Classification of waste by effects, that is, whether it is harmless or hazardous, raises other problems. Not only does it produce two cumbersome categories, each requiring further breakdown, but it depends for its accuracy on our ability to distinguish between the two. How, in fact, do we determine what is 'hazardous', 'dangerous', or 'toxic' waste? WHO suggests a number of criteria: the composition of the waste, its physical form and quantity, its mobility and persistence and the availability and vulnerability of potential targets.Together these determine both short and long-term hazards. So far as composition is concerned, it is more important to know the 'hazard characteristics' than actual make-up, that is, whether it contains posionous matter or matter which, acting on other contents, may become dangerous. The physical form is relevant for both short- and long-term effects, for example, liquid or sludge is more likely to affect water than solid waste; asbestos fibres are more dangerous than asbestos cement; and finely divided metals are hazardous while the same material in massive form may be harmless. The importance of quantity is obvious. A one-off dumping of toxic waste in the sea, however undesirable, may be less detrimental than the continuous outpouring of effluent. The most difficult problems are probably those of determining the 'threshold' level at which to set the quantity, especially when there are a number of small, unregulated discharges.[14]

Hazardous effects — the absence of information

This rational, common-sense approach unfortunately breaks down in practice. In view of major advances in medicine and technology generally, it was a shock to discover, during research for this book, that, according to the US Academy of Sciences, by the end of 1988 a proper hazard assessment was possible for fewer than 7 per cent of the 17,202 chemicals known to be in agrochemicals, cosmetics, drugs and food additives. While people had been concerned about the use of pesticides for up to 30 years, some 44 per cent of the resulting commercial products were still without sufficient information for a full hazard assessment, and, for other chemicals, a partial assessment was available for a mere 11 per cent. About 80 per cent had no formal toxicity information of the kind essential for assessment and not a single chemical had the range of information needed for full assessment.[15] These disturbing figures do not, of course, refer solely to waste, but the prospect of farmers spraying their fields with increasing doses of pesticides that are carried away by wind but whose toxicity is unknown arouses not a little disquiet. Almost at the same time, the British Government announced that files on pesticides, previously kept secret on the grounds that the information was the property of the manufacturers and might fall into the hands of rivals, if released, were to be opened to manufacturers 'to increase competition'. They would not, however, be available to the general public.[16]

Almost a year later, in November 1989, the OECD announced a plan to investigate the toxicity and effects on the environment of 1,500 chemical compounds, which accounted for 95 per cent by volume of all the chemicals around the world and were consequently those to which human beings and the environment were most likely to be exposed but about which there was no toxicological data as they were in use long before legally enforced screening of new compounds. In the first phase, due for completion by 1993 at a cost of US$20 million, 147 compounds will be investigated; 70 of them are produced in volumes greater than 10,000 tonnes a year.[17] Unfortunately, there is no information on which of the chemicals concerned appear in waste, though, on grounds of probability, it is reasonable to assume that there are some. The chemicals concerned may be quite harmless, or they may be lethal. The simple facts are that we do not know, and that the makers were prepared to release them in vast quantities, even though they were equally ignorant.

As for the threshold of toxicity, that is the level at which known harmful substances become dangerous, a report by the US National Research Council published just before Christmas 1988 on the effects of exposure to nuclear radiation is instructive. Using data from Hiroshima and Nagasaki, the scientists concluded that the risk of developing cancerous tumours from doses of low-level radiation was three times as great as was previously thought, and for contracting leukemia four times. Children exposed to a given dose of radiation are at twice the risk of contracting cancer as are adults. The net effect of this research into the effects of low-level radiation is to abolish the concept that there is a threshold below which they can be disregarded.[18] Yet for almost half a century the scientific advisers of governments have maintained the opposite; the politicians framed their policies accordingly. In view of our ignorance and the increasing number of substances which, once approved as 'harmless' or 'harmless in small doses', that is, below the threshold, are later discovered to be harmful — for example, lead or the pesticide spray for apples, alar — the distinction 'harmless/harmful' breaks down until we can state with every scientific certainty that the substance will not harm either humanity or other living creatures or in any way affect the ecological balance.

The plan for the remainder of this book is a compromise born of necessity. Chapter 2 on 'Waste makers and their wastes' aims to present a panoramic picture of the production aspect by identifying the major sources and types of waste and describing their characteristics. Beginning with personal waste, that is, individual human excrement, it proceeds to that discarded by the household and municipality, thence to the waste from industry, particularly the chemical industry, with a sub-section on mining and smelting, and so to agriculture, with a glance at waste from modern fish farming. After investigating the production of nuclear waste, including lesser-known sources, together with submarines and satellites, it concludes with a survey of waste gases, ranging from the exhaust fumes of cars and trucks to the eructations of cattle and the now familiar waste gases responsible for the Greenhouse Effect.

Part II, 'What happens to waste', is concerned with two aspects — where the waste goes, and the resultant effects. Chapter 3, 'On the way', deals with what happens to waste during transportation from its source to its place of so-called disposal. Chapter 4 considers the burial of waste in, or dumping of it on to the earth, Chapter 5 its discharge or dumping into Water, Chapter 6 its passage into (and out of) Fire (through incineration) and Chapter 7 the direct discharge of waste gases into the Air.

Part III begins with an examination of positive attempts to solve the waste problem. Chapter 8 surveys technological responses to the challenge from science and industry, while Chapter 9 evaluates the activities of politicians and policy-makers, particularly in the field of legal regulation. Finally, Chapter 10 considers the broader aspects of waste in the context of development and examines the dilemma posed by plans for continued industrial growth when faced with the production of waste that threatens the very existence of life on the planet.

Notes

1. HoC 1989 para. 31
2. ECA 1982 Regulations 1
3. HoC 1989 para. 31
4. ECA 1982 Regulations 1
5. WHO 1983 p.102
6. Ibid.
7. HoC 1989 para. 32
8. Subrahmanyam and Swaminathan 1989
9. *WR 1988 – 89* p.314, Table 20.7
10. Ibid. p.316
11. Ibid.
12. HoC 1989 para. 37
13. Quoted Ibid.
14. WHO 1983 pp.102 – 4
15. Tucker 1988b
16. *Guardian* 12 November 1988
17. *New Scientist* 18 November 1989
18. Ibid. 6 January 1990

2. Waste makers and their wastes

Waste makers range from individual human beings to multi-million dollar industrial corporations, from the solitary gold miner sifting his spoil to the nuclear power station discharging radioactive effluent. This chapter attempts to identify the major sources of waste, to describe its properties and, where possible, to determine its quantities.

Domestic and municipal waste

There are two types of domestic waste — personal and household. The first is what the individual body does not want, the second what the family discards.

Personal contributions

According to World Bank estimates there are now some five billion human inhabitants of this planet and by the year 2000 there will be six billion.[1] Those whose bodies are not affected by disease, malnutrition or starvation discharge unwanted liquid and solid matter which, if quantified on a global basis, evokes a picture of mountains of human waste awaiting disposal. As to the properties of this waste, if we set aside the aesthetic aspects, which arise mainly from turds in the wrong place, for example, on bathing beaches, accompanied by hordes of flies, the only thing wrong with human excrement is the possibility of disease in the human beings who produce it rather than the substance itself.

Everyone knows that, because of the nitrates or phosphates it contains, properly rotted down horse manure is excellent fertilizer, and one organic farmer even claims to use his own excrement for this purpose. Unfortunately, there are three problems:

- without treatment, raw sewage contains disease-causing viruses and bacteria which, if discharged into rivers or the sea, infect those who come into contact with them, a danger that increases with the prevalence of disease among the local population, and is thus more widespread in Third World countries;

- the growth-producing elements in sewage may excel themselves to the extent that, when discharged into water, their demand for oxygen exceeds the supply, thus upsetting the ecological balance and causing a mass slaughter of other plants and animals;
- in developed countries sewage is rarely discharged in its pristine form. The addition of industrial effluent means that, far from being a useful fertilizer, the resultant sludge contains heavy metals — mercury, cadmium, copper, lead or zinc — which, above certain levels, are harmful to all forms of life.[2]

To cope with this waste, societies have evolved systems prescribed largely by density of population and the immediate environment. For a remote African savanna village, where the sun bakes the sandy soil into concrete, a trip to a lonely place in the bush satisfies the needs of hygiene. In populous South American cities open sewers act as 'an immense breeding ground for rats'. While

the well-equipped colonial houses had latrines and septic tanks ... two-thirds of the population lived in shanties at the edge of the swamp and relieved themselves in the open air. The excrement dried in the sun, turned to dust, and was inhaled by everyone along with the joys of Christmas in the cool, gentle breezes of December.[3]

In 1810, London, with a million people, had 200,000 cesspits, traditionally used as receptacles for *all* household waste; when they overflowed, the whole system was flushed into the Thames, just as, in Europe, the Seine or Tiber received its daily loads of human and animal excrement, household refuse and all the detritus of city life. In June 1858 the hot, dry weather caused such a sharp fall in the level of the Thames that the emanating stench was known as 'The Great Stink'. Inhabitants could approach the river only with handkerchiefs clamped firmly to mouths and noses, members of parliament ran up curtains soaked in chloride of lime before they could continue sittings, and it was even proposed to run a pipe up Big Ben to draw off sewer gas.

Not until the 1850s did Sir Joseph Bazalgette's grand 'intercepting sewage system' come into operation. All sewage, except storm water, was conveyed to outfall works north and south of the Thames and stored, to await a suitable ebb tide before it was discharged.[4] Today's practice in countries with 'advanced' sewage disposal is basically an extension of this system. A network of sewers carries the waste, either by gravity or pumping, from household, office or public lavatories to the sewage works. The two major changes are in content and treatment. Sewage has deteriorated in that it no longer consists solely of human waste but includes noxious discharges of industrial effluent. Conversely, its works treatment has improved. The theory is simple: after the filtering out of large objects such as rags or wood, which are taken away and burned or buried, the sewage passes through grit removal channels, where small stones and sand are removed, to be used later for road repair or building. In the preliminary sedimentation tanks the solid material, 'crude sludge', settles at the bottom, while the liquid undergoes chemical treatment, in which microbes destroy obnoxious matter in about eight hours before themselves being separated and re-used. The sludge is subjected to similar treatment, microbes converting part of it into gas containing methane, while the remainder, with more water removed, may be sold to farmers as fertilizer.[5]

Unfortunately, practice rarely conforms to theory. If, as is claimed, the finally treated liquid is so pure that it is discharged into rivers from which drinking water is taken, how does it happen that, in an 'advanced' country such as the United Kingdom, there are outfalls around the coast discharging what is obviously, from sight and stench, faecal matter? And why, if sewage sludge is useful to farmers, is so much of it dumped into the sea?

These problems are exacerbated by neglect of the system, sharp practice by its operators and, in the UK at least, by administrative policy. In August 1987 a report by the Consumers' Association maintained that many of the 150,000 miles of sewers in England and Wales, one out of ten of which was well over 100 years old, were in danger of collapse; 3,500 actually did so every year, and 1,500 blockages needed excavation, problems not helped by the fact that the exact location of some sewers was unknown. While a £40m additional spending to the current £270m was needed merely to keep the system going, the actual level of spending was the same as in 1966.[6]

Administratively, in England and Wales sewage was the responsibility of ten Water Authorities, whose contradictory functions of both gamekeeper and poacher, in that they were responsible for safeguarding against pollution while themselves being polluters, was condemned by both the RCEP and the House of Commons Environment Committee — to no effect. Under the 1974 Control of Pollution Act they operated by 'consents' which laid down the quantity and quality of sewage they were allowed to discharge into rivers or the sea. In mid-1987 a survey by Environmental Data Services (ENDS) stated that 22 per cent of the 4,353 principal sewage works were operating in breach of their consents, which the Secretary of State for the Environment had already relaxed. At the end of 1988 a Leeds University report maintained that 20.5 per cent of 4,355 plants broke their legal limits, and, in October 1989, even the government placed 17 per cent of 4,417 main plants in this category. In 1988, according to the DoE's own statistics, no fewer than 4,578 incidents of water pollution from sewage were reported. The Water Authorities claimed that the main problem was lack of finance; they just did not have the money to do the job properly.

An additional problem concerned the 12,000 'storm sewer overflows', some of which were little more than holes bored into the pipe to conform to regulations, and which periodically spilt their contents into rivers and streams when the antique sewers were overloaded. Thousands were allegedly illegal and badly designed, more than a third unsatisfactory, a situation that would cost £600m to rectify.

The Pollution Inspectorate supported the Water Authorities by claiming that these problems were caused mainly by underinvestment. The government's response was different — when faced with a public service requiring a large injection of public money, get rid of it, in short, privatise and let the new private companies pass the additional expenditure to the consumer. To make the prospect attractive the government ordered a relaxation in consent conditions at 835 sewage works in England and Wales, exempted the new Water Companies from prosecution for breaching consents for a year after their formation, and, to overcome the storm sewer overflow problem, directed the new 'independent gamekeeper', the National Rivers Authority (NRA) to give 'temporary authorisation' to sewer overflows applied for before it took over. As this date, approached, the sudden rush of applications surprised even the DoE, if not the outside observer, who had watched this charade with increasing cynicism.[7]

The USA has the double problem of the Two Cs, combined sewage overflows and corruption. In many of the older cities of the Eastern and Great Lakes region the sewers carry both sewage and storm water so that, after heavy rains, with the sewage plants unable to cope, the contents bypass treatment and head for the nearest river, or urban conglomerate. Of New York City's 6,500 miles of sewers, 70 per cent are combined; in Chicago, the plants are overwhelmed a hundred times a year, and in Long Island and New Jersey, bad planning and unregulated development in the post-war years result in houses being flooded after heavy rain.[8]

Constructing sewage works attracts its share of the incompetent and corrupt. Federal investigators described a US$1,200,000,000 scheme in Suffolk County designed to serve 400,000 people as shot through with 'kickbacks, payoffs and shoddy workmanship':

> In October 1981, a federal grand jury on Long Island convicted an engineering firm, its principal partner, and an attorney for the firm on charges that they participated in a US$900,000 bribery scheme that concerned four federally backed sewer construction projects in three states. One of the projects was in Suffolk County. A few months later, the design engineer for the firm was sentenced to 12 years in prison and was fined US$85,000. He obtained contracts worth nearly US$70m, the government had argued, by arranging for bribes to be paid to government officials and politicians.[9]

Things rarely worked out as they should, When the EPA undertook a construction programme for advanced sewage treatment at an anticipated cost of US$106bn., the House Appropriations Committee that later investigated the project found 'widespread examples of failure' and recommended that no more money be spent on the widely publicised Lake Tahoe plant on the California–Nevada border. It was particularly critical of what it called 'gold-plating', the construcion of 'elaborate, ornamental, and costly aesthetic features which do not contribute to the functional uses of a treatment plant'. Few sewage works are criticised on aesthetic grounds but it could hardly be claimed that the US$7,000 flagpole and the US$5,000 sign identifying the works in Philipsburg, Pennsylvania, contributed to the treatment process.[10]

Household and urban waste

Household waste is the 'rubbish' (US: 'garbage', 'trash') which, in industrialised countries, is deposited in 'dustbins' (US:'garbage cans') and removed by refuse collectors for disposal. Third World domestic waste differs in content and the proportions between types.

In practice the Western consumer is almost always an enforced generator of waste. Contemporary industrial society provides us with a daily intake of plastic wrappings, cartons, glass bottles or junk mail, the greater part of which is discarded. Before World War II, in the U.K the milkman measured out pints from a large can and tipped them directly into the waiting jug, while the greengrocer added onions, cabbage, cauliflowers or bananas to the potatoes at the bottom of the shopping basket. Jam jars were washed out and saved for jam-making, and beer that did not come from a handpump was not 'proper' beer. The curse of plastic may have made for better hygiene, but it has also increased the 'stress factor' as the latest consignment from the weekly shopping fills half the dustbin and adrenalin rises with each unsuccessful attempt at opening plastic packages seemingly designed to make the operation impossible. Today's Western consumer is forced to get rid of more than twice the waste of previous generations before s/he reaches objects that were once readily available. It is her/his task to dispose of it, but it is for the convenience of supermarkets and fastfood stores, or the alleged enhancement of cosmetics and perfumes on display, not for the benefit of the consumer, that industry produces it.

'Domestic Waste' is by and large a myth. It is 'industrial waste' in disguise and 99 per cent unnecessary, if, under present methods of large-scale distribution, inevitable.

Studies for the World Bank into the extent and composition of 'urban solid waste' corroborate what common sense and a little imagination lead us to conclude, namely, that 'urban refuse generation tends to increase with the economic levels of countries and cities.'[11] In modern throwaway economics, the more you have, the more you chuck out. In New York City, the 'going' rate is 1.8kg per person per day, in Hamburg 0.85kg and in Rome 0.69kg. In contrast, the rates for Cairo, Kano (Nigeria) and Calcutta are estimated as within the range of 0.46 to 0.51kg. Singapore and Hong Kong, however, are well on their way to joining the West; the former, with a rate of 0.87kg per person per day, exceeds Hamburg; the latter equals it.[12] A city of a million inhabitants produces 500−850 tonnes of waste a day; smaller cities, irrespective of whether they are in the industrialised world or the Third, generally have lower generation rates than large ones because they have fewer commercial activites.[13] In short, urban waste owes more to commerce than to the individual.

The composition of the waste displays a converse, if not entirely unexpected, characteristic, namely, that the proportion of 'vegetative and putrescible' material tends to increase as the overall economic level decreases. In Brooklyn, NY, only 26 per cent of the waste (by weight) is 'compostable'; in Jakarta it is 85 per cent, in Lucknow 82 per cent and in

Karachi as much as 96 per cent. In contrast, 43 per cent of Singapore's waste and 32 per cent of Hong Kong's is paper, which also accounts for 37 per cent of London's waste and 35 per cent of Brooklyn's. Hong Kong discards a higher proportion of glass and ceramics than either London or Brooklyn (10 per cent, 9 per cent, and 8 per cent respectively), but Brooklyn leads the data given for metals and plastics with 13 per cent and 10 per cent respectively against London's eight and two, a figure that appears somewhat low, when compared with the 6 per cent for both Singapore and Hong Kong, both of which are also leading discarders of textiles (9 per cent and 10 per cent respectively).[14] As percentages of total waste the figures, of course, give no indication of quantity, just as the earlier figures of weight did not indicate volume.

A more recent analysis for the UK gives the following breakdown of waste by weight:[15] kitchen waste (30 per cent), paper (25 per cent), textiles (10 per cent), glass (10 per cent), metals (8 per cent), plastics (7 per cent), and ashes, dust, etc. (10 per cent). According to the same sources, the average Briton dumps one-third of a tonne of unwanted matter into the dustbin every year. For paper alone, the average household throws away the equivalent of six trees annually, while the 4,450,000,000 drink cans disposed of in 1986, placed end to end, would reach to the moon.[16] In the USA as a whole it is estimated that every day about 400,000 tonnes of garbage are discarded, giving a total of over 140,000,000 tonnes for the year.[17] In the UK the corresponding figure for domestic waste is 18 million tonnes.[18]

Solid domestic waste has three characteristics that affect its (and our) future: 1) the sheer volume is already causing disposal problems, 2) while the waste is discarded as what the current owner does not want, almost all the contents are useful to somebody. Glass, paper and scrap metal have obvious uses, discarded clothes ('Textiles') are welcomed by charity shops and those whose income forces them to buy other people's cast offs, while the 'compostable' element of kitchen waste could become useful fertilizer; 3) in contrast to these useful components, household waste includes a number of items that are far from innocuous: plastics because of their persistence and non-biodegradability; batteries which, until recently, contained the heavy metals mercury or cadmium; paint residues, especially those that are lead-based; and unused medical pills and potions.

Household disposal of the latter is small compared with the major source of clinical waste, hospitals. In their investigation of toxic wastes, the British House of Commons Environment Committee was particularly concerned with pathological wastes such as tissues and organs, infectious wastes (from laboratories, surgeries and the treatment of infectious patients) and 'sharps' (for example, discarded syringes, needles, broken glass). All such waste is burned in hospital incinerators, yet HM Inspectorate of Pollution (HMIP) found that 'there is no doubt that a large number of clinical incinerators at hospitals are, by any present standards, inadequate', with problems in both design and operation. While a temperature in excess of 800 degrees C was essential in the after-burner area, most units inspected had 'totally inadequate temperature monitoring', with frequent emissions of black smoke (in infringement of the 1956 Clean Air Act); and there was 'a suspicion that the collection of bags and their feeding into an incinerator is left to hospital staff who are not aware of the need to operate incinerators at particular temperatures, nor how to do it.'[19]

At a different level is the question of liquid waste which, because it goes down the drain and is thus out of sight, is too often out of mind and inevitably avoids inclusion in statistics. Emergence of the clothes washing machine as an 'essential' in modern consumer society (and to a lesser extent the dishwasher) has brought about a change from old-fashioned soaps, made from animal fats and vegetable oils, to contemporary petrochemical-based detergents and washing-up liquids, and, though one is now spared the sight, common in the 1950s, of masses of suds blown in the wind at weirs and locks, in 1989 Britain flushed over 500,000 tons of detergent into its watercourses. The most controversial components of modern detergents are the 'builders', used to precipitate calcium and magnesium ions from the water and prevent unsightly scum. Most commonly used are phosphates, which can make up to half a box of washing powder. Although banned for use in detergents in Switzerland and Holland, and strictly limited in many American states, the use of phosphates is uncontrolled in the UK and the EC. Apart from the production of poisonous cadmium as a by-product of phosphate manufacture, phosphates themselves, as mentioned already in discussing sewage and as will appear later in our examination of fertilizers, can have undesirable effects on the environment as part-cause of algal blooms and in destroying protective oils in seabirds' feathers.[20]

Nor do individual and domestic contributions end here. To the visible solid contents of dustbins and disappearing liquid effluents must be added the invisible or partly visible waste gases from personal and domestic activities; the carbon dioxide that goes out of chimneys or directly into the air from burning fossil fuels, the chlorofluorocarbons (CFCs) from aerosol sprays and discarded fridges, and the nitrous oxides from car exhausts, all of which join emissions from other sources and so become quantifiable only as a whole. Even after death human waste production does not cease. Among recent bizarre and gruesome findings is the discovery of dioxins in emissions from crematoria which were thought to arise from 'incomplete combustion' of plastic bone replacements.[21] And you thought that, once out of this world, at least you would be unable to do it any more harm!

Industry

From a global viewpoint, all figures on industrial generation of waste are suspect, if not open to outright scepticism. In the first place, data are often unavailable; second, figures refer only to solid, semi-solid or liquid forms of waste, and omit gaseous emissions; third, the nuclear industry is either omitted or treated separately; and fourth, there are no uniformly accepted criteria for classifying hazardous or toxic waste.

With these reservations in mind, we learn that, in 1985, the USA led the world by producing some 613m tonnes of 'industrial waste' and 250m tonnes of 'hazardous or special waste', followed by the USSR, Poland and Japan (in 1983) with around 306m, 275m and 221m tonnes of industrial waste respectively. Further comparisons are impossible as figures for special/hazardous waste production for the USSR and Poland are not available, though Japan is credited with 760,000 tonnes. Compared with these giants, in 1982 West Germany produced over 52m tonnes of industrial waste and almost 5m tonnes of special/hazardous waste, the UK (in 1984) 50m tonnes of industrial waste and 1½m tonnes of 'notifiable wastes', and France (in 1985) over 32m tonnes of industrial waste, 2m tonnes of hazardous or toxic and a further 18m tonnes of 'special waste', though why this is separated remains unclear.[22]

If it is impossible to discover the total worldwide production of industrial waste, the figure for hazardous or toxic waste has been estimated at some 325−75m tonnes for 1984, 90 per cent of it from the industrialised world. As the USA is credited with two-thirds − three-quarters of this total and the (then 10) countries of the EC with 8−9 per cent,[23] this leaves only 14−25 per cent for the remaining industrial countries and suggests either that the figures are not available or that the definition of 'industrial countries' is limited in application. The situation is hardly clarified by the assertion that 'conservative estimates put the amount of hazardous waste generated in England and Wales at some four million tonnes',[24] while the official figure given above for 'notifiable wastes in the UK as a whole is 1½m tonnes! In this statistical miasma the only certainties are 1) that no one really knows how much 'industrial' or how much 'toxic/hazardous/special waste' exists; 2) there is far too much already for the health of the planet and its inhabitants; and 3) the amount is daily being increased.

The ramifications of the chemical industry

Central to waste production are the giants of the chemical industry, whose influence extends far beyond actual production of chemicals. Schematically, the industry has two main manufacturing sectors — the production of 1) organic, 2) inorganic chemicals.[25]

Organic chemicals are important because carbon lies at the root of life and modern industrial civilization depends ultimately on the carbon stored in trees crushed deep beneath the surface of the earth millions of years ago to become today's fossil fuels, that is, oil, coal and natural gas. Stage 1 of the manufacturing process is thus the large-scale production of primary organic chemicals from these sources. In stage 2 these chemicals are converted into secondary or intermediate materials, which may undergo further 'in-house processing', be passed on downstream for conversion into final products, or used in other industries. Final products include such familiar objects as dyes, cosmetics, toiletries, pharmaceuticals (including biocides) and plastics;

industrial uses include the application of chemical solvents for degreasing in engineering, degreasing and cleaning of transport fleets, and plant or machinery cleaning in the production of paint or printing inks.

The inorganic sector accounts for nine out of ten major products, including the manufacture of the four main acids, sulphuric, hydrochloric, nitric and phosphoric, the corrosive properties of which need no stressing, and ammonia, lime, chlorine and sodium hydroxide. Sulphuric acid is actually the largest product of the chemical industry. A danger peculiar to the manufacture of phosphoric acid is that the phosphogypsum waste produced may be radioactive on account of the natural uranium found in the mineral itself. In their industrial applications, the greatest acid wastes arise from metallurgical operations in which various acids, or mixtures of acids, are used in etching, electropolishing, anodizing or other surface treatments of both ferrous and non-ferrous metals.

The important point is that each process, at every stage in the manufacture of both organic and inorganic chemicals and in their industrial application, produces its own particular form of waste. As a detailed description would only baffle the reader with science (or at least presuppose a knowledge of chemistry outside that of the majority), we shall consider only the use of chlorinated organic solvents in industry.

Perchlorethylene and trichlorethylene, for example, are used in dry cleaning establishments, in the manufacture of microchips for removing grease, and in the engineering industry, either by dipping the material in a solvent or by passing it through solvent vapour. Both methods produce a waste sump residue containing cuttings, oils, lubricants, fine metal particles and general dirt, which, on reaching an unacceptable level of contamination, is removed for disposal or recovery. Other organic hydrocarbon solvents such as white spirits or kerosene are used for degreasing and cleaning transport fleets, thereby producing an unhealthy waste mixture of spent solvents, often badly contaminated with oil, grease and dirt, and containing phenolic compounds used as degreasants. (Phenols can cause liver damage and some are suspected carcinogens.)[26]

A different, if no less dangerous, type of waste comes from the paint industry in the form of either dirty solvents from plant cleaning or as reject batches of paint. Such waste often contains compounds of heavy metals such as antimony, barium, cadmium, chromium, cobalt, copper, lead, manganese, mercury, tin or zinc (see Box 2.1).[27]

In the manufacture of printing inks, wastes from using solvents to wash down plant or machinery are also contaminated with heavy metals, while the washing down of printing machines using such inks produces wastes that may contain ethanol, butyl acetates and both aliphatic and aromatic solvents. Ethanol, is, of course, ethyl alcohol, butyl compounds are derived from butane, which is more familiar as a gas for heating, while 'aliphatic' and 'aromatic' refer to different combinations of hydrogen and carbon within the hydrocarbon family, of which some of the most complex — polycyclic aromatic hydrocarbons (PAHs) — are known carcinogens.[28]

Organic solvents leading to the production of different forms of waste are also used in the making of adhesives, cleaning materials and polishes, pesticides, food flavourings and toiletries, in the degreasing of fatty skins in tanning, and in the photographic industry.[29]

Box 2.1 : Heavy Metals

Heavy metals, which include antimony, barium, cadmium, chromium, cobalt, copper, lead, manganese, mercury, tin and zinc, vary widely in their chemical properties and biological effects. Of the 'beneficial' heavy metals, copper, manganese and zinc are essential to human diet, while others, such as cadmium, lead and mercury can be poisonous except in very small quantities. In 1988 it was estimated that some seven million tonnes of heavy metals entered the environment annually, three quarters of them being dumped in landfills, the major source being ash from burning coal and the dumping of rubbish. As elements, heavy metals are indestructible and can only be converted from one chemical compound to another. They are thus extremely difficult to dispose of. If burned, they cause air pollution, if dumped at sea, they can accumulate in the water and sediments and enter the food chain of marine animals, particularly shellfish.

Cadmium is present in phosphate fertilizers and is discharged into the environment during their refining, a process that occurs also during zinc or lead smelting, as cadmium is usually present in the ores. Its major industrial uses are in metal plating, as a pigment in certain plastics, and in some rechargeable batteries. High levels frequently occur in the industrial contribution to sewage sludge. Cadmium is toxic to human beings, chronic cadmium poisoning causing damage to heart and kidneys, while prolonged exposure results in loss of calcium from the bones, which become brittle and break easily, as in the Japanese outbreak of *itai-itai*, when an entire village was struck by cadmium poisoning. West Germany has banned the use of cadmium in pesticides and the UK outlawed cadmium plating on food utensils in 1956.

Lead has been used for thousands of years and, despite its known toxic properties, is still in use for batteries, paints, alloys, petrol and in building construction. Lead piping for drinking water has become notorious in that many houses in the UK still have lead levels above recommended standards. Tetra-ethyl lead, added to petrol to prevent knocking, was and, despite legal and financial attempts to popularise lead-free petrol in the USA and EC countries, is still responsible for high concentrations in urban air and dust, and affects food by contaminating leafy vegetables. Acute lead poisoning causes stomach pains, headaches, irritability and, at its worst, coma and death. More insidious, and perhaps more dangerous, are the effects of continued ⇨

⇨ low levels on the brain and nerves. A 1985 study by the Harvard School of Public Health established that these have a retarding effect on the development of young children and cause listlessness, fatigue and apathy among adults, even affecting verbal ability and number memory, defects that persist even when levels of lead are reduced.

Mercury is still used in metallic form in thermometers and barometers and as part of compounds in industrial processes and protective seed dressing. It is highly poisonous, attacking the nervous system, so that small doses cause irritability or headaches, large ones convulsions and death. Organic mercury compounds, such as methyl mercury, which resulted in some 300 deaths at Minamata, Japan, betwen 1953 and 1983, following discharges into the sea by the Chisso Corporation, are more deadly than inorganic (which are nevertheless poisonous) as they are soluble in fat and so readily enter the food chain, and in Iraq hundreds of villagers were poisoned after mistakenly cooking and eating dressed seed cake.

Sources: Goldsmith and Hildyard 1990 pp. 32, 90, 102, 107–8; *Gourlay* 1988 pp. 144–7

Of these activities the most important, quantitatively, is the manufacture of pesticides, or, more correctly, since they are harmful to all forms of life, biocides (see Box 2.2). In 1986 world production was estimated at about 2,300,000 tonnes.[30] Although some of the most dangerous are now banned or severely restricted in the industrialised West, the hazardous waste produced in their manufacture has not disappeared, and production continues in many Third World countries. To the non-specialist the most disturbing feature is that almost all wastes contain residues of the final product. A 1989 study of biocide manufacture in India, for example, shows that production of DDT generates both a tarry waste that includes raw materials, reaction products, and highly acidic waste water containing sulphuric acid and 1.05kg of DDT for every tonne of DDT made. Similarly, the manufacture of HCH generates a waste that contains both the pesticide itself and highly poisonous benzene (now rated as a cause of leukemia) together with lime sludge used to 'neutralise' waste water containing HCH. The making of malathion leads to a waste containing 'complex organic pesticide residue', and the manufacture of carbaryl to a semi-solid tarry residue of carbaryl and intermediate products, while the production of DDT, HCH and carbaryl dusting powders produces a fine dust containing soapstone, HCH, DDT and carbaryl pesticides.[31]

On the inorganic side there are numerous wastes, both before and after industrial application. The Vetrocoke process for removing carbon dioxide, for example, produces a waste that contains about 120kg of arsenic per tonne, while recovery of the catalyst used in extracting metals from their ores leads to an aqueous waste containing 25 per cent sulphuric acid with small quantities of nickel, copper, zinc and iron in solution. Titanium dioxide, which was widely used in the manufacture of paints, paper, rubber and plastics, is produced either by the chloride process or the sulphate process. The former generates large quantities of iron salts as waste; the latter also produces considerable waste.[32] Concern over the disposal of waste from the industry so aroused the EC that a directive of February 1978 introduced strict controls aimed at eventually eliminating the resulting pollution. Also attracting EC attention was the Chlor-Alkali Electrolysis industry in which plants used alkali chlorides to produce chlorine, discharging a waste that contained mercury or its compounds.[33] In the metal finishing industry numerous processes are used for the surface treatment of metals, to protect them against corrosion, to modify their properties or for decoration. Among these are cleaning and degreasing, chemical and mechanical surface treatment, electroplating, chemical and electrolytic stripping, anodizing, galvanizing and chemical or electric polishing. These use a wide range of chemicals which eventually find their way into the resultant liquid, sludge or solid wastes. Redundant lead/tin plating solution, for example, contains compounds of both lead and tin with fluorine and boron, while acid strip solution is 40 per cent nitric acid, together with smaller quantities of sulphuric, acetic and phosphoric acids and dissolved nickel. Spent cadmium plating solution (now, in some countries, on the way out) contains cadmium, sodium hydroxide and sodium cyanide.[34]

Box 2.2 : Biocides/Pesticides

Biocides, literally 'life-killers', more commonly referred to as 'Pesticides', comprise, according to function, *Insecticides* (pest killers), *Herbicides* (weed killers) and *Fungicides* (used against plant diseases and moulds), together with such lesser known groups as *Nematicides* (used against eelworms and similar creatures), *Acaricides* (used against mites) and *Rodenticides* (used against rats).

Chemically they consist of a number of groups, the members of which usually have similar characteristics and are used for similar purposes: In *Chlorinated hydrocarbons* one or more of the hydrogen atoms of the hydrocarbon is replaced by chlorine. Because the resultant products do not occur in nature, the bacteria involved in the natural processes of decomposition and decay have difficulty in coping with them so that they tend to be persistent. Combined with a second characteristic — their ability to dissolve in fat, which enables them to concentrate in the fatty tissue of animals, increasing as they pass up the food chain from lesser to greater — they have caused considerable harm to wildlife. The most widely used, *p.p-dichlorodiphenyltrichloroethane*, invariably referred to simply as *DDT*, has been used throughout the world, causing the thinning of many birds' egg-shells and consequent failure to reproduce. *Hexachlorocyclohexane (HCH)*, ⇨

⬥ originally, if inaccurately known as BHC — benzene hexachloride — is especially toxic to fish and, in its most deadly form, *lindane*, has seriously harmed birds of prey and bats. *Chlordane* (and the very similar *heptachlor*) is absorbed through the skin of human beings, affecting the nervous system and leading eventually to death. Once in the environment, *aldrin*, classified by the WHO as 'highly hazardous', is converted into *dieldrin*, which played a role in the decline of the British otter and, with its closely related compounds, *endrin* and *telodrin*, was blamed for the decline in the Sandwich tern population of the North Sea. Finally, *Pentachlorophenol* is used as a general biocide against fungi, algae, molluscs and other organisms. All hydrocarbons are carcinogenic (cancer causing) to either human beings or animals; chlordane and pentachlorophenol are also teratogenic (causing defects in the offspring of an exposed mother), while chlordane and lindane have both been linked to the incidence of leukaemia. In view of the high toxicity of these substances it is not surprising that many are now subject to regulation. DDT, HCH, Lindane and Chlordane are banned in the USA, France and West Germany, though the UK and the USA did not finally ban Chlordane until 1988, and, while the UK placed a voluntary ban on DDT between 1974 and 1984, even now products containing it are still available. Pentachlorophenol is restricted in the USA, New Zealand and Canada but still available in the UK to people not trained to use it. Regulation of the 'drins' has varied considerably. Data that led the British Pesticides Advisory Committee to consider a ban unnecessary led the French to impose a ban in 1972, while West Germany instituted a series of increasingly stronger restrictions. In 1981 the EC banned the marketing of aldrin and dieldrin in plant protection products and in 1989 there was a final ban on the sale of all products containing dieldrin. This did not, of course, mean an end to the production of chlorinated hydrocarbon biocides and their associated waste. As the home markets closed, those of the Third World, especially countries undergoing a Green Revolution opened. In 1983 99 per cent of the 'drins' manufactured in industrialized countries, almost 5,000 tonnes, were exported, mostly to Third World countries where regulation was less strict or non-existent.

Carbamates are a group of organic nitrogen compounds, many of which are used as insecticides in areas where pests have become resistant to DDT. They range from the moderately toxic *carbaryl*, used in shampoos to kill head lice as well as in gardening and agriculture, to the highly toxic *aldicarb*, a suspected carcinogen, which has been found in drinking water in California and in wells on Long Island, New York. Recent research has linked it to the AIDS virus as its interference with the immune system makes people more vulnerable. In the UK aldicarb is classed as a poison, in the USA it is restricted (if still ⬥

✧ used illegally) and in the Philippines it is considered too dangerous for general use. Another carbamate, *zineb*, a recognised carcinogen and powerful skin irritant, is used as a fungicide. Carbamates are unselective and readily kill non-target organisms by attacking the nervous system.

Organophosphates (organophosphorus compounds), discovered during research into nerve gases and used mainly as insecticides and acaricides, inhibit the transmission of signals along the nerves, thus causing nausea, vomiting, twitching and diarrhoea, and lead to convulsions, coma and death. Because of their high toxicity and low selectivity they have produced devastating effects on wildlife, even if they are not as persistent as chlorinated hydrocarbons. *Malathion*, used to kill insect pests, while unselective and the cause of damage to wildlife, is not generally considered very toxic to human beings. *Dichlorvos*, used as a liquid in agriculture, is more familiar as the poison used in domestic fly-strips.

Phenoxy herbicides, hormone weedkillers, cause weeds to die through overgrowth. Originally thought not to be harmful to human beings because there were no immediate symptoms, there is now concern over the long-term effects. Known to be highly poisonous are *Paraquat*, which has been responsible for more poisonings than any other weedkiller and, though restricted in the UK, USA, Sweden, Finland, Denmark, New Zealand, Turkey and Israel, is still widely used in many Third World countries; and *Dinoseb*, which achieved worldwide notoriety when, in January 1984, 80 drums containing 16 tonnes of the weedkiller were swept overboard into the North Sea from the *Dana Optima* during force 12 storms. Of the more general herbicides, in 1969 a US commission concluded that *2,4-D* was likely to cause birth defects and recommended its restriction, a proposal so strongly contested by the manufacturers, Dow Chemicals, that *2,4-D remains one of the most widely used herbicides in the industrialized world. Controversy surrounds 2,4,5-T*, not only as an ingredient of the notorious Agent Orange used by the US in Vietnam, but over whether it is dangerous in itself or becomes so owing to contamination by highly toxic dioxins during manufacture. Taking a cautionary approach, Sweden has banned and the USA severely restricted its use. The official UK view, however, is that it is not harmful provided it is properly used and the dioxin content does not exceed 0.01 parts per million, a level twice that recommended by the EC.
Sources: Goldsmith and Hildyard 1990 pp. 17, 28, 35, 39−40, 49, 55, 91, 105, 123, 126−7, 129, 162−3; *Gourlay* 1988 pp. 137−8

The list could be continued, but we will conclude with two examples from the consumers' end of the process and glance at one of the more disconcerting products of industry. Car drivers may not have considered that storage tanks for leaded petrol at filling stations eventually produce a waste sludge that contains both organic lead compounds (tetraethyl and tetramethyl lead) and inorganic lead compounds, together with petroleum hydrocarbons and water. Owners of boats in increasingly popular marinas may likewise be unaware that redundant anti-fouling paint, applied to protect the hulls of craft from attack by marine organisms, is extremely hazardous in that it contains not only the sulphides of copper and mercury, together with cuprous oxide, but PCBs. In themselves PCBs are not waste; they only become waste when, at the end of their working lives, the objects of which they form part are 'no longer wanted' (see Box 2.3).

Mining and smelting

Extracting minerals inevitably leads to two forms of waste: 1) since by definition, mining consists of making holes or tunnels in the ground, the unwanted material extracted must be dumped somewhere; and 2) as the substances sought rarely exist in the form in which they are wanted (the nugget of pure gold weighing almost 70kg found in Victoria, Australia, in 1869 and the 500 ton lump of pure copper dug up in Michigan, USA, in 1856 are exceptions)[35] but occur as part of an ore from which they have to be smelted, or are encrusted with other matter that must be 'washed' away, this produces a second form of waste. Not surprisingly, extractive industries have rarely had a favourable reputation. As Georgius Agricola, author of the first mining textbook, *De Re Metallica*, published in 1556, put it:

> The strongest arguments of the detractors are that the fields are devastated by mining operations...the woods and groves are cut down, for there is need of an endless amount of wood for timbers, machines and the smelting of metals....Further, when the ores are washed, the water which has been used poisons the brooks and streams, and either destroys the fish or drives them away....Thus, it is said, it is clear to all that there is greater detriment from mining than the value of the metals which the mining produces.[36]

The intervening four and a half centuries have seen major changes in techniques, but whether the entrepreneur is the solitary gold prospector, albeit operating in their hundreds in present-day Amazonia, or a multinational corporation, such as Rio-Tinto-Zinc (RTZ), with interests in 40 countries, the waste continues to grow, as have the profits. Formed in 1962 by the merger of Rio Tinto Co., a late nineteenth-century enterprise to exploit the Spanish copper mines of that name, and Consolidated Zinc Corporation of the lead-zinc-silver mines at Broken Hill, Australia, RTZ, now a major producer of bauxite, gold, diamonds and uranium, acquired British Petroleum (BP) Minerals in June 1989 for an anticipated US$4.27m. The scale of its current operations can be judged from its 1988 turnover of £4.99bn, with BP Minerals at £673m, their respective profits for that year being £956m and £284m.[37] There is money in mining, if not for those on whose land the mines operate.

Box 2.3 : Polychlorinated Biphenyls (PCBs)

PCBs were first synthesised in 1881 but did not come into general commercial use until the 1930s. Characterized by low flammability, high heat-resisting capacity and low electrical conductivity, they were used in products as varied as fluorescent light bulbs and hydraulic fluid. Their main use, however, was for insulation in electrical transformers and capacitators. They are immensely stable and persistent so that, once released into the atmosphere, they may be around for hundreds of years. The only practical method of destroying them is incineration at temperatures above 1,200°C, a process not without its dangers as, if inadequately carried out, it can lead to the release of even more deadly dioxins and polychlorinated dibenzo-furans (PCDF).

The toxic effects of PCBs were recognized as early as 1936 but only fully appreciated in the late 1960s, when 1,684 Japanese became seriously ill after eating PCB-contaminated rice. PCBs can damage enzymes in human livers, cause neurological disturbances and find their way into breast milk, but they have caused greatest havoc among marine populations, particularly by affecting fertility. While birds lose their eggs through thinning of the shell and PCBs accumulate in the muscles of eels in British rivers, lakes and canals, mammals at the top of the food chain are most at risk (see Chapter 5).

No PCBs have been manufactured in the UK since 1977 when Monsanto, the only manufacturer, ceased production. In 1980, the British Government implemented a 1976 EC directive banning their use except in sealed equipment, but it has been estimated that 90 per cent of the UK's 20,000 transformers are in such poor repair that they regularly leak PCB insulating fluid, and that 69 per cent of the world's 1.2 million tonnes of PCBs produced are still in use, storage or landfills, and thus potentially dangerous. Optimistically, at the March 1990 Conference on the North Sea, the British Environment Minister, Chris Patten, announced a proposal to destroy all PCBs in industrial use in Britain by 1999.

Sources: Goldsmith and Hildyard 1988 pp. 198–9; *Brown, P.* 1989c; *Guardian* 10 August 1989, 8 March 1990

Coal

As a generator of waste, coal must rank among the more unfortunate sources of energy. Mining it leads to huge holes and tunnels in the ground and corresponding mountains of material removed, or, with open-cast production, to great gashes in the landscape; 'washing' it clean of impurities produces unwanted slurry; burning it leads to emissions of carbon dioxide that poison the atmosphere, and, with brown coal (lignite), as in Eastern Europe, a seeping pall of sooty smoke; in the end, one is left with the ash to dispose of. Nevertheless, despite other forms of energy, humanity goes on using coal. In 1986 China produced 23 per cent of the world's coal and North America a further 23 per cent with the USSR producing 16 per cent. All three areas used slightly less than they produced. Consumption rose by only 1.6 per cent, largely owing to low oil prices at the time, but the following year it increased by 3.4 per cent. It is unlikely that there will be any serious coal shortage between now and the end of the century. At 1986 consumption rates North America still has over 300 years' reserves and Europe over 200, as have Asia and Australia.[38]

Much of the world's coal is now obtained by open-cast methods as opposed to the deep mines of Victorian Britain. Australia and the USA started early in the century and open-cast mining now accounts for half the coal used in the USA. In Colombia and Venezuela all coal production is open-cast. Technically the method uses mechanical scrapers to strip the soil, subsoil and bedrock, collectively known as the overburden, to reach the seam, which, on average, is found at a depth of 150 metres. Soil and subsoil are separated and transferred to storage dumps or mounds, and hydraulic grabs or draglines using buckets through the seam are used to extract the coal. Up to 30 tonnes of overburden are removed for every tonne of coal extracted. In theory, the site is filled in after use and the soil returned. Unfortunately, storage greatly impoverishes it by reducing the number of organisms, especially worms. In many Third World countries, however, where environmental regulations are less strict than in the West, many mining companies simply move on or make a perfunctory attempt to clean up the site.

The greatest waste comes from the use of water, sprayed to keep down dust and to wash the coal, which results in a coarse refuse (chitter) and fine slurry (tailings). These were formerly dumped in rivers and streams, thus increasing acidity. In the West they are now placed in large settling ponds to allow the water and impurities to separate. The water is then returned to streams and the solid residue used in restoration.[39]

Among contemporary projects to be watched is that in Kalimantan, Borneo, Indonesia, where BP Minerals and Conzinc Riotinto of Australia (CRA) (49 per cent owned by RTZ; in short, the whole is now an RTZ project) have established a US$500m joint venture, Kaltim Prime Coal (KPC) to produce seven million tonnes of high grade steam coal by 1991. The scheme will use the truck-and-shovel technique, not dragline, and a 17km conveyor will take the coal to a wharf with facilities for loading ships of up to 180,000 tonnes. The whole industry is thus geared to export; it is also a threat to the last virgin rainforest in the region.[40]

Copper
The ancient Egyptians extracted copper from its ore by smelting, that is, heating the ore with charcoal in a fire to leave a spongy mass of metal that could be beaten into weapons, tools or ornaments. Modern methods add the ore to an aerated, frothing liquid containing a chemical 'collector' which enables mineral particles to cling to air bubbles on the surface, while the

waste is wetted and sinks.[41] The result is an undesirable waste of copper tailings.

Agricola's warning against poisoning brooks and streams is only too evident in their disposal. Copper, along with zinc, lead and cadmium, now pollutes many Australian rivers,[42] and in Chile copper tailings have led to 'high mortality among marine organisms, hindrance of harbour activities and recreation, and geomorphological coastal modifications'.[43] In short, they have spoilt the coast and ruined fisheries and leisure activities.

Two Third World examples aptly illustrate the dangers. In the Philippines the Marcopper Mining Corporation, a joint venture of Performance Investment Corporation (48 per cent of stock), formerly owned by Marcos with 28.2m shares and now government property, and Placer Development Ltd. of Vancouver (40 per cent of stock), established an open copper mine on a small island in 1960. When production began in 1969, tailings were dumped in a pond reserved for that purpose. Discovery of high-grade copper beneath the pond led to mining of that area and discharging wastes directly into the sea, with disastrous results.[44]

Events at the Panguna mine in Bougainville, Papua New Guinea, were even more dramatic as they affected the root of local culture — rights to the land. The mine is operated by Bougainville Copper Ltd. (BCL), in which CRA is a major shareholder, and provides 16 per cent of internal government revenue and 44 per cent of exports.[45] Its annual capacity is estimated at 550,000 tonnes of copper concentrate, which also contains significant quantities of gold and silver. In 1988 both its earnings (Australian $299m) and material mined (89.8m tonnes) reached record levels.[46]

The price of this commercial success was paid by the local Nasioi and Rorovana peoples, 10,000 square miles of whose land was alienated under a 1966 Act agreed with the then Australian administration holding the territory in trust on behalf of the United Nations. Following independence, the new Papua New Guinea (PNG) Government of Michael Somare took a tough line in renegotiating taxation and royalty payments but failed to secure adequate compensation of those who had lost their land, or to provide for its rehabilitation.

Events reached a climax after November 1988, when sabotage and unrest at the mine culminated in armed struggle between the guerrilla Bougainville Liberation Army and the company, backed by the PNG Government and supported by military aid from Australia. Bougainville, which, ethnically, belongs to the Solomon Islands and only found itself in PNG as part of the colonial spoils, has always fostered separatist movements, but the root cause of the rebellion was the destruction of the land. In May 1989 BCL was forced to shut down the mine as inoperable and at the end of the year, CRA, disturbed by losses of A$16.5m, announced that they were pulling out.[47]

Whatever the mine's ultimate fate, little can be done about the waste. In the ten years to 1983 768m tonnes of ore and waste were processed, approximately half (395m tonnes) being deposited in waste dumps in the Kawerong Valley, which connects with the Jaba Valley. Of the 373m tonnes of ore processed, 366m tonnes were deposited in the Jaba Valley, where half the tailings remained while the rest, rich in copper and sulphur, were carried into Empress Augusta Bay.[48]

Gold

A ton of ore is needed to obtain just over a third of an ounce (10 grams) of gold. The rest is unwanted waste, making gold extraction the most uneconomical form of production of a mineral of minimum utility. Today the old-fashioned gold prospector's method of panning, that is, swirling the dirt from the bed of a stream in a pan of water until the lighter gravel is washed out and the denser gold left,[49] is superseded by chemical methods that turn the 'waste' into 'hazardous waste'. Cyanide solution is pumped into a slurry of crushed, concentrated ore; the cyanide dissolves the gold, enabling its later recovery. The operation takes place either in a sealed vat (vat leaching) or in the open air (open-heap leaching) with the ground protected by an 'impermeable' polythene pad about one eighth of an inch thick. Most dangerous of all is 'solution mining', pouring the cyanide solution directly into the ground to permeate the ore and dissolve the gold, which is either collected downstream or pumped out of the ground. Nor is crushing and concentrating the ore without hazard, as it may liberate heavy metals, for example arsenic and lead, to dangerous levels, especially if, in the process, particles of waste become airborne.[50]

An alternative method is to use mercury. With the aid of motor pumps, divers or mechanical dredgers bottom sediments are removed from a river bed and, after concentration, amalgamated with mercury in large pans. In the process between 5 and 30 per cent of the mercury is lost or discharged directly into the river, while, in the final recovery of the gold by burning the amalgamate in pans on riverbanks or even in boats, up to 20 per cent of the mercury is released to the atmosphere.[51]

The greatest quantities of toxic waste from gold mining inevitably occur in the Third World: in Amazonia, where, in Brazil alone, more than 650,000 people are directly involved,[52] and where 45,000 miners, employed by large companies, using heavy machinery to destroy the rainforest, cut roads through the jungle and construct illegal airstrips, have occupied Yanomami tribal lands, bringing previously unknown diseases, alcoholism and prostitution to a forest people who have lost their gardens, their game, their fish and their water;[53] in Papua New Guinea, where the OK Tedi mine in Western Province, owned jointly by Broken Hills Proprietary (BHP), Amoco and a West German consortium, has discharged highly toxic tailings directly into the Fly River after one of the frequent earthquakes destroyed the site of the dam intended to contain them,[54] where a prospective clash between local landowners at Mt Kare in the Highlands and CRA, who have acquired prospecting rights, threatens another Bougainville, and where, at Lihir Island off the north-east coast, what has been described as the world's richest gold deposit outside South Africa, RTZ, on taking over from BP Minerals, have an 80 per cent share in the project and Niugini Mining 20 per cent. The prospect of using cyanide leaching to extract gold from a collapsed volcano offers possibilities of hitherto unknown forms of waste whose only foreseeable destination is the surrounding ocean.[55]

Uranium

Uranium is arguably not only the most deadly but also the most wasteful form of waste production. The ore contains only 0.1–0.2 per cent uranium metal, leaving 99.8 per cent of the mass, and 85 per cent of the radioactivity, as waste. These tailings continue to emit radon gas for thousands of years. Current disposal practice is to build a dam and cover the heaps with either clay or water to minimize escape of the gas. The process is not always effective. In Colorado, a centre of uranium mining, over 40 per cent of the houses have radon levels above safe limits.[56] Breaches of the dams also occur. In 1971 monsoon rains caused a breach in the tailings dam at Rum Jungle, Northern Territory, Australia; in February 1984, a million litres of radioactive liquid were deliberately released from ponds at the Mary Kathleen mine, Queensland, into a nearby creek during the wet season; and at Port Pine, South Australia, site of the military plant for Radium Hill mine, the tailings dams were left unfenced; children played and swam in them. According to the US Nuclear Regulatory Commission, radon emissions from tailings should not exceed two units per metre; at Mary Kathleen, following seepage through broken rock, emissions rose to 18 units.[57]

Uranium mining, in which Canada leads production for the West, followed by the USA, with other sources in South Africa, Namibia, France and Australia,[58] has two other deleterious aspects, which, if not directly the result of waste, cannot be ignored: first, the hazards undergone by mine-workers, with lung cancer in Canada 4.8 times that of the general population, while in the USA, statistics dating back to the 1930s show that half those employed in the mines eventually died of lung cancer;[59] second, mines tend to be situated in what, to governments, are more remote parts of their territory but which, in practice, are often lands of extreme importance to the original inhabitants, the Navaho in the USA or the Aborigines in Australia, for example, where conflicts have arisen over sacred burial sites. In 1989 environmentalists united with the local Jawoyn group to oppose re-opening the disused uranium mine at Coronation Hill, a conservation zone in the Kakadu National Park in Australia's Northern Territory. The government eventually reduced the 2,252 sq km, which, in 1986, BHP had won the right to dig, to 37 sq km and in June 1991 pronounced in favour of a ban on mining in the park.[60]

In India uranium is mined in the Singhbhum region of Bihar under highly unsatisfactory working conditions. At the Jaduguda mill tailings are dumped into a 25-hectare pond at the rate of 325,000 tonnes annually. The tailings are decanted and the fluid channelled into a nearby ravine, which also receives water discharged from the mine, containing uranium, radium and manganese.[61]

Conditions were little better in developed parts of the world. The

Jachymov uranium mine in Czechoslovakia, three miles south of the East German border and less than 30 miles from West Germany, was notorious. In the last century it provided the uranium that aroused the interest of Henri Becquerel, thus leading to some of the first experiments conducted by Marie Curie, but in the post-World War II era political prisoners condemned to work there after the early 1950s show trials called it 'hell on earth'. Although the mine was closed in 1964, radiation levels in the town are more than double those permissible in the West, especially where townspeople have helped themselves to building materials from the old mine works.[62] Of the eleven mines in Bohemia, which, according to the Chinese, provided the USSR with one-fifth of its uranium in the mid-1970s, only two will remain in operation by 1995. In former East Germany also, Chernobyl and the 1989 popular revolution have brought about cutbacks in uranium mining. The mine and processing plant at Crossen, Oberrothenbach, near the Czech border, will close before 1995, but the meadows of the Mulde river are too contaminated for reclamation, and radioactive slag heaps dominate the nearby town of Ronneburg. In September 1989 the Hungarian Government announced the closure of the country's only uranium mine in the Mecsek Hills, near Pécs in the south, after 30 years' working, during which shafts that started at 150 metres reached over 1,000 metres, making the cost of extraction at US$90 a kilogram uneconomic against a world price of US$30−70. The authorities are reportedly examining the possibility of turning the disused mine into a receptacle for waste from the nuclear power station at Paks, 60 miles to the north, which reprocesses all fuel elements from East European nuclear power stations. One can only hope that the scientific advice behind this suggestion is sound.[63]

Mining waste, and its impact, is too often ignored as a necessary evil. Whether it comes from phosphorite mines, as in Estonia, where its effects have still to be assessed,[64] or the search for diamonds, titanium and tin in the homelands of the Yanomami Indians of Amazonia,[65] the results are the same and occur in the most unexpected places. In Kenya, liquid effluents contain cyanide from mining and smelting operations;[66] in British Colombia, mine tailings from uranium mining pollute the north-east Pacific;[67] and, though the bottom fell out of the tin market in October 1985 and prices were almost halved, in the big tin-producing countries of Malaysia, Indonesia, Thailand, Bolivia and Brazil the waste from extraction remains.[68]

Agriculture and fish farming

Farming has always produced waste — the inevitable 'slurry' from cattle sheds, pig sties or hen coops and the leftover stubble when a crop has been harvested. But the greater part of present agricultural waste arises not because the farmer does not want it, but because he fails to use it, or at least uses it in such quantities that wastage is inevitable, for example, the artificial fertilizers and biocides that have become the hallmark of modern intensive farming. Nor does waste end here; the waste gas from paddy fields in rice production and from cattle in their normal functioning, methane, is now recognized as an important contributor to the Greenhouse Effect (see Waste Gases and their Makers below).

For the UK, intensive farming dates back to World War II when, isolated by Hitler's conquest of Europe and a naval blockade at sea, the country set about feeding itself, extending land under cultivation, expanding mechanization and ripping up traditional hedgerows as part of the same war effort by which iron railings were carted away for scrap. For the rest of the world the starting point was the Food and Agricultural Organization's (FAO) first World Food Congress of 1963, when, faced with expanding global population and the spectre of hunger, it launched its Freedom from Hunger campaign and followed it with the Indicative World Plan for Agricultural Development, the Green Revolution. The plan was based on the introduction of high-yielding varieties of cereals from hybrids developed by the International Rice Research Institute (IRRI) in the Philippines and a similar institution in Mexico. These were short-stemmed (to prevent being blown over by the wind) and quick-maturing, making possible the growth of three crops on the same land every year.

Only later, from the viewpoint of Third World peoples whom the scheme was allegedly intended to save from hunger, did the disadvantages become apparent:

- Only cereals, easily stockable and saleable on the world market, were affected; locally grown fruit, vegetables and other staple foods were outside the scheme.
- High yields were possible only on good soils and not on the marginal lands, where most people lived.
- Such yields occurred only with heavy, and increasing, applications of fertilizer.
- As the hybrids proved vulnerable to pests and diseases, farmers were forced to apply more and more pesticides, especially when the original pests acquired immunity.
- The need for irrigation water led to the construction of large-scale dams, leading to ejection of people from their land, increased water-borne diseases and salinization.
- The costs of chemical farming caused many to fall into debt, or, worse still, become landless labourers and drift to the city, while giving up traditional crops has led to a loss in genetic diversity and a corresponding increase in vulnerability to pests, which in turn leads to an ever greater application of pesticides.[69]

What, then, are these wastes that present agricultural methods inflict on the world?

Slurry is more dangerous than is generally appreciated, being 100 times more toxic than sewage, while silage effluent is as poisonous again.[70] In the UK, reports of slurry pollution rose from 61 in 1974 to 2,961 a decade later.[71]

Artificial fertilizers, designed to make crops grow, are wasted when applied in such quantities that they go beyond their targets, to enter the soil and so reach the water system. Even before this, production of fertilizers, based mainly on nitrogen or phosphorus, is itself a source of waste. An Indian example cites the nitrogenous fertilizer industry as a source of arsenic and chromate wastes, the latter being toxic to fish, a possible carcinogen and the cause of skin ulcers and kidney inflammation in human beings. The phosphatic fertilizer industry generates about five tonnes of wet phospho-gypsum for every tonne of fertilizer produced; in 1980 11 major plants generated some 3.5m tonnes of this byproduct, about a fifth of which was used to produce ammonium sulphate, while the rest, containing thousands of tonnes of heavy metals and toxic substances, such as cadmium, chromium, copper, lead, manganese and fluorides, was used as landfill or, as slurry, dumped in lagoons.[72]

World use of fertilizer has shown a remarkable increase from some 14m tonnes in 1950 to 57m in 1970 and an estimated 143m for 1989. Use of nitrogen fertilizer more than doubled between 1970 and 1985. (31.8m tonnes to 69.9m) while that of phosphate fertilizer rose by almost a third (25.3m to 33.4m). As nitrogen fertilizer use in OECD countries over this period rose by only 32 per cent, while consumption of phosphate fertilizer actually fell by 2 per cent,[73] the greater proportion of these increases would appear to be in Third World countries following Green Revolution policies, where less adequate technology can lead to greater waste.

Data on pesticide use are less adequate. The world market reached an estimated US$18 million in 1987 with Brazil, India and Mexico the leading consumers.[74] When Rachel Carson published *Silent Spring* in 1962, she recorded that production of pesticide active ingredients in the USA had risen from 124.3m pounds in 1947 to 637.7m in 1960. By 1988 the EPA maintained that production for the same range of products was 1,500m with US actual usage at 1,090m pounds. If wood preservatives (fungicides), disinfectants and sulphur are added, the figure for US usage becomes 2,700m. Excluding these three categories, and assuming that US production is about a quarter of the world's total, then the earth as a whole must receive about 6,000m pounds of these products.[75]

In Box 2.2, we surveyed the major pesticides and their characteristics. Two questions remain — the extent to which pesticide spraying produces waste, and the deadliness of the pesticides in use, particularly in countries where environmental regulations are lax or non-existent.

Pesticides, by definition, are intended to kill pests. They are wasted when they fail in this objective. We saw above that, as pests become immune, greater quantities of pesticide or more deadly pesticides are applied, leading to waste that may be carried away by the wind, remain on the crops, or fall to the ground, whence it may be swept by rain into surface water or leach into underground aquifers. Obviously it is extremely difficult to discover how much is lost. According to one estimate, a billion gallons of crop sprays were poured on to the British countryside in 1986, of which approximately one fifth, two hundred million gallons, would drift.[76] The scientific explanation is that droplets less than 100 microns in size (a micron is a millionth of a metre) become unstable and are prone to drifting. The Soil Association argue that as little as 1 to 5 per cent of the quantity actually sprayed is sufficient to do the job. Most fields are sprayed many times, and even winter cereal crops have four or five applications. Airborne spraying accounts for only 2 per cent of the total, but there are grounds for believing that, because of the shortness of the spraying season, many cowboy operators cut corners in their activities.[77]

Even when spray drifts, or is deliberately and often illegally discharged, so that it affects human beings, there is the further problem, from the viewpoint of legal action, of establishing a connection between cause and effect. A blood test is necessary within 48 hours. Documents compiled by the British Agricultural Inspectorate reveal that, in 1985, at least 327 people were involved in 230 incidents investigated by the inspectors. Fewer than half the incidents were officially confirmed, partly because the inspectorate, itself understaffed, arrived too late to gather the evidence. Examples included schoolchildren who became ill when a cloud of spray used on a neighbouring wheat field drifted in through the windows, two children playing in their garden who were covered in pesticide sprayed from a tractor in the next field, a pensioner sprayed without warning from a helicopter, and seven golfers sprayed from an aircraft. The inspectorate's memorandum of 18 June 1986 stated blandly:

> It has been decided nationally that [the inspectorate] will not investigate complaints about crop spraying unless there is at least a suggestion that a person's health has been affected. Cases where people have been thought to be affected, and any others which appear to have a real potential for political repercussions, will normally need to be investigated, but being as economical of resources as possible.[78]

Presumably the only certain way to get your case investigated is to ensure that there will be 'political repercussions'.

If this is the situation in an advanced Western country, it must inevitably be worse in Third World countries where pesticides leave not merely waste, but deadly waste, for many of the older pesticides, now banned or restricted in the West for their toxicity, are still in use. In India, for example, where pesticide use increased from about 2,000 tons annually in the fifties to more than 80,000 tons in the mid-eighties, while the area affected rose from 6 million hectares of cropland to 80m, DDT, HCH (BHC) and malathion account for the bulk of consumption in crop spraying and also form the base for public-health sector programmes. The first two are banned from use in the USA and restricted in many European countries, though the ban does not extend to their manufacture, or their export. In 1976 approximately 30 per cent of US pesticide exports were of products prohibited in the US; for example heptophos, regarded by the WHO as 'extremely hazardous', has been exported to Third World countries, including India, under the brand name Phosvel. As for spraying, whether in anti-malarial public health work or on farms, since few workers use either gloves or face masks, this must rank as one of the highest occupational hazards in the world. A survey of farm workers in Gujarat revealed that they were not provided with face masks, only half of them covered their nose and mouth with a cloth, and a fifth failed to wash afterwards. It is not surprising that a 1965 report maintained that the accumulation of DDT in the body tissue of Indians was the highest in the world.[79]

Ironically, increased use of pesticides has led to diminishing returns. By 1980 Gujarat cotton farmers needed to spray their fields 20 to 30 times more often than before; in Maharastra, expenditure on chemicals has risen 340 per cent since 1954 without increasing the average yield; and in Andra Pradesh, with the highest pesticide use of an annual 15,000 tonnes, at least 15 species of pests have become resistant to all commonly used pesticides.[80] So much for the Green Revolution.

Elsewhere the same policies are in operation. In East Africa, aerial spraying of DDT on cotton crops is extensive in Kenya, Mozambique and parts of Madagascar. Products containing DDT and dieldrin (see Box 2.2) are sprayed aerially to control tsetse fly in Kenya, Somalia, Tanzania and Mozambique. DDT is used to disinfect harbours in Kenya, and unsafe herbicides such as 2,4-D and 2,4,5-T are still used in all four countries.[81] The application of pesticides to harbours needs come as no surprise. In Britain, of the 26.5m kilograms of active ingredient used, the equivalent of a quarter of a pound per head of population, one of the major users is British Rail. Vast quantities are sprayed on the tracks to keep them clear of weeds.[82] Cynics have been known to suggest that, with more trains, the weeds would have little chance to grow!

The trouble with fish
Modern technology has brought about a revolution in fishing similar to that in agriculture. Two techniques, at opposite ends of the spectrum, namely the use of driftnets in deep-sea fishing and the rapid growth of fish farms in coastal waters or inland valleys, are not only disturbing in themselves but sources of highly dangerous forms of waste.

Traditional fishing nets were made from hemp, cotton or flax. Because of their fibre size they could be detected visually and acoustically by diving birds and sea mammals, which could avoid becoming ensnared. If lost, or discarded, they would sink and rot away. Modern monofilament nets, made from extremely fine plastic, float overnight like a ghostly curtain, 40 miles long and dangling 15 metres below the surface, entrapping everything in their path until hauled in next day. In the Pacific the Japanese red squid fleet sets up to 30,000 miles of monofilament nets every night for seven months of the year. It is estimated that 100,000 seals, dolphins and turtles and perhaps half a million albatrosses tangle to death in the nets, while the Japanese high-seas salmon fishery kills up to three-quarters of a million puffins, shearwater, dublets and other sea birds every year. These are the hazards of 'normal operations'. According to the International Maritime Organization (IMO), discarded fishing nets, the industry's waste, are responsible for the deaths of up to 10 per cent of North Pacific fur seals.[83] And the practice looks set to continue. When 20 South Pacific nations met in Wellington, New Zealand, in November 1989 and signed a convention to exclude drift netting from their territorial waters and ban use of the nets by signatories, the two largest users refused. Japan with a fleet of 20 vessels (60 the previous year) argued that there was no evidence that the species most at risk, albacore tuna, faced extinction, while Taiwan, with 24 vessels (also 60 the previous year), pulled out of the conference, to announce later that it would halt drift-netting operations if Japan did, a safe enough offer in the face of Japan's statement that 'there was no possibility'. Not surprisingly, their reaction to the South Pacific Forum Fisheries Agency's assessment that albacore tuna could vanish in two years provoked a comment from the Australian delegation that they refused 'to accept any evidence until all the fish are gone'.[84]

Of the 30,000 miles of driftnets put out by Japan nightly, it is estimated that ten miles are lost each night.[85] Simple multiplication suggests that, at the end of the season, some 2,000 miles of waste nets are drifting throughout the region on their insidious trail.

In contrast, the newly developed farming of salmon, particularly in sea inlets such as Scottish lochs or Norwegian fjords, shows every prospect of thriving. In Scotland even the more remote waters now support huge rafts to which are attached the cages packed with Atlantic salmon. In 1984 the Scottish farms produced a mere 2,500 tonnes of fish; in 1988 production had risen to 19,500 tonnes; the forecast for 1990 shows an exponential increase to 54,000 tonnes.[86] Only Norway, with 747 fish farms along the coast and applications flooding in, exceeds this, having reached the 80,000 tonnes figure in 1989 and, with over 90 per cent of farmed salmon and trout earmarked for export, earned itself US$320 million in 1987.[87]

In Britain the small entrepreneur has already been taken over by the big food conglomerates, including Unilever and Booker McConnell. UK salmon and trout farming are now valued at some £100m annually compared with the £400m for conventionally trawled fish caught in 1988.[88] By the end of 1989 there were 460 coastal salmon farms and 400 onshore trout farms in Britain. The salmon farms contain between 50,000 and 500,000 salmon in rafts of cages that at times are as large as several football pitches.[89] To feed the fish the Scottish industry alone will need 184,000 tonnes of sand eels, sprats and other prey essential to wild salmon. Compressed into pellets, the sand eels are not as nourishing as when fresh, so each pellet contains a supplement of 15 vitamins, 11 minerals and a synthetic colouring to make the fish pink rather than 'hatchery grey'. The fact that this chemical, canthaxanthin (E161g), is banned in the USA suggests that we are reaching a 'danger zone' in the process.

The fish and the cages are kept clean with chlorine, sodium hydroxide, iodophors [a solution of iodine] and calcium oxide. Disease is kept at bay with formaldehyde, malachite green and four common antibiotics. *No one knows what the combined effects of these substances might be, but the use of another chemical, Nuvan, is giving cause for alarm.*[90] (my stress)

Nuvan, or Aquagard, is the trade name for a pesticide containing dichlorvos (see Box 2.2), now listed among 23 other 'Red List' chemicals which the DoE wishes to eliminate. Dichlorvos is needed to overcome the lice to which crowded salmon become extremely susceptible. The snag is that dichlorvos is highly toxic to other forms of sea life, a fact which, though known and accepted, did not prevent the Ministry of Agriculture's Veterinary Products Committee from disregarding DoE advice and, in July 1989, approving its use for a further year.[91]

At this point the question of waste becomes crucial. As with the spraying of pesticides on land, there is an inevitable surplus that fails to make its target. In practice, according to observers, the average fish farmer in Scotland doses his stock with Nuvan every three or four weeks by putting a tarpaulin round the cage for an hour or two, then flushing out the contents. The difference between this and aerial spray is that it is obvious where the residue will go — into the water and so to the seabed. But this is not the only waste travelling this path. According to one study, for every 200 tons of food fed to the fish, 40 tons fall to the bottom as waste and about 3 tons of this wasted food consists of nitrogen compounds.[92] Nor is waste food the end of the story. There is also waste from the fishes themselves, which in one respect resembles that from human beings — it is rich in nitrogen and phosphorus, some of which is dissolved in the water, while the rest falls as small particles. Ackefors and Enell have investigated the respective contributions of nitrogen and phosphorus from fish farming and other sources in Sweden and concluded that 'the nutrient load from aquaculture is obviously negligible in comparison with other nutrient sources'. They add that 'local effects on coastal areas can, however, be of importance'.[93] Whenever scientists use the word 'local' to describe effects one immediately recalls that the *Exxon Valdez*, like the *Amoco Cadiz* before it, was the cause of what, in global terms, is only a *local* catastrophe. Comparisons can often be framed in comforting terms. Fish farmers will be relieved to learn that 'rain over the sea area surrounding Sweden adds about 140 times more nitrogen than the production of 40,000 tons of trout or salmon' and that the 'phosphorus input from rain is about 20 times greater than the load from 40,000-ton fish production'.[94] The receiving waters still have to put up with both forms of waste, and, in Britain, a highly undesirable dose of Nuvan is added for good measure.

The nuclear sector

The nuclear industry's origins in the production of the atomic bomb have by and large determined its attitude to the non-nuclear world. The industry, whether civilian or military, owes its existence to the basic instability of the uranium atom. When neutrons, tiny particles much smaller than atoms, strike the nucleus (central core) of the atom, they cause it to split (nuclear fission) and, in so doing, release huge amounts of energy. The energy can be used for destructive or peaceful purposes — in the atomic bomb or the nuclear reactor. In the latter, fuel assemblies, rods or thin tubes containing pellets of uranium dioxide, are stacked in vertical bundles with spacers to separate them. The energy generated is controlled by withdrawal or insertion of the rods, and used to heat water, the steam from which drives a generator to produce electricity. A small handful of uranium can allegedly provide as much electrical energy as 70 tons of coal or 390 barrels of oil, while 3 kilograms of uranium a day are enough to operate a power station able to supply a city of a million people.

Since reactors generate large quantities of heat, they must be prevented from overheating. The method used gives the reactor its name: Advanced Gas-cooled Reactors (AGRs), first built in Britain, use carbon dioxide gas as a coolant; in Pressurized Water Reactors (PWRs), the most common throughout the world, the reactor is cooled by water under high pressure, which does not boil, but which then passes on heat to a second, non-pressurized water circuit that boils to produce steam and so drive a generator.[95]

How, then, does waste arise, and what are its characteristics? We must guard against being deceived by terminology, for what is normally referred to as radioactive waste is only part of the unwanted product. Waste is broadly classified according to the danger it presents from radiation, that is, the discharge of different types of rays which inevitably accompanies all nuclear activity. All radiation is harmful in that, depending on the quantity, nearness to the source and the means by which the radiation is absorbed, for example, externally or internally, it can affect living creatures, including human beings. Low-level waste (LLW) consists mainly of discarded clothing, gloves, wrappings and worn-out equipment. Intermediate-level waste (ILW) includes irradiated cladding from around nuclear fuel, reactor components and various process residues, resins and filters, which emit more powerful and penetrating gamma rays. High-level waste (HLW), which includes a reactor's spent fuel, though by comparison small in quantity, for example, a plant generating 1,000 megawatts of electricity produces only two cubic metres a year, is lethal; a person standing 20ft away from a small amount of such waste for ten minutes would have only a 50 per cent chance of survival. What is more, its components, especially when enriched uranium and moderators, such as graphite, are used to slow down neutrons and so increase their chances of further fission, include products such as plutonium, strontium and caesium whose rate of radioactive decay ensures that the waste remains dangerous for thousands of years.[96]

Decay is measured in terms of 'half-life', that is, the period over which *half the material* will have decayed. Thus a gram of radium-226 will be reduced to half a gram after 1600 years (its half-life), to a quarter of a gram after twice that period (3200 years) and to an eighth of a gram after 4800 years.[97] Decay may also lead to the production of 'daughter products' with half-lives that are considerably longer than the original substance. Thus thorium-234, with a comparatively short half-life of 24.1 days, decays, through a short, intermediate stage, to uranium-234 with a half-life of 250,000 years.[98] From this perspective HLW becomes a distinctly more sinister component of our future. If it is any consolation, natural uranium has a half-life of 405 billion years, or roughly the age of the Earth.[99]

In practice, these wastes are supplemented by others generated during the nuclear process. In the first place, there are the radioactive tailings from uranium mining considered earlier, while the actual operation of nuclear reactors leads to two further types of waste, which, because they do not remain as residues for disposal, tend to escape inclusion. While the fuel rods are at work inside the reactor, by-products begin to accumulate. Solids such as caesium, strontium and plutonium either remain in the chamber or, as particles, are (in theory) prevented from escaping into the atmosphere by means of filters. Waste gases, however, know no such restrictions; instead of 'waste', however, they have become 'emissions'. In the UK alone such emissions include strontium-90, caesium-137, krypton-85, argon-41 and tritium from the Sellafield complex, tritium oxide and inert gases from Winfrith and Harwell, radon-220, radon-222 and tritium from Amersham International plc and argon-41 from nuclear power stations.[100]

In addition, stations built for convenience of supplies on rivers or the coast, operate a thermal opening for discharging used (and contaminated) water, and pipelines for highly contaminated water from storage ponds and washing-out operations.

Finally, owners of nuclear power stations are faced with the greatest waste problem of all, that is, getting rid of the reactor, and any stored waste, at the end of the reactor's useful life. It was the costs of decommissioning, previously glossed over in discussions of nuclear power, that eventually persuaded the British Government that privatization of the industry was impossible. There would be no takers, certainly not for the older Magnox reactors now nearing the end of their useful lives, because profits would not cover essential expenses. The problem threatens to become one of the major waste disposal issues in the remaining years of this century and the first decade of the next.

Despite this, supporters of nuclear power continue to play down the waste issue. Zhu and Chan, for example, argue that, of the 4 million cubic metres of toxic waste produced annually in the UK, only 1.1 per cent is radioactive, and of this small amount 88.8 per cent is characterized as LLW, 11.1 per cent as ILW and only 0.1 per cent, a mere 0.0011 per cent of the total, as HLW.[101] In their view, the nuclear industry places emphasis 'upon demonstrating that all radioactive wastes, even the most highly radioactive wastes, can be safely isolated for the required time period from man and the environment'.[102] And in the British House of Commons, the then Environment Undersecretary, Virginia Bottomley, poured scorn on the 'common misconception that there were vast amounts of radioactive waste awaiting disposal. By the year 2030 all the radioactive waste would be the equivalent of only two to three weeks' domestic production. Much of it was low-level waste which could be handled with gloves. High-level, heat-generating waste, keeping its radioactivity for centuries, would by the year 2000 be only enough to fill two large rooms'.[103] While the 'required time period' has become the more precise, if still vague, 'centuries', one would like to know in what ways the radioactive waste is 'equivalent' to domestic and how 'large' is a 'large room'.

The plain fact is that, having persuaded themselves that reprocessing would 'solve' the waste problem, the nuclear industry, as Lord Marshall, former chairman of the Central Electricity Generating Board (CEGB), eventually admitted, preferred to shut its eyes to the difficulties that lay ahead and is now faced with a question to which it has no answer. Cynthia Pollack sums up the situation:

> The Nuclear Energy Agency in Paris projects that nearly 160,000 metric tons of spent fuel will have accumulated in countries belonging to the Organization of Economic Co-operation and Development (OECD) by the year 2000. Existing utility holding ponds are not large enough to accommodate this increase, nascent away-from-reactor storage techniques are unlikely to be sufficiently developed and permanent repositories i.e. deep underground mines in appropriate geological strata, will probably be stalled by political and technical obstacles.[104]

What are the facts? In October 1989, despite increased opposition in the post-Chernobyl era, 31 countries had 531 nuclear power reactors in operation or under construction. In 67 countries, 356 research reactors were in operation, under construction or planned, with 239 units in 'shutdown status' at the end of 1988. In addition, nearly 100 'nuclear facilities' were in various stages of being decommissioned in 17 countries.[105]

In the USA alone, at the end of 1989, there were approximately 110 commercial reactors and over 100 defence-related or smaller research reactors 'on line', with 21,000 tonnes of radioactive waste currently stored at nuclear plants and being added to annually at the rate of 2,000 tonnes. The cost of decommissioning spent reactors and carrying out essential environmental clean-ups at numerous sites is estimated at anything between $80bn and $120bn.[106] In practice, the waste continues to be left in storage ponds as one proposed disposal plan after another is eventually rejected as unsuitable.

In the USSR, where, as in the UK and the USA, nuclear power for civilian purposes is only 40 years old, there were, at the beginning of 1989, 47 reactors supplying 13.6 per cent of the country's electricity. Half of these were PWRs, the remainder BWRs (Boiling Water Reactors), similar to the ill-fated Chernobyl model. Plentiful supplies of uranium have so far made reprocessing of spent fuel unnecessary and thus helped to cut down waste.[107] The Soviets, however, at least in the early days, were considerably more cavalier in their treatment of waste, simply dumping it in lakes and rivers until the situation became intolerable. From 1955 onwards they adopted the policy of storing HLW in special concrete underground tanks lined with steel.[108]

The world's third largest 'nuclear economy', France, with 34 900-MW reactors and 8 of the larger type under construction, despite evidence of oversupply, generates more than 70 per cent of the country's electricity and, until recently, had acquired an image of success. This was distinctly dented at the end of 1989 when Electricité de France (EDF) was forced to admit that the previous 12 months had been financially 'disastrous', while the leaking of a report by Philippe Rouvillois, since appointed head of the Commissariat for Atomic Energy (CEA) and the publication of a second report by Pierre Tanguy, chief inspector of nuclear safety at EDF, only increased public anxiety about the future, not least in Britain. Cutting costs by building reactors to a common design doubtless contributed to economic success, but it also ensured that major design errors or faults, such as damage to tubes in steam generators, would proliferate throughout the industry. The Tanguy report attacks the reassuring French official estimates that an accident on the scale of the 1957 Windscale fire or the 1969 Three Mile Island near-disaster is likely to happen only once in every 100,000 years of reactor operation by suggesting that, 'in the present situation of EDF's reactors', the chances over the next 20 years amount to 'several per cent'. With six large reactors at Gravelines, 30 miles across the Channel and less than 100 miles from London, this is disconcerting news for the British, especially as there are seven other and larger reactors along the Channel coast, giving a productive capacity of nearly twice that of the entire British industry.

The Rouvillois' report is much broader and, while arguing that the existing prog.amme cannot be halted because of the effect on manufacturers, sees the key to continued public acceptance in solving the problem of waste disposal. It, therefore, recommends that sites for underground storage should be found and used quickly 'to avoid any build-up of public opinion against the choice'. The Prime Minister, Michel Rocard, responded by witholding the report from members of parliament, then ordering a moratorium for at least a year on the finding of new sites in response to rising public concern. Finally, on decommissioning, the report notes the absence of joint procedures for co-operation between different parties concerned and concludes that only the outlying areas of plants can be removed, the reactors themselves remaining untouched under costly guard.[109]

The country with the world's fourth largest nuclear industry, Japan, with 37 reactors generating 27 per cent of the country's electricity, has also felt the effect of people's power. The emergence of women as a majority force in the anti-nuclear movement shook the male-dominated establishment. In Tokyo a demonstration on the first anniversary of Chernobyl attracted around 2,500 people; the following year 20,000 attended, organized by 150 local groups.[110]

During the 25 years of its existence, the Japanese nuclear industry has accumulated about half-a-million 200-litre drums of LLW, mostly asphalt, clothing and liquids, which is at present stored on site pending the building of a repository. High-level waste, growing at the rate of 700 tons a year and at present sent to the UK or France for reprocessing, must eventually be returned to Japan, where the plutonium produced will be used for its Fast Breeder Reactor programme, due to begin in 1992. Japan's own reprocessing plant, scheduled to begin operations in 1997, was still, by mid-1990, awaiting approval for construction to start. A major problem is ensuring the safe return of the reprocessed plutonium. Since 1969 ships have carried spent fuel to Sellafield, whose contract until 2002 is worth £2.5bn to British Nuclear Fuels (BNF); but returning the plutonium is a different matter. Japan planned to reduce the risk of hijack by using air transport with non-stop flights over the North Pole by Boeing 747s, but the US administration effectively stopped this, when, after a series of tests on proposed containers that would survive a plane crash, it finally refused to set specifications. It also blocked proposals for sea transport on the grounds that these would need an armed escort. As Japan's constitution prohibits it from maintaining land, sea and air forces, a condition that has not prevented the building of 60 warships for 'self-defence', the Japanese gave the task to their coastguard force, the Maritime Safety Agency. The depressed ship-building industry was delighted with the news; it had the task, backed by 20bn yen (£90m) of building a new armed escort ship capable of sailing round the world nonstop.[111]

Like other countries, Japan also faces the prospect of decommissioning older power stations, the first being the Tokei reactor, north-east of Tokyo, possibly as early as 1996. Estimates that this will cost 30bn yen (£130m), which the industry must find for itself, are considered optimistic; they are less than half the British estimates for its own similar Magnox reactors.

Meanwhile, the British suddenly realized that the world may not come to an end in the year 2000 or even 2030 and that increased decommissioning would lead to even greater waste. In August 1990 the DoE produced revised estimates of waste from BNF operations at Sellafield. Operational LLW from reprocessing were upped from 560,000 cubic metres to 732,000 cubic metres, decommissioning wastes from 50,000 to over a million (to include wastes arising after the year 2030), while corresponding figures for ILW rose from 107,000 cubic metres to 127,000 (operational) and from 47,000 to 128,000 (decommissioning).[112] When estimates of waste increase by more than a million cubic metres overnight, comment is superfluous.

Lesser-known generators of radioactive waste
In 1983 a British comparative research project led to the surprising discovery that levels of radioactive iodine-125 were as high in the thyroids of both

animals and human beings in the 'safe' area of Weybridge, Surrey, as in the neighbourhood of 'contaminated' Sellafield. The isotope occurred in local drinking water, supplied from the River Thames, and was also found in swans living on the river.

The source of this contamination, officially confirmed some seven years later by a research team from London's St Bartholomew's Medical College, was a group of organizations, hospitals, research centres and industry, allowed to dispose of low-level radioactive waste, usually by flushing it down the lavatory or sink. Hospitals used radioactive isotopes in cancer treatment, research institutes in tracing chemicals in experiments, while industry applied them in manufacturing materials such as luminous paint for clock dials. The levels of iodine actually found were extremely small, if sufficiently high to cause an increase of 1 per cent in the number of cancer cases in the Greater London area. The disturbing feature is that, while we know that some 181 organizations in London and about 1,600 non-nuclear institutions in Britain as a whole are legally permitted to dispose of radioactive waste in this way, no one knows the actual quantities of waste involved. While discharges from nuclear power stations are fixed, if at times somewhat arbitrarily, by law, non-nuclear sources, licensed under the 1960 Radioactive Substances Act, are not only not obliged to reveal the type and quantity of radioactive waste discharged but, under the secrecy clause, actually forbidden to do so. The Government does at least publish a list of licence holders, which, in addition to major hospitals, includes such well-known companies as Kodak, IBM, Fisons, British Telecom, Marconi, Shell UK Ltd., Colgate-Palmolive Ltd., ICI and Unilever. Control is exercised through the Inspectorate of Pollution which, in 1987, announced that new applicants would have to produce a full environmental impact assessment. Officially the Inspectorate monitors disposal by twice yearly checks, but a spokesman admitted that, because of staff shortages, it was possible to make visits only once every three years. An internal report by the former director, Brian Ponsford, revealed that only 35 people were involved in inspecting sites licensed under the 1960 Act and that, of 1,900 inspections considered necessary for effective regulation, only 850 were likely to be carried out in 1988/89. Other reports from the former Radiochemical Inspectorate reveal examples of mismanagement, bad record-keeping so that it was impossible to tell whether the organization was complying with discharge limits, and even examples of theft or loss of radioactive substances.

The secrecy that has surrounded the nuclear industry from its inception has found worthy successors to the founding fathers of Windscale, Aldermaston and Harwell. Whatever happens, the public must be kept in the dark. There is, however, one major discrepancy that demands immediate investigation. While the National Radiological Protection Board (NRPB) produced its usual anodyne assessment in its 1988 report: 'the radiological impact of these disposals is negligible compared with those by the nuclear industry', the independent Holliday Report of 1984 informs us that:

about 87% of the radiation to which the population of the UK is exposed comes from natural sources....The remaining 13% is manmade resulting from the treatment of cancer and medical diagnosis (11.4%), fallout from atmospheric weapons testing in the 1950s and 1960s (0.5%) and routine power plant operations and uses in scientific research, defence and industry (1.1%).

The figures refer to exposure, not to quantities discharged, but they are sufficiently disparate to suggest the need for an explanation.[113]

What happens in Britain presumably also takes place throughout the remainder of the industrialized world and, to a lesser extent, in the Third World. Without even the legal guardianship of the NRPB and the monitoring, however ineffective, of the pollution inspectorate, the quantities and destinations of these radioactive wastes remain hidden from public view — at least until drinking water is affected and another 'mystery disease' makes the local headlines.

Of subs, satellites and space

There are yet other nuclear reactors at work, in the earth, oceans and in the sky, each generating its own waste, contaminating its surroundings and ultimately requiring disposal, if it does not dispose of itself meanwhile. In addition, there are nuclear weapons which, whatever category one assigns them to in their 'active' state, become waste if the vessel carrying them is lost.

Outside the American and Russian military establishments no one can write with certainty about this most secretive of all nuclear sectors. Three reports published between March 1988 and June 1989 are hardly reassuring. An internal analysis carried out by the Royal Naval College at Greenwich, and obtained by the *Guardian* newspaper, revealed that, during their first 16 years of operation (1962–78) nuclear reactors in British submarines were involved in 712 'incidents'. Independent assessment of these by the US Institute of Policy Studies suggested that 'probably no more than a dozen were significant in that they resulted in the release of radioactive material', but strongly contested the Pentagon claim that 'in over 3,100 reactor years of US naval reactor operations there has never been a reactor accident or a problem resulting in fuel damage', while estimating the Soviet incident rate at 200 over ten years. One problem common to all navies is that at times safety at sea necessitates running a reactor to maintain power in circumstances when, on land, it would be shut down. Moreover, because there is no readily available 'public' to suffer the consequences, military personnel being by definition expendable, some safety features are dispensed with.[114]

Using documents obtained under the US Freedom of Information Act, in May 1988 the Institute of Policy Studies and Greenpeace published an inventory of nuclear weapons at sea which revealed that they were more extensive than previously supposed. Between them, the Western and Soviet naval forces possess about 16,000 nuclear weapons, almost a third of the world total; these are carried on some 1,100 ships and submarines and nearly 3,200 naval aircraft which can deliver or transport them. Britain alone has some 128 strategic nuclear weapons and 198 tactical warheads aboard 30 nuclear-capable ships and aircraft, including four Polaris submarines, three aircraft carriers and 23 destroyers and frigates. The report argued that the most dangerous group comprised sea-launched cruise missiles, the numbers of which had risen to 550 on 75 surface ships and 94 submarines of the Russian and American navies.[115]

In June 1989 the same sources published a further report on naval accidents between 1945 and 1988. This covered some 2,000 incidents of which 345 involved the Royal Navy, and included 15 sinkings, 129 collisions, 86 fires, 28 explosions and 25 groundings. Submarines were involved in 108 accidents, and aircraft carriers in 40. Obviously not all these involved nuclear vessels, though there have been eight serious fires aboard Royal Navy submarines since 1972, including one aboard *HMS Warspite* in Liverpool docks in 1976. Ten major US and Soviet mishaps have resulted in 50 sunken nuclear warheads and eight discarded reactors, including the twin reactors aboard the Soviet Mike class submarine that sank in the Norwegian Sea on 7 April 1989.[116]

A final problem awaits all users of nuclear vessels — what to do with them when the reactor reaches the end of its life and the submarine, like the land-based power station, needs to be decommissioned. In October 1987 Britain had only one such nuclear submarine on its hands, *HMS Dreadnought*, moored at Rosyth dockyard, Fife, Scotland, but has still to decide. Six months later, with the first fleet approaching the end of its active service, the Ministry of Defence (MoD) admitted that, beyond removing the reactors, it did not know how it would dispose of the contaminated hulls. Suggestions that the ministry had not considered the problem when the submarines were built merely elicited the reply that there were enough problems to think about in the 1950s.[117] In August 1989 the MoD, having run out of storage space for nuclear waste but needing it for the ILW from refitting and decontaminating operational submarines, announced proposals for two new stores to meet its requirements for the next 20 years, one at Rosyth, a mile from the town, the other in the middle of Plymouth, 50 yards from the main London–Penzance railway line. Meanwhile, the *Dreadnought* is still tied up at Rosyth, making it difficult to decide which set of operators is the less successful at coping with radioactive waste — the MoD or the CEGB.

There are two related problems of waste in space: the use of nuclear reactors or plutonium in satellites as large as a London bus, and, at the other end of the scale, the ever-increasing quantities of debris, estimated, according to one count, as 60,000 or more invisible and undetectable, but none the less lethal, fragments hurtling round the earth at up to 11,000 miles an hour. In the 30 years between *Sputnik I* in 1957 and the end of 1987 there were up to 3,000 launches and 3,600 satellites in orbit; there were also spent satellites, upper stages of rockets and fragments of both.[118]

Proportionally the number of nuclear-powered satellites is small. The USA has launched at least 23, all except one powered by radioisotope thermonuclear generators (RTGs), essentially lumps of plutonium that generate heat as they decay and so produce electricity; the USSR has reputedly launched 31, including some RTGs, but the majority fission-powered Radar Ocean Reconnaissance Satellites (RORSATs) with reactors containing 50kg of enriched uranium, designed to separate from the main body of the spacecraft on re-entry. Unfortunately, out of this 54 nuclear-powered satellites at least nine have been disasters, the best known, on the US side, being the navy navigational satellite, *Transit 5BN* in which, as the result of human error, the booster misfired some 30 miles above the Indian Ocean on 24 April 1964, and it crashed. The RTG, with one kilogram of plutonium, burned up in the upper atmosphere, but the intensity of atmospheric global plutonium levels increased three times as a result. On the Russian side, in January 1978, *Cosmos 954* re-entered the atmosphere before its reactor could be ejected into higher orbit, scattering a quarter of its canister of highly enriched uranium-235 over Canada's sparsely populated Northwest Territories; in February 1983, *Cosmos 1402*, launched to provide a view of the Falklands War, burned up over the South Atlantic, south of Ascension Island, leaving a radioactive trail behind it; and in September 1988 *Cosmos 1900* re-entered the atmosphere, its reactor fortunately boosted to 'storage' orbit over 700 km above the earth.[119] The waste stays, we hope, in space.

In short, somewhere, above our heads, there is about a ton of nuclear material going round the earth, arousing concern among leading scientists, if not politicians. In May 1988 the Federation of American Scientists and the Committee of Soviet Scientists against the Nuclear Threat jointly proposed a ban on orbiting nuclear reactors. This would have stopped both the Soviet RORSATs and the US Strategic Defense Initiative (SDI), or 'Star Wars', but not scientific missions into 'deep space'. The only response was that a ban would harm commercial as well as military activity, though the US agreed to test its Star Wars system at low altitudes so that debris would fall rapidly to earth. In practice, 'testing Star Wars' means increasing the quantity of small-scale debris by destroying old satellites, each of which breaks into 1,000 tiny fragments, which, on striking each other, break into smaller fragments. At speeds of 11,000 miles an hour even the most minute can do untold damage. Paint seems to be a particular problem. In 1983 the windscreen of the space shuttle *Challenger* was struck by a speck of paint a fifth of a millimetre across, but was so badly chipped as to need replacement. And when, after four years in orbit the Solar Maximum Mission aluminium panels were repaired by a US shuttle crew, they contained 331 tiny craters, 20 of them with traces of meteorites but over 150 smeared with traces of spacecraft paint.[120] The problem is simply that space is no longer space; it has become a junk yard.

Waste gases and their makers

Gases, like radioactivity, are insidious forms of waste. As many are neither seen, nor, except in the more obnoxious cases, smelt, it is not surprising that we have taken so long to credit their effects. The only merit of the filthy smoke from a diesel-powered heavy goods vehicle (HGV) is that we recognize it immediately, if only because, in the traffic jams of the modern world, we are unable to avoid it. Today, when the Greenhouse Effect, the hole in the ozone layer and, currently less popular, acid rain, have received so much media attention, it may seem that yet another account is unnecessary. Our concern is to demonstrate that these phenomena are part of the wider problem of waste and that their fate depends on humanity's reaction to that problem as a whole.

The infernal combustion engine

There are allegedly 350m cars in use throughout the world. On average each takes 335 gallons (1,500 litres) of oil to manufacture and uses at least 2,250 gallons (10,000 litres) of fuel before it is scrapped.[121] In the UK there are 330 cars for every 1,000 people, in France 400, in West Germany 500 and in the USA 575. British vehicle use (in 1990 of over 21.5m cars) is expected to rise by up to 142 per cent by the year 2025;[122].

The consequences were foreseeable. In West Germany, which invests more on transport than any other European country and has the best road system, serious traffic jams have risen from 1,000 in 1986 to 20,000 in 1988, and that excludes jams under three kilometres in length which are no longer reported.[123] The car, in fact, is becoming less a viable means of transport than a symbol of affluence or status, with the two-car family vaunting its superiority over the one, and with large, powerful cars preferred to more serviceable small vehicles. The Third World has been infected by the contagion. In India, according to the National Transport Policy document (1980), there were 3.7m motor vehicles on the roads, including 840,000 cars and jeeps, 44,000 trucks, 24,000 buses and 83,000 taxis.[124] Between 1971 and 1978 the number of registered vehicles increased by 49.6 per cent in Bombay, by 51.3 per cent in Calcutta, by 64.5 per cent in Madras and by 120.0 per cent in Delhi, and the numbers have doubtless risen even more in the last decade.[125] Even in China where, in the early 1980s there were only 1.5m motor vehicles and bicycles outnumbered cars by 250 to one,[126] the numbers are increasing by 20 per cent a year and will keep up this rate as new plants producing Chinese Volkswagens and Renaults enter the market.[127]

Each of these vehicles is powered by an internal combustion engine that puffs out through its exhaust a mixture of waste gases: carbon monoxide, which is odourless and highly poisonous and which, on entering the air, is quickly transformed into carbon dioxide; nitric oxide (NO), rapidly converted to nitrogen dioxide (NO_2) in the atmosphere (hence NO_x to denote these two nitrogen oxides, which are inevitable products of high-temperature combustion); and hydrocarbon particulates, incompletely burned specks of matter that form part of the visible smoke and give exhaust gases their unpleasant smell. In addition many car engines still emit lead, which is added to petrol to improve its performance and is dispersed as fine particles.[128]

Diesel engines, mainstay of taxis, buses, dustbin lorries and, above all, HGVs, do not use a spark but rely on compression. Squeezed sufficiently, diesel obligingly explodes. Properly tuned, a diesel engine gives off less carbon monoxide than a normal petrol engine and 30 per cent less carbon dioxide than a petrol engine fitted with a catalytic converter. Conversely, a diesel engine gives off more nitrous oxides and, because of the high sulphur content of diesel fuel, sulphurous oxide, but the most immediately obnoxious feature is the black smoke from particulates, which are very small and so penetrate deeply into the lungs, aggravating conditions such as asthma and bronchitis. In 1981 American research confirmed that diesel particulates carry polyaromatic hydrocarbons, which are known carcinogens. The main cause of the poisonous waste is undoubtedly human: failure to maintain diesel engines to high standards, especially on HGVs; failure to enact protective legislation and, where it is adopted, continued use of old and the potentially most dangerous engines; and government policies encouraging use of road transport.[129] While European politicians welcome the opening up of EC trade in 1992, in practical terms this means a liberalization of road haulage and the introduction of cabotage, that is, the freedom of a lorry from Country A to operate without hindrance in the domestic market of Country B. From 1992 onwards there will be no capacity restrictions on the number of lorries that can trade internationally.[130] Each of them will be armed with a powerful diesel engine.

How much of this waste gas entering the atmosphere can be blamed on road transport? So far as Britain is concerned, in 1988 smoke from diesel engines accounted for 34 per cent (184,000 tonnes) of atmospheric soot, 42 per cent (223,000 tonnes) being from domestic chimneys and bonfires. But while the domestic share has decreased by a third since 1978, that from diesel engines, which is three times blacker than coal soot, has risen in the same proportion. The government's response is to launch a £12 billion road-building programme that will enable the use of diesel fuel to rise by 50 per cent in the last 20 years of this century.[131]

As for waste gases from non-diesel sources, in the EC motor vehicles account for about half the emissions of NO_x and in the United States about 45 per cent of the total. In Britain the proportion rose from 37 per cent in 1980 to 42 per cent in 1985, in France from 56 per cent to 66 per cent and in Japan from 40 per cent to 49 per cent over the same period. Fewer data are available for carbon monoxide; in 1985 the transport sector was responsible for 70 per cent of emissions in the USA (some 67,500,000 tonnes), 84 per cent in the UK and 59 per cent in West Germany, while emissions of hydrocarbons in the UK rose by 12 per cent between 1975 and 1985 but declined by 22 per cent in the USA over the same period; only 28 per cent of these in the USA and 26 per cent in the UK were from motor vehicles.[132]

Waste gases do not 'disappear' with their discharge into the atmosphere. Under the influence of sunlight NO_X and hydrocarbons react with carbon monoxide and oxygen in the troposphere (lower atmosphere) to produce ozone (0_3). This tropospheric ozone must be distinguished from the stratospheric variety in the now familiar ozone layer that protects us from ultraviolet radiation. It occurs as a component of that familiar urban phenomenon, photochemical smog, and can actually form at street level when nitrogen oxides and hydrocarbons from vehicle exhausts interact in the presence of sunlight. Ironically, under certain conditions nitrogen oxide can destroy ozone so that city streets filled with traffic fumes may actually have lower ozone levels than downwind rural areas. As a strong oxidizing agent, ozone can cause dramatic changes in the biochemistry of the lungs of people exposed to it. The WHO's Air Quality Guidelines for Europe state that ozone levels should not exceed the band between 76 and 100 parts per billion (ppb) averaged over an hour. Research in progress suggests that the current US limit of 120ppb (raised from 80ppb ten years ago) is far too high and that more sensitive equipment has made it possible to detect effects at 60ppb, a figure that may shortly be reduced to 20ppb. Recent long hot summers in Britain have underlined the danger. In the summer of 1989 levels of 100ppb were recorded on the Norfolk coast. At the beginning of May 1990 levels reached 117ppb in West London, while on the south coast a low threshold of 60ppb was exceeded for 16 hours.[133] Ozone is, of course, yet a further danger; it is one of the greenhouse gases.

Burners of fossil fuels
Fossil fuels, namely, coal, oil and natural gas, are basically carbon, but certain types of coal contain large quantities of impure sulphur. In burning such fuels for domestic use, in motor transport, in power stations to produce electricity or for smelting non-ferrous ores, the carbon and sulphur enter the atmosphere as the waste gases carbon dioxide (CO_2) and sulphur dioxide (SO_2).

Carbon dioxide
As a natural component of air, carbon dioxide is not only in itself relatively harmless but essential to some forms of life. Plants use it as food and, with the addition of water and sunlight, convert it into sugars by photosynthesis. Human beings have taken advantage of its antipathy to combustion by using it in fire extinguishers. Its present greatest cause for concern to life on this planet is that, quantitatively, it is the most prolific of the greenhouse gases.

In 1987 fossil fuels accounted for 88.1 per cent of the world's energy consumption as opposed to the 11.9 per cent produced by hydroelectric or nuclear power. Oil had become the major fuel and satisfied 55.1 per cent of Japan's energy needs, 45.1 per cent of those of Western Europe and 41.3 per cent of those of the USA; in the USSR its primacy was ousted by natural gas which provided 36 per cent as opposed to oil's 31.1 per cent[134] Among industrializing nations, China depends for 70 per cent of its energy on coal; most of the billion tonnes burned in 1989 in large power stations, small local heating stations or as charcoal was of low quality and high ash producing.[135] The demands of industrialization have made China the world's largest coal producer; so great, however, is the demand that, despite an annual output of more than 900m tonnes, China needs to import coal to meet its requirements.[136]

How much carbon dioxide does this reliance on fossil fuels produce and who is responsible? In the following survey it should be noted that, where figures are given for carbon, each ton of this is responsible for producing 3.7 times its own weight of carbon dioxide. In 1988, burning fossil fuels accounted for some 5.66bn tons of carbon, while the cutting down and burning of tropical rainforests released another 1–2bn tons into the atmosphere. Not surprisingly, carbon has been called 'one of the largest waste products of modern industrial civilization'.[137] Even more disconcerting is the rate at which these emissions have increased and, unless action is taken to stop them, will go on increasing. In the post-war period it took ten years for emissions of carbon to rise from 2bn to 3bn tons, but only six to reach the four billion mark. In 1988 global carbon emissions rose by 3.7 per cent, the largest increase for almost a decade, at a time when politicians and industrialists were talking in terms of a reduction.

There can be no doubt which countries lead the world in the production of this waste. In 1987 the United States was responsible for 1,224m tons of carbon, the USSR for 1,035m and China for 594m.[138] Beyond this we reach the stage where statisticians, and government scientists, introduce their Fun with Figures game. Stressing, quite rightly, that, since these countries occupy large areas of the earth's surface, the results are not entirely unexpected, they introduce other, allegedly fairer, methods of comparison. Suppose, for example, one considered emissions not in absolute terms, but on a per capita basis, that is, in relation to population. This still leaves the USA heading the list with 5.03 tons per person, but it is now followed by Canada (4.24) and Australia (4.00), while the USSR has sunk to fourth place (3.68) and China disappeared behind Western Europe, South Korea and even Mexico. If, however, we consider emissions in relation to each dollar of the GNP, a different picture emerges: the Chinese (2.024 grams) are more than three times as responsible (or irresponsible) as their nearest rival, India (655 grams), while the USA drops to 276, Canada to 247 and France to a modest 133 grams.[139]

Percentages can be equally obliging. Giving evidence to the Hinkley C Inquiry, the chief scientist at the British DoE, David Fisk, pointed out that, between 1950 and 1980, emissions of CO_2 rose by 586 per cent in developing countries and by 337 per cent in the USSR and Eastern Europe, compared with 91 per cent in North America and 125 per cent in Western Europe,[140] that is, the Third World and the wicked Reds had greater responsibility for any unfortunate effects than the more abstemious West.

On the UK itself he was more precise. British emissions rose by 18 million tonnes to 171 millions between 1984 and 1987 but remained below the peak of 190 millions reached in 1979. In 1987 power stations were responsible for 37 per cent of the total, industry for 20 per cent, transport for 16 per cent, domestic fires 14 per cent and offices and other sources 13 per cent.[141]

Scientists at the US Oak Ridge National Laboratory viewed the matter differently. The increase in British emissions in 1987 from 152.5m to 156.1m tonnes of carbon, that is, an increase of 2.6 per cent, exceeded the world average of 1.6 per cent, while those of West Germany had fallen by 2.2 per cent and France, with its concentration on nuclear power, by 3.2 per cent.[142] Even less kind critics suggested that the increase was not due to coal burning, which had remained largely static, but to petroleum combustion from increased use of cars and an increase in gas for central heating owing to the poor insulation of houses built swiftly during the construction boom.[143] Undeterred, perhaps even unaware, planners at the DoE produced predictions by which carbon dioxide emissions would rise by 37 per cent by the year 2005 and by 73 per cent by 2020. While this was not a 'final scenario', any changes in these 'Energy Pollution Projections' were 'likely to be small'.[144] One can only wonder on which planet these 'planners' are living, though doubtless they would accept, as only to be expected, Oak Ridge's latest calculation that, in terms of the amount of carbon dioxide emitted per head of population, East Germany was now marginally ahead of the USA, each with more than five tonnes of carbon per person.[145]

One could continue. The plain fact is that, however one projects the figures, there is still too much carbon dioxide entering the atmosphere for the good of the planet.

Sulphur dioxide

Sulphur dioxide has no merits. It is highly corrosive, hazardous to human health and, in conjunction with the nitrogen oxides, responsible for acid rain and subsequent harm to the environment. It can be produced naturally by decaying organic matter or volcanoes (the eruption of Mount St Helens in the USA in the early 1980s increased emissions in that country by about 1 per cent) but the main causes are the burning of sulphur-containing fuels and the smelting of non-ferrous ores. In industrialized countries, electricity generation is the largest single source, contributing 69 per cent of the USA's 20,700,000 tonnes in 1985 and 71 per cent of the UK's 3,580,000 tonnes (fuel sources only).[146]

Ironically the well-intentioned 1960s policy of building industrial smokestacks higher to avoid polluting the immediate neighbourhood merely resulted in spreading the problem. Cases are on record of sulphur dioxide compounds travelling 1,000–2,000 kilometres in three to five days. The nickel and copper smelting plant at Sudbury, Ontario, where one 400-metre high stack belches out more than 650,000 tonnes a year, has the dubious distinction of being the largest single source of sulphur dioxide waste gas in the world,[147] though as more and more reports arrive from Eastern Europe, where the prevailing brown coal (lignite) emits 20−30 per cent more sulphur dioxide than 'black' coal, this record may not be unassailable. In Czechoslovakia, around the four cities of Ústi, Teplice, Chomutov and Most are power stations generating 60 per cent of the country's electricity. Not suprisingly the atmosphere over Prague contains 20 times officially permissible amounts of sulphur dioxide.[148]

Globally, emissions have been rising for over a century, from under 10m tonnes in 1860 to over 150m by 1980, but from 1970 onwards a move away from heavy industries to the service sector, mandatory installation of 'scrubbers' to filter out toxic gases, and the use of lower-sulphur grades of coal have combined to produce an actual reduction in some countries. Coal used for generating electricity in the USA, for example, caused 44 per cent less sulphur dioxide to be emitted per unit of electricity in 1987 than in 1975.[149]

CFCs and halons

Perhaps the most remarkable fact about CFCs is that in Britain by mid-1990 one could collect an accurate and informative handout, *CFCs and the Ozone Layer*, at the local Tesco supermarket. CFCs, it would appear, had arrived, together with 'ozone-friendly' or even 'environment-friendly' substitutes, which the customer was exhorted to buy. Rarely have arguments in favour of the environment been so openly directed at a popular audience.

CFCs had, in fact, arrived nearly 60 years earlier, when, in 1930, their inventor, Thomas Midgley, demonstrated their safety, to human beings, by inhaling vapours from a beaker and then blowing out a candle. There is no doubt that CFCs have been useful in boosting the consumer society, as propellants in aerosols, coolants in refrigerators, in the manufacture of foam packaging, in air-conditioning and in washing microcircuits. But the final result is that they end up in the stratosphere as a persistent and damaging waste gas.

Two facts to consider about CFCs are that 1) since they are man-made, the natural world is not equipped to cope with them and, in consequence, they can survive in the atmosphere for more than a hundred years, and 2) on reaching the ozone layer in the stratosphere, between 10 and 15 miles above the earth, ultraviolet radiation breaks them up, freeing chlorine atoms to destroy ozone in the thin layer which blocks and absorbs the sun's most damaging radiation. Since each molecule can destroy 100,000 molecules of ozone, it is not surprising to learn that chlorine, which once occurred at a ratio of two parts per billion, now occurs at three and may rise to seven. Even if planned reductions in the use of CFCs take place, the amount of chlorine in the stratosphere is expected to double in the next 50 years.[150]

The CFCs considered most responsible for damage, namely CFC-12, sold under the trade name of Freon, and CFC-11, were the subject of the 1987 Montreal Protocol to save the ozone layer (see Chapter 9). Yet, while concentrations of CFC-11 and CFC-12 are increasing at the rate of about 5 per cent a year, those of CFC-22, which was not included in the protocol because it lasts only 20 years and is destroyed in the troposphere, have increased at an annual rate of nearly 8 per cent.[151]

This leads to the third important fact: not only are CFCs deadly in their destruction of the ozone layer but they contribute to the Greenhouse Effect (see below and Chapter 7) at an effectiveness more than 10,000 times that of carbon dioxide. Put at its simplest, if we do not get rid of CFCs, they will get rid of us.

Britain is the largest producer and exporter of CFCs in Europe, with Imperial Chemical Industries (ICI) playing a leading role, while Dupont dominate the US scene with an estimated 50 per cent of the home market and 25 per cent worldwide. In 1988 Britain produced some 105,000 tonnes, almost half of which (48,146 tonnes) was exported, a third (16,514 tonnes) going to other European countries.[152]

The unresolved question is what will happen in the Third World. Developing countries such as India, Taiwan and South Korea, which are large producers of CFCs, argue that they cannot afford to buy alternative technology without financial help from rich countries that have enjoyed the benefits for years, and China has announced a plan to increase CFC production to ten times its present level so that, by the year 2000, it will equal 1989 US production.[153]

The second group of chemicals, halons, differs in that they are based on bromine instead of chlorine and are made in smaller quantities for use in hand-held fire extinguishers, or for fire-suppressing systems that protect bank vaults, computer rooms and telephone exchanges. In the stratosphere they act in the same way as CFCs, except that bromine atoms destroy the ozone instead of chlorine.[154]

Questioned on this issue in the House of Commons in February 1989, all that the Environment Secretary, Nicholas Ridley, could offer was that such equipment should not be used in fire-fighting *practice*. Until a substitute was found it was difficult to deny the use of such equipment in fire-fighting.[155] The choice would appear to be between allowing someone's house to burn now and all of us to burn later.

The mysteries of methane

Methane (CH_4), in its pure form a colourless, odourless and highly inflammable gas, occurs naturally, but is also a waste gas from human and animal activities. While scientists have been able to calculate that atmospheric concentrations of methane remained steady at 0.7ppm between 1500 BC and 1700 AD, when, with the industrial revolution in Europe, they began to rise, have now reached 1.7ppm and are increasing at the rate of 1.2 per cent annually, they are less certain about where methane actually comes from or what happens to it in the atmosphere.[156]

Major problems are the number of sources and lack of data on some of those. The earth's five million square kilometres of bogs and marshes produce methane naturally, but we know little about the quantities generated by the two largest northern wetlands, the Siberian lowlands and the

Hudson – James Bay lowlands of Canada.[157] No one has successfully calculated the quantity produced by termites as no one knows the world termite population, and the seemingly bizarre research of the German chemist, Dieter Enhalt, to measure the methane in cow's farts (despite suggestions that he is examining the wrong end of the cow) appear less absurd when we realize that the world's cattle population has doubled in the last 40 years and there is now one cow for every four human beings, converting 3 – 10 per cent of the food eaten into methane in its guts.[158]

Human-related sources include putrefying waste tips (an estimated 2.2m tonnes escape from British landfill sites annually), burning forests and grassland, and the 1.5m square kilometres of rice paddies. There are grounds for supposing that, thanks to changes in the activity of microbes in the soil, grassland burning may produce larger releases than the rainforest, but data are sparse. As for rice paddies, it appears that at certain seasons the roots of rice plants capture methane from the muddy bottoms and transport it through the plant to the air, thereby avoiding microbial attack in the water. This may, in fact, be the world's most important man-made source of this waste gas, emitting up to 150 million tonnes a year.[159]

What happens to methane in the atmosphere is even more problematical. Every year 50 million tonnes more methane enter the atmosphere than leave it, the result of increased emissions but also due to the fact that the methane is lasting longer than the previous average of ten years before oxidizing bacteria consume it or it is removed by chemical reaction with hydroxyl. This 'free radical', consisting of one oxygen atom and one hydrogen, occurs in minute quantities in the atmosphere where it acts as an important oxidizing agent in removing pollutants such as methane and carbon monoxide. Concentrations of both gases have increased and, in its efforts (and failure) to cope with this, the amount of hydroxyl in the atmosphere fell by a quarter between 1950 and 1985. As 80 per cent of the hydroxyl is required for reaction with the carbon monoxide, increased quantities of methane are left in the air.

And the cause of increased carbon monoxide? Once again, we are back to car exhausts. As Fred Pearce puts it succinctly: 'In an unpolluted world, there appears to have been a balance between methane and carbon monoxide in the air. The balance was managed by hydroxyl. But vehicle exhausts have upset that balance .... Cars could be more damaging than cows'.[160]

The damage arises because methane is another greenhouse gas, 20 – 25 times as effective in its warming properties, molecule for molecule, as carbon dioxide. It has been increasing at the rate of 1.2 per cent since 1950, four times the rate of increase of carbon dioxide. In another 50 years methane could become the most important of the greenhouse gases, and cars, rather than the rainforest, become the prime concern in the survival of the planet.[161]

The evils of co-operation

Innocuous or harmful in themselves, the waste gases examined above are invariably damaging in combination. The two most important results of such combination — the formation of acid rain and the Greenhouse Effect — are now so well known that only a brief explanation is necessary.

Sulphur dioxide and nitrogen oxide emissions from burning fossil fuels or vehicle exhausts combine with water vapour, sunlight and oxygen in the atmosphere to produce a diluted 'soup' of sulphuric and nitric acids which return to earth as acid rain, hail, snow, sleet or fog (wet deposition). Near the source of emissions they may combine in gaseous form to return in the form of gases and particles (dry deposition). Additionally, in some heavily industrialized areas, hydrogen chloride gases are mixed in with this soup to produce hydrochloric acid, which then becomes an ingredient of acid rain.[162]

The greenhouse gases — carbon dioxide, methane, CFCs, nitrous oxide and ozone — derive their name from their function. Incoming radiation from the sun is reflected by the surface of the earth and begins its return to space. While some 70 per cent ultimately escapes, infra-red heat is absorbed by the gases, which form a layer around the earth, and so warms the troposphere, which in turn passes on the heat, so keeping the earth warmer than it would otherwise be, hence the Greenhouse Effect. As long as the amount of water vapour and carbon dioxide in the air remains constant and the heat arriving from the sun does the same, an equilibrium is set up by which the amount of long-wave radiation leaving the earth balances the amount of energy coming from the sun.

What has happened is simply that humanity, in its unwisdom and ignorance, has upset this equilibrium. Increased concentrations of carbon dioxide and other, even more effective gases, by absorbing infra-red radiation, and preventing its escape to space, warm the earth more effectively than present conditions require, if the climate is to remain stable.[163]

We shall examine what has already happened because of acid rain and what we can expect if the Greenhouse Effect is allowed to continue when we consider what eventually happens to waste gases that go 'Into the Air' (Part II, Chapter 7).

Notes

1. *Guardian* 15 September 1989
2. See also Gourlay 1988 pp. 119–22
3. Marquez 1989 p. 106
4. Charlesworth 1989; Reader's Digest 1990 p. 47
5. Reader's Digest 1990 p. 47
6. Consumers' Association *Which*? August 1987
7. *ENDS Report* No. 146; *Guardian* 15 May 1987, 4 and 20 October 1989, 16 November 1988; *Observer* 4 December 1988, 2 July 1989, 12 November 1989; DoE 1989a Table 3.5b
8. Powledge 1982 p. 160
9. Ibid. pp. 162–3
10. Ibid. pp. 163–4
11. *WR 1988–89* p. 45
12. Ibid. p. 46, Table 3.8
13. Ibid. p. 45

14. Ibid. p. 47, Table 3.9
15. *Observer* 24 September 1989
16. Ibid.
17. *Newsweek* 27 June 1987
18. Consumers' Association *Which?* March 1990
19. HoC 1989 paras 82−3
20. Anon 1989a
21. Goldsmith and Hildyard 1988 p. 165
22. *WR 1988−89* p. 314, Table 20.7
23. Goldsmith and Hildyard 1990 p. 89
24. Ibid.
25. Outline based on WHO 1983
26. Goldsmith and Hildyard 1990 p. 40; WHO 1983 p. 106
27. WHO 1983 p. 106
28. For more details on hydrocarbons see Gourlay 1988 pp. 84−5
29. WHO 1983 pp. 106−7
30. Goldsmith and Hildyard 1988 p. 197
31. Subrahmanyam and Swaminathan 1989 p. 13 Table 3
32. WHO 1983 p. 105
33. ACOPS 1985−86 p. 88
34. WHO 1983 pp. 109−10
35. Reader's Digest 1990 p. 102
36. Quoted Gooding 1989
37. Suttill 1989
38. *WR 1988−89* pp. 110−11 and Table 7.2
39. Laidler 1989
40. *Parting Company* Winter 1989
41. Reader's Digest 1990 p. 103
42. *WR 1988−89* p. 137
43. *TAO* 1983 p. 172
44. Manz 1989; *TAO* 1983 p. 173
45. *Australia* 20 December 1988
46. Hammond 1989
47. *Financial Times* 8 March 1990; *Parting Company* Spring 1990
48. *Parting Company* June 1987; Moody 1991 pp. 68−9
49. Reader's Digest 1990 p. 103
50. *Parting Company* Spring 1989, Autumn 1989, Spring 1990
51. Malm *el al.* 1990
52. Ibid.
53. Nicholson 1990
54. Gourlay 1988 p. 168
55. *Parting Company* Autumn 1989; Partizans' *Special Report* 1990
56. Goldsmith and Hildyard 1988 p.227
57. Partizans 'What is BP up to?' April 1988
58. Goldsmith and Hildyard 1988 p. 228
59. Ibid.
60. *New Scientist* 14 October 1989, 22 June 1991
61. Agarwal and Narain 1985 p. 288
62. *Guardian* 2 November 1989
63. Thorpe 1990a
64. *Observer* 17 September 1989
65. Goldsmith and Hildyard 1988 p. 98
66. Borgese and Ginsburg 1985 p. 175
67. *TAO* 1983 p. 172
68. *Labour Research* May 1986 p. 16
69. Goldsmith and Hildyard 1988 pp. 157−8

70. Lean 1987b
71. *Guardian* 15 November 1986
72. Agarwal and Narain 1985 pp. 199–200
73. *WR 1988–89* p. 135, Tables 8.3, 8.4; Brown and Young 1990 p. 67
74. *WR 1988–89)* p. 135
75. Briggs 1990 p. 54
76. Peckham 1989 p.45
77. Harrison 1990
78. Lean 1987a
79. Agarwal *el al*. 1982 p. 141; Postel 1988 pp. 120–21; for further details on pesticide use in the Pacific see Gourlay 1988 pp. 163–8
80. Agarwal and Narain 1985 p. 201
81. *RSRS 8* 1982 p. 28
82. Peckham 1989
83. Smith, M. 1989
84. *New Scientist* 9 December 1989
85. Parker 1990 p. 23
86. Mills 1989
87. Sattaur 1989
88. Erlichman 1989c
89. Cook and Halsall 1989
90. Mills 1989
91. *Guardian* 4 July 1989
92. Cook and Halsall 1989
93. Ackefors and Enell 1990 p. 28
94. Ibid. p. 34
95. Reader's Digest 1990 pp. 121–2
96. Ibid. p. 122
97. Holliday 1984 p. 6
98. Gourlay 1988 p. 175
99. Zhu and Chan 1989 p. 6
100. DoE 1989a Table 4.1
101. Zhu and Chan 1989 p. 5
102. Ibid.
103. *Guardian* 29 October 1988
104. Pollock 1986 p. 19
105. Zhu and Chan 1989 p. 7
106. *Guardian* 1 December 1989
107. O'Neill 1989
108. Medvedev 1990 p.25
109. Hughes 1990; Lean and Schneider 1990
110. Cross 1990a
111. Cross 1990a, 1990b; Holliman 1989
112. *Guardian* 29 August 1990
113. Holliday 1984 p. 6; Gourlay 1988 pp. 174–5; Green and Young 1990 pp. 22–5; Bennetto 1990
114. *Guardian* 3 March 1988
115. Ibid. 25 May 1988
116. Ibid. 7 June 1988
117. Ibid. 31 March 1988
118. Radford 1988a
119. Booth 1989
120. Radford 1988a; *New Scientist* 11 August 1988
121. *Green Magazine* January 1990 p. 57
122. Department of Transport figures in *Guardian* 1 May 1990 and 13 May 1990
123. *Guardian* 24 November 1989

124. Agarwal *el al*. 1982 p. 77
125. Ibid. p. 102
126. Smil 1984 p. 126; Lowe 1990 p. 121
127. Silvertown 1989
128. Goldsmith and Hildyard 1988 p. 114
129. Anon 1990a pp. 22−4
130. Whitelegg 1989
131. Anon 1990a, 1990b
132. *WR 1988-89* pp. 165, 169 and Table 10.1
133. Reed 1989; Brown, T. 1990; *Green Magazine* December 1989 p. 34
134. Patterson 1989
135. Long 1990
136. Patterson 1989
137. Flavin 1990 p. 18
138. Ibid. p. 19
139. Ibid.
140. *New Scientist* 18 March 1989
141. Ibid.
142. *Observer* 9 July 1989
143. *Guardian* 10 July 1989
144. Ibid. 17 November 1989
145. *New Scientist* 1 April 1989
146. *WR 1988−89* pp. 163−4 and Table 10.1
147. Goldsmith and Hildyard 1988 pp. 67-8
148. *Guardian* 18 June 1987
149. *WR 1988−89* pp. 164-5
150. *Guardian* 6 March 1989
151. *New Scientist* 25 February 1989
152. *Guardian* 1 October 1988, 1 March 1989
153. *New Scientist* 11 February 1989
154. Ibid. 25 February 1989
155. Ibid. 11 February 1989
156. *WR 1988−89* p. 171; Gribbin 1988
157. Gribbin 1989
158. Pearce 1989
159. Ibid.
160. Ibid.
161. Ibid.
162. Hinrichsen 1988 pp. 67−8
163. Gribbin 1988

Part II:

What happens to Waste

3.   On the way

Gaseous wastes go directly into the air; some liquid wastes enter water as effluent; others, like solid waste, are either stored on site or taken elsewhere for disposal. The emerging pattern is that the more hazardous the waste, the further it goes. Domestic waste may travel only a few kilometres to the local rubbish dump; hazardous wastes, as in the *Lynx-Makiri-Zanoobia* saga, may travel over 17,000 miles, only to return to their starting point.

The most disconcerting feature about the carriage of waste is that the means used, whether road, rail or ship, and what actually happens are often only revealed by chance. In 1976 a chemical explosion at Seveso released a cloud of dioxin and caused the evacuation of over 900 people, but it was only eight years later that 41 barrels of the dioxin waste, removed for disposal and 'missing' in France, turned up in an abandoned abattoir at Aguilcourt-Le-Sart in northern France.[1] They had apparently been taken there and just dumped. But for the sinking of the *Herald of Free Enterprise* the British people would never have known that it contained chemicals for disposal, as the items were mislabelled and only in extremity did the truth come out.[2] Only when, on 21 October 1986, a lorry owned by the West Germany company, Transnuklear, skidded off the road near Mol, Belgium, and irregularities were discovered in the paperwork and packaging were investigations started that culminated in the Nukem corruption scandal (see below).[3] The sinking of the *Mont Louis* with its cargo of uranium hexafluoride off Ostend on 25 August 1984 caused port authorities in Panama to refuse services to the *Pacific Fisher*, a British ship carrying spent nuclear fuel from Japan to Sellafield. The action shocked BNF, but only because they had used this mode of transport 'for years'.[4] It shocked others, because they became aware of it for the first time.

The transport of toxic waste, both chemical and nuclear, offers opportunities for sharp practice and double dealing found in few other activities, and, as rising disposal costs, more stringent environmental regulations and a decrease in the number of available sites add to the pressure, the corner cutting and underhand practice increase.

According to the Federation of American Scientists, the USA produces 275 million tonnes of industrial waste annually, of which 135,000 tonnes are exported. Ninety per cent of the exports of hazardous waste goes to three sites in Canada, the nearest facilities licensed to handle it.[5] Yet in mid-1989 the Canadian Government closed 94 of its 125 border crossings with the USA to tanker traffic when it discovered that millions of litres of toxic waste had been disposed of over the previous four years by mixing it with fuel oil. The shipments included PCBs, industrial solvents such as perchloroethylene, heavy metals, sulphur-bearing pesticides and phenolic by-products from fuel refining.[6]

It is not always necessary to go to such lengths; misleading paperwork or mislabelling of waste are often more convenient. In August 1989 the South Yorkshire firm, Wath Recycling, discovered that 20 containers with a total of 530 tonnes of toxic waste received from the FMC Corporation, Baltimore, contained highly toxic xylene and furan, which Wath has no licence or facilities to handle and of whose presence it claimed to be unaware. FMC retorted that the waste was exactly as described to Wath and that it must have been mixed with other waste when the British firm put it into 2,700 barrels. The incident received major publicity when the newly appointed Environment Secretary, Chris Patten, anxious to display his green credentials, broke off his summer holiday and promised that the waste would be returned to the USA, only to learn from his own civil servants that the UK had no powers to do so as, under British law, the 'legal holders' of the waste were an intermediary company.[7]

In February 1990 a quarry in a suburb of Swansea, South Wales, found itself the unlikely recipient of 75,000 tonnes of soil and rubble from a Stuttgart building site contaminated with PCBs to a maximum level of 10 milligrams per kilogram. According to Swansea City Council test samples sent by the German waste disposal company had proved clear and the council was only put on the alert when the Stuttgart waste export licensing authorities approved the waste's actual contents. Whether the quarry operators, Max Recovery, whose licence for the site is for 'inert waste' only, hoped to get away with it, and make a large profit on the deal, or the Germans had deliberately deceived Swansea Council over the contents, remains one of those mysteries too often encountered in waste disposal practice.[8]

Investigations by Greenpeace and the London *Independent* in mid-1990 reveal an even more complex method of by-passing EC and British regulations on the transport of hazardous waste. In 1987 a Hanover firm making cleaning products, Kertess, went bankrupt, leaving behind barrels of contaminated chemicals, including chlorine and sodium-related compounds and a selection of acids. The resultant disorder, in which much of the waste was not clearly labelled, with mixtures of chemicals lying around in plastic sacks, was sufficient to dispel hopes of acceptance for recycling, and in 1988 the waste was put out to tender for disposal, the contract going to Recycling-Centrum Seevetal. After failing to receive authorization to ship the waste to the Netherlands and the UK, Seevetal cleared the site in April/May 1990 and despatched the waste for storage at Brunsbüttel, near Hamburg, clearly labelled as hazardous waste. Along with wastes from other sources, shipment was then organized by the inevitable middlemen and reached the UK through the ports of Felixstowe, Harwich, Ipswich and Immingham on the Humber. What had begun as 'hazardous waste' was now, however, 'goods-in-transit' or 'non-ferrous metal residues'. The advantage of the former is obvious — waste is not entering the country, merely passing through it; of the latter, that they can be recycled. Technically, however, under British regulations this is still hazardous waste and its movement must be notified to the local councils responsible for their implementation. Unfortunately, a lorry loaded with large bags of the waste, which had been stored at a warehouse in West Thurrock, Essex, reached the Manchester waste processing company of P.J. Collier, where the staff, suspecting that it had been imported from overseas without correct documentation, alerted Essex County Council.[9] Once again, it was almost by chance that the nefarious practices of the waste disposal trade came to light.

Such actions are only to be expected when British firms are actively encouraged to import hazardous wastes for disposal. The official line, that the UK has the technical ability to handle the most toxic wastes, for example, the capacity to destroy PCBs by incineration, masks the more obvious inducement to the world market, that British disposal costs are considerably lower than those of their European and US competitors and that there are high profits to be made in an industry with a £5bn a year turnover.

In 1981—82 the official figure for the import of 'special wastes', that is, notifiable hazardous waste, was 3,800 tonnes. By 1985—86 it was 24,500 tonnes, in 1986—87 52,000, and in 1987—88 it had risen to 80,000 tonnes, though there was a decrease to 52,000 tonnes the following year. Non-special wastes, for which no accurate figures were available, imported for direct landfill, had also increased. The DoE told the House of Commons Environment Committee that, while 'in earlier years', imports, mainly of fly ash, gypsum and contaminated soil, 'had amounted to only a couple of hundred tonnes...in 1986 the figure was 130,000 tonnes'. Although the Hazardous Waste Inspectorate estimated the import of less hazardous waste in 1987 as 180,000 tonnes, some of it unlabelled, the official figure somehow fell to 10,000 tonnes in 1987—88 with a further fall to about 5,000 tonnes in 1988—89. In short, no one really knows the answer.

Significantly, most of the special waste came from Europe. In 1986 55 per cent of imported waste came from the Netherlands, 12.5 per cent from Ireland and a further 12.5 per cent from Belgium, with Portugal, Canada and the USA each contributing 2.5 per cent. The remainder came from West Germany, Denmark, Norway, Sweden, Spain, Italy and Switzerland in Europe, with Australia, Singapore and Hong Kong supplying long-distance contributions.[10] Concern at this traffic was not limited to environmental groups. In June 1988 the chairman of the RCEP, Sir Jack Lewis, took the unusual step of writing to the environment minister: 'The commission suspects that waste producers are seeking the easier option for disposal rather than the best',[11] that is, they were dumping it in Britain because it was cheaper.

Government embarrassment over the *Karin B* episode in August 1988 led to implementation of the EC Directive on the Transfrontier Shipment of Hazardous Waste and the issue of regulations to take effect on 14 October and 14 November 1988. As the directive had already been in force elsewhere for a number of years, it was not surprising that the EC Commissioner criticized the British Government for its tardiness.[12]

The issue refused to go away. Eleven months after the *Karin B*, on 28 July 1989, the DoE announced that it had agreed to the import of 1,500 tonnes of toxic waste for disposal at the Rechem plant in Pontypool, South Wales. The 88,000 litres of PCB-contaminated waste oils came from a fire that destroyed the Slt Basil-le-Grand warehouse in Montreal and caused 3,000 nearby residents to be evacuated.[13] Unfortunately, Rechem (see also Chapter 6) was already the subject of strong local opposition, which accused it of discharging dioxins into the air during the incineration of PCBs. Even more unfortunately, the local opposition leader had received a letter from the Canadian Environment Ministry, dated 31 January, stating that 'PCB-contaminated remains' of the fire would 'not be exported from Canada'. The situation was thus ripe for a display of public anger and, if necessary, trade union muscle, similar to that at the time of the *Karin B*.

On 7 August it was reported that the *Madezha Obukhova* of the Balt Canada Line of Leningrad, with a first consignment of 100 tonnes of the waste, was expected to dock in Liverpool between 5 and 9 August, to be followed by a sister ship, the *Khudozhnik Saryan* and 13 others. At this point an element of black comedy enters. The *Khudozhnik* arrived first, having sailed from Rotterdam; its proposed port of entry was not, however, Liverpool but Tilbury, where the Port Authorities refused to handle it because of 'public concern and the environmental issues', doubtless much to the relief of the local dockers whose zest for action had been seriously undermined by the sacking of its shop stewards during the recent dock strike. Rechem announced that the cargo was not for them but for another company, which they refused to name, though the ship's manifest gave it as the Grosvenor Power Services Company of Carrington, Manchester, which in turn stated that, after stripping down disused equipment, it would send the PCB-contaminated remainder to Rechem! In fact, the vessel contained only six tonnes of PCBs and the seven drums containing these remained on it, unhandled 'because of public concern'. Twenty-four hours later, the ship, and its cargo, was on its way back to Canada. By that time 38 ports had announced their refusal to unload PCBs, though the largest British port employer, Associated British Ports, stated that it had no ban on handling them. Inevitably, when the *Madezha Obukhova* eventually reached Liverpool, it was forced to return with its cargo intact. Quebec's Environment Minister, Mme Lise Bacon, announced that the waste would be stored at a special high security site in Canada; Canadian dockers retaliated by proclaiming that they would refuse to offload the cargo on return. The affair was embarrassing for both governments, the British because they supported entry but did not override public protest, the

Canadian because Canada had already banned the import of PCBs. Ironically, facilities for destroying PCBs existed in Canada but, because of over-demand, the only plant, in Alberta, refused to accept PCBs from outside the province.[14]

Even before the tumult and shouting died, three cargoes containing PCB-contaminated waste had been quietly unloaded, the first two, from Greece and Ireland, at Liverpool, the third, from Uruguay, at Tilbury, within hours of the *Khudozhnik Saryan*'s departure. The Liverpool dock authorities said they could not give details of PCB shipments for the period in question, while Tilbury maintained that no PCBs had left the vessel; conversely, 'if the PCBs had not been declared, they could have been unloaded'. The method is even simpler than misleading labels: ask no questions and you'll be told no lies. You will not be told the full truth either. Where PCBs are concerned, the best way to avoid trouble is obviously to keep one's mouth shut. The episode would doubtless have had greater public impact had the ships not been Russian. Unlike the *Karin B*, or even the *Zanoobia*, no one could remember their unpronounceable names.[15]

The transport of toxic waste from the West to the Third World did not begin with the *Khian Sea*, nor did it end with declarations from the OAU or the Basel Convention on Toxic Waste of March 1989. Among the more notorious merchants of waste in the USA were the New York-based Colbert brothers, Jack and Charles, and the Florida businessman, Maxwell Cobb. The Colberts collected huge volumes of explosive and poisonous wastes, including outdated pesticides and industrial chemicals, which they stored in 20 warehouses along the east coast before shipment to India, South Korea, Nigeria and Zimbabwe. Half the waste came from the federal or state governments, the rest from private industry. As the Colberts were quite open in their dealings, one can only assume that the official bodies preferred not to know what was happening. The brothers overreached themselves when they relabelled a consignment of waste as pure dry cleaning solvent and shipped it to a firm in Zimbabwe that had paid for it with funds provided by the US Agency for International Development (USAID). In July 1986 a Federal Court in New York sentenced them to 13 years imprisonment for fraudulent practices. Their most bizarre deal, revealed only after the authorities seized a warehouse in Newark, New Jersey, was the prospective sale to an African country of lead-contaminated engraving paper from the Treasury Department's Bureau of Engraving; the buyer proposed to sell it as toilet paper!

Maxwell Cobb's firm, American Electric of Jacksonville, obtained much of its waste from East Coast military establishments under a large contract with the Defense Department. In 1984 he tried to sell PCB-contaminated wastes to Honduras, but was prosecuted, and acquitted, on insufficient evidence. He eventually went to gaol, on a drug conviction.[16]

Africa was not the only continent considered a potential dustbin. The US-based Abbott Laboratories in Puerto Rico, where pharmaceutical dumps were full, exported wastes containing antibiotics and fish oil to the Dominican Republic for use as cattle feed and fertilizer, which resulted in the death of one animal in 1985. TRW Inc. of Redondo Beach, California, hired the transport company, Eco-Therm, to ship 205 cylinders of poisonous corrosive gases to Costa Rica, where the government, after contacting the EPA, refused to accept them. The Bergsoe Metal Corporation of St Helens, Oregon, attempted to send 700 tonnes of crushed battery plates containing lead to the Kwang Shin Industrial Company of South Korea, where the government's opposition to importing 'such harmful waste' resulted in the EPA withdrawing export approval. Three further attempts to different companies in Taiwan followed the same pattern of rejection by the government and withdrawal of approval by the EPA.

The cover of importing waste under the guise that it was for 'recycling', so that technically it was no longer waste, also failed. In 1981 an American, Charles Nugent, was arrested in Mexico for exporting 'hazardous waste' to a 'mercury recovery plant' in Zacatecas. In reality the waste was simply dumped and burned. In the Pacific, the Marshall Islands, now threatened with inundation from rising seas, have received at least two offers. Western Pacific Waste Repositories, of Carson City, Nevada, have proposed the building of a hazardous waste storage and treatment plant on the uninhabited Erikub atoll in return for cash payments and development of the nearby Wotje atoll. Admiralty Pacific's offer may be even more attractive. The company propose to send the islands 25m tonnes of rubbish over five years from 1990, which could be used to protect the atolls against rising tides.[17] No such ethical motives lay behind the shipment of thousands of falsely marked containers of toxic waste that lay unclaimed for years in Bangkok's Klong Toey Port after being shipped from Singapore to bogus companies in Thailand. According to a United Nations expert, the rusty and broken containers had contaminated the water supply of the adjoining, densely populated slum area.[18]

The waste merchants have not entirely given up Africa, they have merely acquired greater sophistication. In March 1989 the London *Observer* reported a £130m scheme, allegedly the brainchild of Roger Cottenie, head of the Belgian project promotion company, Sport and Import, to ship millions of tons of the West's household rubbish to the port of Pepel, about 62 miles from Freetown, Sierra Leone. Phase One of the scheme would involve the establishment of a waste dump of between 8 and 12 acres for the generation of methane gas, either for bottling or for fuelling a small power plant. Phase Two included construction of a high-technology rubbish incinerator, the heat from which would drive a steam turbine power station of 90–120 megawatts. Cottenie insisted that, by producing electricity and using only non-toxic household waste, his scheme differed completely from previous waste dumping. The Euro-MP, François Roelants de Vivier, who exposed earlier machinations, regarded it, however, as 'simply a waste dumping scheme dressed up as a high technology venture'.[19] If the plans fail to reach the heights of Künzler's grandiose vision, that may well be because the merchants of waste have learned from the dangers of excess.

Despite the OAU resolution, a Guernsey Company, Prodev, formed in 1986, whose four listed directors all have South African addresses, attempted to persuade the governments of Botswana, Zambia, and Mozambique to import and bury millions of tons of American hazardous wastes. These included highly dangerous pesticides, chlorine and phosphorus compounds, lead sludge, heavy metal oxides, asbestos, pharmaceuticals and effluent sludges. Under the Botswana plan the waste would be imported into South Africa and sent by rail to Botswana for burial at a site in the Kalahari Desert in trenches 400 ft long and 6 ft deep, with 3 ft of toxic sludge covered by a 4-ft mound of earth planted with grass. Once the waste was buried, the company would return the land to the government for agriculture. One of the directors claimed that several sites where the hydrology would allow the waste to remain undisturbed for up to 1,000 years had been identified. All three governments rejected the proposals, but the company, conceding that, politically, it was too much of a problem, remained convinced that, commercially, it would be a good thing! The question was — for whom? 'Commercial secrecy' would doubtless have kept the whole affair under cover had not leaked papers from the Botswana Ministry of Local Government and Land reached the British press.[20]

In May 1989 another scheme also became public. The British consortium, Midco, planned to import 2,000 tonnes of toxic waste a day through Tarfaya in southern Morocco, where incinerators would generate enough electricity to produce cement, gypsum and road-building aggregate from the residue. Mott MacDonald, designers of the British end of the Channel Tunnel, were approached to design the scheme and a Canadian employee of the consortium, Claude Cornet, who had a family connection with King Hassan, attended meetings at which they presented their proposals, while Pat Dolan, a Midco director and regional vice-president of the ruling Canadian Progressive Party in Saskatchewan, declared that people in the EPA were committed to the project and only awaited the King's approval. The visit to Morocco of the British Prime Minister, Margaret Thatcher, to promote British interests, gave the consortium a boost, at least in its own eyes. (Downing Street refused to confirm that Midco was mentioned.) At this stage Cornet began to have doubts; he felt that Midco had not been honest with the King over the type of waste to be imported, was unhappy about the ability of the local workforce, and began to question the company's expertise when it sent an employee to Britain to dig out over-the-counter information on incinerators and waste quantities. Published in the British press, these reservations were immediately sent to Rabat, where the Moroccan Government, facing an imminent Arab summit, promptly vetoed the whole scheme.[21]

If Britain, rather than Third World countries, is already the dumping ground for the world's hazardous waste, by the turn of the century it will hold a second title, for the dumping of nuclear waste. As the first generation of reactors reaches the end of its working life, the amount of spent fuel and radioactive waste will increase out of all proportion to what has happened in the past. One major industrialized country after another has rejected the traditional answer to what should be done with it, namely, reprocessing, while Britain, against the advice of environmental groups and the House of Commons Environment Committee, has gone ahead with the construction of the huge Thermal Oxide Reprocessing Plant (THORP) at Sellafield. Due to open in 1992, in the first ten years of its operation it is scheduled to reprocess 7,000 tonnes of spent fuel. Half the capacity for the second ten years is already booked by the West German Government, under a series of contracts worth £750m, after Germany decided to close down its Wackersdorf reprocessing plant when faced with public opposition and stringent environmental rules that allegedly made it uneconomic.[22]

There is no doubt where radioactive waste reaching Britain will go. To Sellafield. The questions are: how will it get there, and how safe is its mode of transport? According to the consultant, John Large, imports of irradiated fuel sent by ferry from Europe have risen 18-fold from the two flasks of 1988 to 16 in 1989 and a planned 37 for 1990. By 1992 there will be 59, and over 50 a year until 1995. At Barrow, Cumbria, about 100 spent fuel flasks are imported annually from Japan, Italy and Spain, using one of the six purpose-built vessels of BNF's subsidiary, Pacific Nuclear Transport Ltd. But at Dover the flasks arrive on ordinary freight ferries of the ro-ro type that sank at Zeebrugge in 1987 and at Harwich two years earlier, and which are also particularly vulnerable to fire. The British Government has apparently stated that it is prepared to allow transport of nuclear waste through the Channel Tunnel at the operator's discretion, a prospect that should finally deter any potential travellers and one that will further add to the load on Dover. From here the flasks proceed by rail through London, Northampton, Birmingham and Stafford to Sellafield; the onlooker with a taste for horrors can watch them as the train sneaks its way past suburban houses or city slums. BNF is adamant that its flasks can withstand a fire at sea or a rail accident on land; as a consulting engineer, John Large is less sanguine. So far the public has not been exposed to the test but the increased traffic means greater possibilities of accident. The public has, at least, received one assurance; BNF has pledged that the waste will not be carried on passenger ferries.[23]

Europe has had other troubles with its nuclear waste, in particular the great corruption scandal which dates back to October 1986 when the lorry carrying waste from West Germany to the Mol plant, near Antwerp, Belgium, overturned, and it was found that the quality of the waste did not conform to consignment notes. At the end of 1987 allegations appeared in German publications, to be followed in January 1988 by similar reports in Belgium, that, contrary to regulations, the German firm, Transnuklear, had transported 2,400 barrels of highly radioactive material, falsely labelled as low-level waste, from German power stations to Mol for treatment, and that, instead of processed waste being returned, there were consignments of plutonium; second, that Transnuklear had allegedly bribed staff at Mol to cover up these irregularities. Subsequent concern involved not only both governments but extended to the EC, the European Parliament, the 1957 European Atomic Energy Community Treaty (EURATOM) and the International Atomic Energy Authority (IAEA). Apart from the alleged corruption, there are four alarming aspects:

- the fate of the potential weapons-grade plutonium, some of which, in October 1987 was alleged by a British TV programme, 'The Plutonium Black Market', to have been sold illegally to Libya and Pakistan through a secret bazaar in Khartoum;
- the inherent danger of transporting highly radioactive substances over land and by sea;
- the emerging picture, which left a European Commission official 'aghast', of an industry unable to cope with the huge problem of disposing of vast quantities of nuclear waste; and
- the inevitable secrecy surrounding the activities of the nuclear industry with its international ramifications, especially in matters of waste disposal.

On this occasion the police were ahead of investigative reporters. A criminal inquiry started in April 1987, when Nukem admitted that it had found evidence of systematic bribery, embezzlement and deception in Transnuklear's activities, which included paying out DM21 million (£7m) in bribes. One million Belgian francs and a car went to the head of the Mol plant, Norbert Van de Voorde, who was sacked. The Transnuklear official responsible for arranging this and apparently hundreds of other similar transactions in France, Italy and Switzerland, Hans Holtz, was arrested on 11 December 1987 after detailed enquiries but apparently committed suicide in prison three days later. He left behind a detailed statement of the bribes, visits to brothels, free holidays and electrical goods used to secure nuclear waste transport contracts.

The corruption scandal should not have come entirely as a surprise. The Hanau complex near Frankfurt houses the Nukem atomic fuel company, the Transnuklear transport company, and the nuclear fuel element factory, Alkem, both of which are Nukem subsidiaries. At the beginning of March 1987 Nukem admitted that one of its employees had been contaminated with a small amount of plutonium 'mixed' with uranium, and that it had closed the section of the plant concerned. On 16 March the Hesse Government revealed that in fact 9 workers had been exposed and 70 undergone checks as a result of the incident. On 28 April the government ordered an investigation into a leak of 'hex' (uranium hexafluoride) from the Hanau fuel fabrication plant run by Reaktor Brennelement, 40 per cent of which is owned by Nukem, and temporarily closed the section. In August the Hesse Environment Minister ordered the temporary closure of Nukem on the grounds that its safety provisions were inadequate; and on the 10th of the month the trial opened in Hanau of two executives of Alkem, charged with illegally operating a nuclear installation, and three officials of the Hesse Environment Ministry accused of aiding and abetting them.

While the British Prime Minister dismissed a request to raise the bribery and corruption issue at a meeting of the European Council of Ministers on the grounds that it was solely the concern of Belgium and West Germany, the UK cannot divorce itself so easily. Under agreements between the UK Atomic Energy Authority (UKAEA) and EURATOM, the UK has exported at least 180kg of British plutonium to Mol and, since 1973, 200kg of plutonium to Nukem. Nukem reportedly owns two-thirds of the shares in Transnuklear, the remaining third being owned by Transnucléaire of France, which, in turn, is involved, with BNF and Transnuklear itself, in Nuclear Transport Ltd. The wider implications of international secrecy became apparent when the EC's committee of inquiry into the affair was refused permission to see the agreement between EURATOM and BNF for reasons of 'commercial secrecy'. The EC revealed, however, that the British Government had forbidden release of details of reprocessing at Sellafield on the grounds that 'national security' was involved.[24] When BNF goes ahead with its full programme of nuclear waste imports, it should at least know the type of firm with which it may have to deal. Past experience suggests that it should be up to the task.

The above examples, and the events outlined in the Prologue, show how the transport of waste, particularly hazardous and nuclear wastes, lends itself to all forms of malpractices: the mixing of highly contaminated and less contaminated wastes; the mislabelling or inaccurate descriptions of waste; causing waste to 'disappear' by making it 'goods-in-transit' or turning it into recyclable material; eliminating it by failing to declare it to authorities which, in turn, ask no questions; and, at the upper end of the scale, outright bribery and the offer of sweeteners, especially in dealings between middlemen and Third World partners, or within the secret operations of the nuclear industry. This is a sordid business in which Britain and the USA occupy special places, the first for actively encouraging the import of waste for disposal, the second for using all means to get rid of it. When spent nuclear fuel is brought in for reprocessing and the public given the impression that contracts stipulate that any resultant waste will be returned, only to discover that this does not apply to agreements made before 1976, passive acceptance is no longer possible, and, faced with the growing piles of radioactive waste, the public and their representatives in parliament demand the return of such waste to the countries from which it came. But this does not eliminate the waste; it merely displaces it. Before, however, deciding what should be done, it is necessary to find out what is happening now and what occurs when, at the end of its journey, waste is 'disposed of'.

Notes

1. Goldsmith and Hildyard 1988 p. 214
2. Brown, P 1988
3. *Guardian* 9 January 1988
4. Gourlay 1988 p. 203
5. MacKenzie 1989a
6. *New Scientist* 3 June 1989
7. *Guardian* 15 November 1989
8. *Observer* 18 February 1990
9. Schoon and Bridge 1990
10. DoE 1989a pp. 57, 89 Table 7.7. HoC 1989 para. 250; *Guardian* 31 August 1988
11. *New Scientist* 23 June 1988
12. HoC 1989 para. 256
13. *Guardian* 7 August 1989
14. *Guardian* 7 August 1989, 9 August 1989, 10 August 1989; *Observer* 13 August 1989, 20 August 1989
15. *Observer* 20 August 1989
16. Weir and Porterfield 1987 pp. 26−7; Milne 1989b
17. Weir and Porterfield 1987 p. 20; MacKenzie 1989a
18. TWN 1989 p. 11; *The Nation*, Thailand 18 June 1988; *The Star*, Malaysia 26 June 1988
19. *Observer* 12 March 1989
20. *Guardian* 31 May 1989
21. Ibid. 15, 16 May 1989
22. Ibid. 25 April 1990
23. Ibid. 25 April 1990, 11 June 1990; *Observer* 10 June 1990
24. Lowry 1988; *Guardian* 9 January 1988, 23 Feburary 1988, 11 March 1988; Keesing's *Contemporary Archives* 1988 pp. 35725−6

4. Into (and Onto) the Earth

All types of waste, not merely domestic rubbish or industry's unwanted by-products, go into the Earth. Surplus spoil quarried from one hole in the ground is dumped in another, the less contaminated products of the nuclear process are consigned to a ditch, while the intensive farmer's excess pesticides and herbicides leach their way into the soil to join the superabundance of nitrate-bearing fertilizer already there.

Domestic waste

Over 90 per cent of domestic waste, in some cases the whole of it, in both the industrialized world and the Third, is taken away and dumped in holes in the ground or added to growing mountains of existing refuse. The remainder is either burned or dumped at sea. In larger cities collection and disposal is a municipal responsibility, to meet which there are official refuse collection and waste disposal services, with the actual business of disposal often contracted out to private firms. Ironically, while, until recently at least, the industrialized world aimed simply at getting rid of the waste, the Third World, through poverty and necessity, was more inclined to make use of it.

New York City, for example, is building its own mountain range, the 3,000-acre Fresh Kills landfill, Staten Island. Bulldozers pile layer upon layer of reeking garbage to form giant mounds of earth that by 1998 will rise to 500 feet, the highest coastal point between Maine and the tip of Florida. Tractors haul 26,000 tons a day up the slopes, while giant cranes scoop up garbage from incoming barges. The site symbolizes the final waste crisis of the US eastern states. When all the space is used up, 7.1m people will have nowhere to put three-quarters of their rubbish. Some states have already reached this point. New Jersey, for many years a dumping-ground for other states, has almost run out of space in its most heavily populated north-eastern region and is forced to send more than half its waste to Pennsylvania, Ohio and West Virginia. Philadelphia attempted to get rid of its municipal ash on the *Khian Sea*; others, less scrupulous, dumped it directly into the sea so that, in the summer of 1988, a filthy tide of medical and other waste was washed up on beaches from Massachusetts to North Carolina.[1]

In contrast, some Third World countries have turned the perennial scavengers of refuse heaps into collectors or sorters of usable waste. In Medellin, Columbia, about 4,000 people earn a living from scavenging and recycling household wastes; in India 1–3 individuals per thousand collect and dispose of refuse; in the eastern Sudan the Regional Ministry of Health contracts out the task of house-to-house collection of dry refuse and rubbish in small towns to sweepers with donkey carts; and in Bangkok refuse collection crews add to their income by sorting recoverable materials and selling them to dealers.[2]

Smokey Mountain is to Manila what Fresh Kills is to New York, namely a great pile of the city's detritus, heaped up over the years, only a ten-minute walk from the Marcos' former palace. But there is one big difference:

> A micro-economy subsists within the garbage. The dustcarts arrive in the early morning, pursued up the smoking mound by a herd of scavengers who fall, locust-like, upon the cascading filth, fighting for the privilege of being first amid the rubbish. Each has a special line: old tin cans, bottles, wiring, clothes, plastics, shoes, cardboard boxes. Middlemen from the Tondo slum purchase the scavenged items at wholesale prices to sell them one rung up the Filipino social ladder. A man kneels in the sulphurous shallows of Manila Bay, washing plastic sacks he has retrieved. A thousand sacks earn him one hundred pesos, about £3.[3]

Perhaps the best-known collector-scavengers are the Zebaleen people of Cairo. Members of the Coptic Christian minority, they migrated from upper Egypt over 50 years ago and have collected the rubbish from the city streets since they arrived. Their donkey carts took the rubbish out to the Maqattam hills, where the women sorted out paper, plastics and metal for sale to the recycling industry. This traditional picturesque method not only conflicted with the authorities' image of a modern city but also raised problems of its practical ability to cope with the city's rapid growth. The Zebaleen community association drew up a plan for progressive mechanization; with the help of a Cairo professional organization, Environmental Quality International (EQI) and a grant from the US Ford Foundation, they competed aganst major companies for the right to operate a motorized collection service, and won. Trucks are gradually replacing donkey carts and, with assistance from Oxfam and the Ford Foundation, the Zebaleen have set up their own recycling plant.[4]

Holes in the ground

At its simplest, landfill means tipping waste into a hole in the ground and covering it up. The theory is that, through the process of 'dilute and disperse', natural chemical and biological processes will render the waste harmless as its seeps through underlying soils. The problem is that, before this occurs, seepage has already taken place and this leachate affected the groundwater system on which many people depend for drinking water. To avoid this, modern containment landfills are lined with non-porous clay, divided into cells, covered daily with plastic, inspected regularly and any leachate drained off and tested. Even this has not solved the problem. Heavy rain can cause the landfill to overflow, and research confirms that it is almost impossible to avoid seepage.[5]

A recent five-year project by the Leichtweiss Hydrology Institute in Brunswick, West Germany, suggests both that the landfill concept requires further study and that domestic waste may not be as innocent as it appears. Rubbish of different types, such as compressed household refuse, household refuse and water or sewage sludge, some in soil through which air could permeate, some between impermeable strata, was stored in ten cylinders, each six metres tall and five metres in diameter, with access from all sides, inspection valves and flexible outer walls. The results were disconcerting: 'Seepage was found to occur from all garbage tips, the exact amount depending on how densely or thickly packed the garbage is and how moist the subsoil is', particularly disturbing features being that the first seepage could take up to a year to occur and that the extent of the seepage *increased* once the tip was closed. The report continues: 'All seepage contains germs: in waste from doctors' surgeries, in sewage sludge or in such mundane items as disposable nappies that are dumped straight onto local authority garbage tips untreated along with other household wastes'. Germs were quickly killed, but only 'in the middle of the dump where temperatures of over 60°C are reached due to decomposition'. In consequence the scientists were unable to forecast when dumps would cease to be health hazards.[6]

The problem, as the European Environmental Bureau sees it, is that 'household refuse does not only consist of organic components but also contains harmful products such as plastics, batteries, paint remnants and medicine', which may pollute the soil and groundwater beneath a waste dump.[7] One need not be reminded that batteries contain (or contained) mercury or cadmium, or that paints were lead-based.

It is the organic component, however, that could prove more immediately dangerous, especially where conscientious site operators have provided waterproof cells and quickly covered a tip to protect it from the rain. This provides ideal conditions for generating highly explosive methane gas, which escapes through the surrounding soil to build up in nearby houses. The problem aroused public concern in 1986 when a bungalow at Loscoe, Derbyshire, England, was blown apart, seriously injuring three people, after methane had built up and ingited when the central heating came on automatically during the night. In March 1987 houses on an estate in Surrey were evacuated following a methane build-up from a nearby tip, and in January 1988 a night storage heater caused a gas explosion in an office at Appley Bridge, Lancashire. A survey by the DoE's Inspectorate of Pollution estimated that 1,300 tips posed a potential hazard to public health with gas building up in or near housing at 100 of these. At least 600 tips required anti-gas safeguards. The Derbyshire County Council, responsible for the Loscoe tip, maintained that most authorities 'were not aware of the problem of landfill gas migration' and felt that the DoE or the Inspectorate of Pollution should have warned them. The House of Commons Environment Committee commented drily: 'We regard the general lack of awareness of this issue to be a symptom of the immaturity, lack of professionalism and low status of waste management'.[8]

In Britain the problem is further exacerbated by the practice of co-disposal, that is, the dumping of domestic and industrial waste in the same landfill. The domestic waste is deposited first, trenches dug in its surface, and the industrial waste in liquid form pumped into them. Obviously this requires skill to avoid exceeding the site's capacity to absorb the liquid and to ensure that incompatible wastes, which may release toxic or inflammable gases, do not come into contact with each other.

Those favouring co-disposal argue that the domestic waste is capable of absorbing a reasonable volume of the liquid, thus preventing run-off, that the resulting biological processes eventually render the hazardous waste safe, that there are significant economic advantages, in that joint burial is considerably cheaper than separate disposal, and that there is little evidence of the process affecting the quality of the groundwater. Those opposing the practice point out that co-disposal has been studied only since the 1970s and that it is too early to assess the long-term environmental problems, that there is the protential to spread contamination over a large area, and that, even if the biological processes do reduce toxicity, there is inadequate information on determining the capacity of the landfill in this respect and consequently a continuing element of risk. Above all, co-disposal depends on the principle of 'dilute and disperse', which can be faulted as potentially dangerous to groundwater and a source of future soil contamination. In the USA arguments against have so far prevailed and co-disposal is not legally permissible; only the UK continues to champion the practice.[9]

The House of Commons Environment Committee investigating toxic waste was 'extremely concerned by the evidence...received about the wide variations in standards of co-disposal in the UK'; while a large number of landfills, in the words of the government's Inspectorate of Pollution, were 'exemplary in the controls they provide', the great problem was 'a lack of consistency'; in short, as a Cheshire County Council officer put it, 'thousands of tonnes of hazardous waste were improperly going to landfill'.[10] In plain language, highly poisonous toxic waste was dumped in co-disposal sites in excess of their hypothetical capacity to cope with it.

Landfill operations in a developed country such as the UK leave little room for complacency. According to the DoE, the 1989 market price for landfill disposal of household waste was between £2 and £5 per tonne. This contrasted with an ideal price, that is, one taking into account the construction of adequate protection against leaching, restoration after use

and proper aftercare, of £9 per tonne.[11] If, under the highly competitive
free-for-all British system, contractors were charging between a quarter and
half of what is actually necessary, it would suggest that, at some point, there
is a certain amount of dubious corner-cutting. The history of landfill, in
both the USA and Western Europe, is, in fact, marked by the discovery of
malpractices due to, at best, ignorance of the limitations of the practice at
worst, to criminal negligence by site operators and quick-fix disposal
merchants.

Landfill in the USA

Symbolic of these is the now notorious Love Canal in Niagara City.
Excavated in the late nineteenth century by an eccentric entrepreneur,
William T. Love, the 'canal' was used by Hooker Chemicals and Plastics
Corporation from the 1940s to 1952 for dumping over 20,000 tonnes of
chemical waste, much of it carcinogenic. In 1953 Hooker sold the site to the
local Board of Education on condition that the company was absolved from
future liability for any injury resulting from leakage. The Board built a
school on the site, and a housing estate followed shortly. By the end of the
1970s cases of cancer and child malformation were linked to the foul-
smelling liquid and sludge that seeped into the basements of houses. In 1978
some 237 families were forced to leave their homes, the dump was cordoned
off and the site declared a Federal Disaster Area. By 1980 anxiety among the
remaining 710 families increased when an EPA report revealed that some
residents had damaged chromosomes and there was a further evaluation. By
1988 three other Hooker dumps in the area were known to be leaking,
including Hyde Park, which contains the largest deposit of dioxin in the
world and from which waste oozes directly into the Niagara River, and
Bloody Run Creek, which is sited across the road from a water-treatment
plant for 10,000 people.[12]

That it took over 20 years for Love Canal to reveal itself is significant. The
first problem in any survey of landfill sites is to discover where they are; the
second to estimate their toxicity; the third to estimate the cost of cleaning
them up.

Attempts to discover the extent of these problems in the USA have led
only to further uncertainty and confusion. According to one report, the EPA
has identified 74,000 sites, of which 32,000 are rated as bad as, or worse
than, Love Canal.[13] According to another, by the end of 1985 the EPA
considered 21,512 sites to be 'potentially dangerous', with 1,750 'in urgent
need of repair'.[14] Other estimates give a total of 50,000 hazardous waste
landfills, of which 20,000 pose a potential threat to human health and 2,000
require immediate clean-up.[15] Yet a further source states that, by October
1987, the EPA had designated 951 landfills and other waste sites as needing
urgent attention and estimated that the list would grow to not more than
2,500 sites with total clean-up costs of US $23bn. Finally, the Congressional

Office of Technology Assessment (OTA) assesses the ultimate number of 'priority sites' as 10,000 and the overall cost of clean-up as $100b, or $400 for every US resident.[16] The only realistic conclusion is that no one knows how many toxic landfill sites exist in the USA, what proportion of them are hazardous and how much it will cost to clean them up.

Nor is this all. In addition to landfills, there are some 170,000 industrial impoundments, used for dumping liquid wastes, and countless deep wells with their own problems (see Box 4.1).

The scandal of Love Canal and increased public anxiety had one potentially good result. In 1980 the Comprehensive Environmental Response, Compensation and Liability Act (CERLA), the last bill signed by President Carter, set up the 'superfund' to clean up contaminated sites. Originally conceived at $4,200 million, under pressure from industry, which was to provide 88 per cent of the cash, this figure was reduced to $1,600 million and claims by which private citizens could sue the fund for damage caused by improper dumping were dropped.[17] What followed, according to William Drayton, assistant administrator to EPA under President Carter, was 'a classic Greek tragedy; enter stage right the Reagan revolution with its enormous ideological antagonism to regulation of any sort. You have a leader who just doesn't understand what all these Latin-named chemicals are and what they do. On this subject he just stopped learning'.[18]

Reagan's choice of top EPA officials to administer the fund was disastrous. In 1981 Anne Burford, a Colorado lawyer and Republican Party fund-raiser, took over the agency and, prompted by the White House, approved the selection of Rita Lavelle, a Californian publicist who had worked for the chemical company, Aerojet General Corporation, to direct the superfund. Lavelle was later convicted of perjury for denying involvement in EPA's dealings with Stringfellow Acid Pits, a notorious Californian waste dump, where Aerojet General and others had over the years dumped tons of caustics, cyanides and heavy metals. Burford was charged with contempt of Congress for refusing to give it internal EPA documents and resigned in March 1988. Meanwhile the White House imposed funding cuts on the EPA that resulted in a loss of 23 per cent of its budget and 19 per cent of its employees. The recall of William Ruckelhaus, the agency's first director under the Nixon administration, did something to restore its image and effectiveness.[19]

Box 4.1: Deep-well injection

Both municipal and hazardous liquid wastes are injected under pressure into porous rocks, usually at depths of 600–1,800 metres (2,000–18,000ft), displacing any liquid or gas in the rocks, before being trapped by the pressure of the rocks above. In the USA in 1981 an estimated 3,600 million gallons of waste from the oil and gas industries, the pharmaceutical industry and the chemical and steel industries were disposed of in this way in 70,000 deep wells. ⇨

⬦ According to the EPA there are in all some 500,000 injection wells in the USA, most of them on farms and oilfields, operating with low pressure. Some 500 high-pressure industrial wells, of which 200 hold hazardous waste, are potentially dangerous.

There are three problems: 1) The permanent threat that the wastes may migrate into deep aquifers and so contaminate water supplies. This is most likely to occur as the result of improper plugging or where the rocks fracture under pressure. 2) If wells are over-pressurized they can erupt, as happened at Eries, Pennsylvania, in 1968. 3) They can cause earthquakes. The controversy here centres on which earthquakes. Scientists agree that deep injection of waste from a paint works caused an earthquake of magnitude 3.6 at Ashtabula, Ohio, on 13 July 1987. There had been no previous earthquakes within a 35km radius and the epicentre was only 700 metres from the well, which had begun operating a year earlier. In the early 1960s the US army caused an earthquake by injecting nerve gas deep into very hard rock in an earthquake-prone area at its Rocky Mountain arsenal, Colorado, and in the early 1970s hundreds of small earthquakes, caused by injecting oilfield wastes near Buffalo, New York, stopped when pressure was reduced. More controversial is the 31 January 1986 earthquake at Perry, Ohio, which registered 4.9 on the Richter scale and shook a nearly completed nuclear reactor 17km from the epicentre without damaging it. Eleven kilometres from the epicentre are two injection wells, operated by Calhio, a division of Stauffer Chemicals, working at pressures of around 100kg per square centimetre and injecting liquid waste to depths of about two kilometres. Geologists at Ohio University in Athens, Ohio, claimed to have demonstrated, by computer model, that pressure from the wells spread through hard igneous rocks to cause slippage on a fault not evident from the surface. Geologists elsewhere argued that the earthquake was similar to one in 1943, which registered 4.7 and occurred long before injection, and, since the energy resulting from high-pressure injection was insufficient to cause a large earthquake, the Perry incident was due to natural causes. Yet a further view was that, while injection in itself could not cause the quake, the pressure may have been the last straw which triggered it off in strained rocks. Once again we are in the realm of uncertainty that teaches caution. In July 1988 the EPA ordered well drillers to judge whether earthquakes could result from their activities.

Sources: Goldsmith and Hildyard 1988 p. 129; *Hecht* 1988

Even so, during its first five years, critics maintained that less than 20 per cent of the $1,600 million was spent on clean-up operations, and the National Campaign Against Toxic Hazards claimed that fewer than 10 per cent of the 850 sites then listed received remedial attention. Reporting in 1985, the OTA concluded that, despite EPA monitoring of sites suspected of endangering underground water supplies, of the 1,246 hazardous waste dumps it surveyed, nearly half showed signs of polluting nearby groundwater. The EPA's monitoring was 'inaccurate, uncomplete and unreliable'.[20] As for clean-up, the solutions were often merely stop-gap transference of wastes to other areas. 'Risks are often transferred from one community to another and to future generations'.[21] In the meagre six sites officially cleaned up in the first five years of the fund's operation, the allocation of priorities and action taken were hardly encouraging.

Why two of them were chosen for quick action remains a mystery. The Mississippi state authorities considered 226 drums of chemicals such as tetrasodium pyrophosphate and formic acid, stored in a warehouse for failure to pay taxes, a fire hazard rather than a contamination threat, but asked the EPA for priority status. The agency solved the problem by carting the drums off to an approved landfill at Emelle, Alabama. Similarly, 700 drums of chemicals in a Cleveland warehouse of Chemical Minerals Recovery Co. and another 700 stored outside, none of which had sprung significant leaks, were taken to a licensed landfill in Geneva, Ohio.

Other sites at least justified action. In Pennsylvania contamination of the Susquehanna River led to the discovery of illegal dumping of toxic waste into shafts that led to the Butler Tunnel, an outlet for waste water from disused coalmines near Pittston. Three men were convicted under the state's Clean Streams Act, one sent to prison, and the men and their company fined $750,000. The EPA supervised the river clean-up and in 1982 removed the site from its primary list. Despite the 'cleaning', when Hurricane Gloria led to heavy rains, 100,000 gallons of oily, smelly chemical wastes rushed back up to the surface and into the Susquehanna.

In Baltimore, where strong acids and corrosive *aqua regia* had been stored throughout the 1970s so that local residents complained of eye, nose and throat irritation and in July 1979 eight people were burned when chemicals leaked into a playing area, the EPA removed 1,500 drums and up to 12 inches of topsoil before sloping and sodding the land for use as a playground. Critics maintain, however, that tests revealed contamination 15 feet below the surface and that there was no attempt to prevent these deeper chemicals from seeping into groundwater or a nearby river.

Near St Louis, Michigan, from the 1930s onward, the Velsicol Chemical Company has dumped and burned toxic industrial chemicals on a 3.5-acre site along Pine River, where a county golf club adjoined the dump. By the mid-1960s fish in the river were discovered to contain dangerous pollutants such as PCBs and DDT. Together with the EPA, in 1982 the company spent $38.5 million on a clean-up operation that included the removal of all soil from the golf course to a depth of three feet below any signs of contamination, some 68,204 cubic yards in all, and pumping 1.25 million gallons of contaminated groundwater into a 3,400ft cement-lined well. The soil was transported across the river to the plant's property and the golf course declared cleaned up. Delighted as were the golfers, cynics maintained that the problem had merely been transferred elsewhere.[22]

In October 1985 the original superfund legislation expired with Congress and the Reagan administration arguing over the amount to be allowed for the next five years. Congress wanted up to $10,000 million, the administration suggested $5,300 million. By 1986 both had accepted the figure of $8.500 million.[23] Whether this will be enough to clean up existing dumps, let alone keep pace with new additions, is anyone's guess, but with environmental regulations becoming more strict and the cost of burying hazardous waste rising from $15 per tonne in 1980 to $250 in 1989, while incineration has reached $1,500 per tonne, it is not surprising that US companies look overseas for a solution.[24]

The problems of hazardous waste are without end and survive their generators. At the heart of 'Chemical Valley', a 12-mile stretch along the Kanawah River, West Virginia, which houses two dozen chemical plants, including the only US producer of methyl isocyanate, the chemical whose leakage caused the Bhopal disaster, is the small town of Nitro (population 9,000), site of the Artel Chemical Company's works. In June 1988 a federal judge ordered the site closed when the company could not pay its workers. The company's bequest to the town included over 3,400 drums and barrels, many of them unidentified or rusting, or both, foremost among them a tank of hydrogen cyanide, 50 milligrams of which are fatal to human beings. In October 1988 over 3,000 residents of the town were evacuated from an area within 1,000 metres of the plant, while the EPA blew up the tank and the resulting fire burned off its contents. Other problems facing the EPA included disposal of a 9,000-gallon tank of toxic and highly flammable methylmercaptan, and of a bunker full of sodium, which explodes on contact with water, a situation reminiscent of the Sandoz fire at Basel in November 1986.[25] Was it coincidence that the Artel Chemical Company was previously owned by the progenitor of Bhopal, Union Carbide?

Landfill in Western Europe

Western Europe had a less spectacular but equally significant awakening to the dangers of old landfill sites when 870 people in a housing estate at Lekkerkek, Holland, were forced to leave their homes owing to the presence of some 2,000 drums containing 500 tonnes of waste. A total of 150,000 tonnes of earth had to be moved at a cost of some US $70 million.[26]

The outcome was a search for disused and contaminated sites, the legacy of a 'carefree' past, when millions of tonnes of dangerous waste were dumped without precautions. In Holland 4,300 potentially contaminated sites were listed in 1980, but five years later the figure had risen to 5,000, of which 1,000 required immediate clean-up. A Danish survey of 1980−82 found 3,115 sites containing chemical waste, of which 114 threatened groundwater. West German investigators revealed around 50,000 waste dumps at the beginning of the 1970s, more recent research suggesting that 35,000 were potentially contaminated and 5,400 required treatment. In

France an initial 1978 survey of old dumps containing dangerous waste identifed 450, with 80, since increased to 140, listed as 'serious' or requiring immediate action. In the Walloon part of Belgium alone 8,363 dumps were identified in 1982 of which 148 contained chemical or infective waste. The European Environmental Bureau (EEB), which provided these figures, concluded its analysis:

> The problem of old waste dumps appears particularly daunting from another point of view: industrial activity over the last 25 years has seen the production in the EEC of at least 300 million tonnes of dangerous waste, the majority of which has 'naturally' been dumped without special precautions.[27]

The figures for Denmark, Holland and West Germany suggest either that the French were considerably more efficient in matters of waste disposal or somewhat less diligent in their search for truth than their European neighbours.

The prize for absence of information must, however, go to the UK. When I began writing this book, I had anticipated that, apart from a DoE assessment that in England there were possibly 10,000 hectares of contaminated soil, i.e. soil posing a danger to planned future use,[28] I would repeat previous statements that 'No one knows how many polluting dumps exist in the United Kingdom. The British Government has yet to undertake a survey' and quote the independently obtained figure of 600 potentially dangerous sites.[29]

In February 1990 the *Observer*, in co-operation with Friends of the Earth (FoE), revealed that one of these statements was untrue. Like its European neighbours, in the early 1970s the British DoE compiled a list of landfill sites in England and Wales from a survey carried out by the Institute of Geological Sciences, but never revealed its contents until a copy eventually passed to FoE. Working from this and information available at 149 different local authority offices, it was possible, after three months' research, to produce for the first time a comprehensive list and map of locations. Estimating that there are more than 4,800 toxic tips scattered across mainland Britain, more than a quarter of them receiving wastes before there were any safety controls, the *Observer* report maintains that 1,300 sites threaten to contaminate groundwater and that 59 of these pose a 'serious risk'.

Comparison of these figures with those given previously suggests that the report is wise to add 'but the full extent of the peril to our drinking water remains unknown. Most of the tips are now hidden, covered over with earth and scrub and abandoned by their operators'.[30] Allowing for different standards of assessment and unreliable data, what are we to conclude from the fact that, in the Netherlands the proportion of sites requiring 'Immediate Attention' to those described as 'Contaminated' is 20 per cent, in Denmark 32 per cent, in West Germany 15 per cent, in France's old sites 17.8 per cent, and even in the USA 8 – 10 per cent, yet in a country with possibly the most lax regulations in the EC and a 'shambolic' disposal system, the 59 British sites listed as a 'serious risk' are a mere 4.5 per cent of the 1,300 threatening to contaminate groundwater. One must at least consider the possibility that further research will raise the number of highly dangerous sites to some figure between 200 and 400.

Investigation of the Flitwick, Bedfordshire, site and Ty Llwyd Quarry, neither of which was included in the 59, though at the time of the survey oily waste was leaking from the first and PCBs escaping from the second, confirms the possibility and reinforces the inevitable conclusion that, while we may now know where the sites are, if not always their precise extent, even in the 1990s no one knows how many are, or may become, dangerous. Nor is confidence increased when we learn further that the DoE carried out studies of the Flitwick leak in 1974 and 1978, concluded that it threatened a major underground water system, and that, when the second survey showed that the poisons had travelled only 125 yards from the tip, did nothing, a policy followed by the local County Councils responsible until the unsought-for publicity.

Given the system of waste disposal in Britain, can we expect otherwise? Until 1972 there were no regulations and 16 years after the passage through Parliament of the 1974 Control of Pollution Act (COPA) relevant parts of the Act have still not come into force on grounds of cost. The 199 Waste Disposal Authorities (WDAs) in Britain (District or County Councils according to region) are not only empowered to provide waste disposal themselves but have the regulatory duties of issuing licences to private site operators, monitoring site operations and enforcing licence conditions.[31] In short, they not only have the same 'poacher/gamekeeper' functions as did the Water Authorities before privatization but must use public money in direct competition with private contractors working for profit. Not surprisingly, the House of Commons Environment Committee reported in February 1989:

> against this *laissez-faire* background...there is no consistency of standards between one Waste Disposal Authority and another. In many the standards are extremely low encouraging the operation of contractors who have no regard for the potential dangers to the environment...we feel that we must warn the Government that by continuing to ignore previous recommendations it is playing – sometimes literally – with fire.[32]

The Committee's plain speaking was reinforced by evidence from experts who pointed out discrepancies and variations in licence conditions 'which are so markedly different that they actually distort the market that operates in waste disposal',[33] while, in management, authorities varied from 'literally a man and a dog...fully occupied in writing licences... to those who have a team of multi-disciplinary staff'.[34] As for monitoring waste disposal, 'A number of... authorities... spend very little time actually in getting out of the office to see whether the licence conditions are actually being applied.'[35] Finally, the WDAs suffered from lack of clear guidance from an understaffed DoE and, at local level, 'their political masters have little concern over a subject which has a low political profile and little electoral appeal and neglect this important service'.[36]

With 98 per cent of toxic waste dealt with by private firms in a £5bn a year business,[37] the result exemplifies the application of Thatcherite market economics. Companies inevitably look for the cheapest way of getting rid of their waste, public authorities are unable to compete with the private sector, and the cheapest prices are available only by using the lowest standard of safety, including, as is widely recognized, infrequently penalized (the law demands being caught red-handed), illegal dumping.

Fifteen months after the Environment Committee's Report, a survey commissioned by the DoE and undertaken by scientists from the UKAEA's Environmental Safety Centre, revealed that, in May 1990, of 100 tips investigated, operators on more than half were not checking groundwater under and around the tips; of those that did, more than half found contamination. Additionally, at 62 per cent of the sample there were no means of preventing groundwater from entering the tips. Presumably what could get in could also, with unwanted and unwelcome additions, get out. Two-thirds of the tips were near houses, three-quarters near farmland. 'Very few' were in impermeable ground as now recommended by the DoE. According to the report's authors, the true picture was probably worse as the survey had an 'unavoidable bias towards the larger, newer and better-managed sites'.[38]

Supporting evidence was already to hand. The names Helsby, Frodsham and Alvaney do not appear in the *Observer*/FoE list of 59 sites posing a 'serious risk', or even in the 1,300 at 'some risk'. Yet in August 1989 it was reported that toxic waste containing PCBs (see Box 2.3) was leaking from a site at Helsby, near Frodsham, Cheshire, owned by Britain's largest electrical equipment company, BICC Cables. The company began dumping PCB waste at the site in the 1960s before its toxic properties were recognized. It claimed that, when the leak was discovered in 1988, it informed the relevant authorities, including Cheshire County Council and North West Water, and had spent £1 million on constructing concrete and plastic barriers to stem the leakage. It refused, however, on grounds of commercial confidence, to make public both its knowledge of the extent of the danger or the results of tests on cows grazing near the site to determine whether PCBs had entered the food chain. It admitted that it had also dumped PCB waste at a tip at Alvaney, four miles away, which drains into the same watercourse, the Hornsmill Brook, as the Helsby site. The Alvaney site had been disused for ten years but, before that, there were no restrictions.

Granted that BICC Cables acted responsibly in its efforts to stem the Helsby leakage and had the law on its side over disclosure of confidential commercial information, local fears were far from stilled. Why, if all test results were available to the appropriate authorities, as was claimed, could not the public also be given concrete evidence instead of verbal assurances? What, in short, were BICC hiding, unless it was the situation at Alvaney, where North West Water had found low levels of PCBs in the Hornsmill Brook.[39]

At the end of June 1990, a further FoE report corroborated the UK AEA findings, and demonstrated the risk to drinking water. Seven hundred and twenty-six supplies of groundwater, a third of the total in England and Wales, came from within 3,000 yards of a toxic tip and 215 from within 1,000 yards, three times nearer than would be allowed under a proposed EC directive. Should any of the tips leak, drinking supplies would be endangered.[40]

While the National Rivers Authority, the government's recently appointed pollution 'watchdog', took these findings sufficiently seriously to consider a follow-up, the government itself rejected the Commons Environment Committee's proposal to set up a national register of 'blighted land'. The Environment Protection Bill, then going through Parliament, would enable local authorities to survey their regions, thereby adding to responsibilities for which finance was already inadequate. The reason given was the fear that 'planning and development' would suffer if too many sites were identified as contaminated. Interpreted, this meant priority for speculators to build houses and office blocks on top of potential British Love Canals rather than safeguard the health, and drinking water, of the country's inhabitants. One could, at least, take warning about development in Cheshire, home of the chemicals industry, where an unpublished report identified 1,577 'problem sites', some of which were discovered only after a search through museum archives on the growth of the industry.[41]

Actual and potential disposers of toxic waste move in mysterious and secret ways, but few were as secret as the planners of what became known as the Big Hole. The idea was simple. Why bother with the expense of constructing special sites for waste disposal when certain areas of the UK were already riddled with holes in the ground, the disused mines of former industry, that were almost begging to be filled with waste. The Big Hole project itself was the brainchild of two Swiss entrepreneurs, Heinz Wienbrauck and Maurice Jud, whose Zürich-based company, Industrie Projekt Management (IPM) sent out strictly confidential invitations in November 1987 soliciting additional waste to the 300,000–500,000 tonnes of toxic dust allegedly available from an unnamed German firm. Among those contacted were Basel chemical industries, including Sandoz, and the City of Zürich Authorities, both of whom later dissociated themselves from the affair. In the plan's first phase up to 20,000,000 cubic metres of toxic waste would be deposited in the Big Hole, which, in its second phase, would become an industrial park for stocking and recycling waste (including up to 50,000 tonnes of highly poisonous chemical residues) and create 150 new jobs over 15 years.

The Big Hole itself was none other than a disused coal mine in Fife, on the Forth estuary. The British Chamber of Commerce in Zürich was instrumental in enabling IPM to approach British Coal (but was later less forthcoming); further approaches were made to Fife Regional Council and Locate in Scotland, the investment agency run jointly by the Scottish Development Agency and the Scottish Office. Despite proferred investment of £8,000 a month for six to nine months 'to overcome the political resistance of certain politicians' and the prospect of 150 new jobs in an area of high unemployment, the project was greeted with scepticism and British Coal, who later preferred not to talk about it, eventually claimed it unrealistic and incompatible with its plans to restore the mine.

Disappointed at rebuttal of a proposal which they claimed would bring not only waste but work to the region, Wienbrauck and Jud consoled themselves with the thought that there was still hope for a Big Hole in Scotland − when British Coal was privatized! Meanwhile, there were, in Jud's view, other holes available − in Africa.[42]

Toxic tips elsewhere

Inevitably the countries with the most advanced industrial systems, and the greatest quantities of waste, have attracted most attention, but the over-rapid industrialization of Eastern Europe under the former Stalinist regimes has inflicted even greater evils on its peoples. Unfortunately, Western visitors are so impressed by the more obvious aspects of pollution, such as the thick, black, sulphurous clouds of smoke from which escape is impossible, that they have given less attention to the ground beneath their feet. Such facts as have emerged are sufficiently disturbing to suggest that worse disclosures will follow.

Czechoslovakia, for example, produces 23 tonnes of waste per square kilometre per year, and 40 times the quantity produced in Sweden, 75 per cent of which was dangerously stored. According to a senior Communist Party official, in power at the time, one third of the country was 'contaminated'.[43] In Hungary, where, at the beginning of 1990, a hazardous waste dump was at last being built, local waste was inadequately stored and waste from the West, imported to obtain hard currency, stored dangerously.[44] East Germany, where mining is thought to have laid waste 60,000 acres of land,[45] also earned hard currency through imports from the West of four million tonnes of domestic and toxic waste annually. The dump at Vorketzin, near Berlin, and the incinerator at Schoeneiche, received a million tonnes of domestic rubbish from West Berlin each year, together with 35,000 tonnes of toxic waste. Europe's largest dump at Schoenberg, which received a million tonnes annually, was responsible for contaminating groundwater, and near Vorketzin eight sources of drinking water have had to be closed. One ambivalent result of unification is that West Germans can no longer dump waste for DM40 a tonne, about a tenth of the cost in the Federal Republic. East German resentment against their former rulers was hardly assuaged by the discovery that, of the one billion West German marks received for accepting waste, only DM125 million was invested in waste-handling facilities.[46]

Elsewhere in Europe information only reaches the public when conditions become sufficiently outrageous to provoke protests, as happened when Greenpeace and the World Wide Fund for Nature (WWF) drew attention to a dump in northern Spain, where a pesticides plant owned by Inquinosa and sited at Sabinanigo, and one of the two in Europe still manufacturing the insecticide lindane, had dumped 30 tonnes of toxic waste daily since 1976. In 1980 the company began using a public waste tip a few metres from the River Gallego, where, by 1989, concentrations had reached 2.3 micrograms per litre, 23 times the approved EC limit, while soil from the previous site contained almost 80 milligrams per kilogramme, enough to merit treatment as toxic waste.[47]

Of the Third World, where increased industrialization generates growing quantities of waste, data are sparse. Sandra Postel sums up the situation:

> Few have implemented regulations controlling this waste, and even fewer have the advanced technologies needed to do so adequately. Industries typically send it to unsecured domestic landfills, stockpile it, or dump it indiscriminately into the environment.[48]

She instances China, 'where some 400 million tonnes of industrial waste and tailings are generated annually, much of it undoubtedly hazardous', and where 'mounds of potentially harmful waste reportedly occupy some 60,000 hectares of land today'.[49] She could have added Morocco, where waste from a lead works was dumped in the middle of a village and 31 children died from lead poisoning.[50] Or Malaysia, which produced 377,000 cubic metres of toxic waste in 1987 and where, in Jelutong, Penang, toxic waste was used to reclaim land.[51] From East Africa a United Nations team gave a discomfiting description of the uncontrolled landfill at Makupa Creek, Mombasa, Kenya: an amalgam of 'broken glass...metal containers, paper and cardboard...hazardous wastes, used lubricating oils in containers, expired medicines from hospitals, old toxic chemicals and animal cadavers', used 'for reclamation of wasteland and swamps'. There were 'no precautionary measures...to prevent landfill leakages from polluting the adjoining creek water nor to circumvent run-off of leachates during the rainy season'. A second tip, also with no control over leachate, accepted solid wastes from foreign ships and unclaimed cargo containing toxic chemicals.[52]

The situation was no better elsewhere. Solid wastes of all types, including hazardous substances, were dumped at 'the crude tip' at Tabala in Dar-es-Salaam, Tanzania, where seepage and leaching occurred during the rainy season. In Mauritius, commercial and industrial solid wastes were dumped 'crudely' and incinerated in the open air at the Roche Bois tip; this one-hectare site received about 70 tonnes of solid waste daily and has operated since the late 1940s. And at Mogadishu, Somalia, a large tipping site was located right on the coast, close to the city abattoir. 'The tip is uncontrolled and infested with vermin'.[53]

Perhaps there are two types of tips in the Third World, those like Smokey Mountain, Manila, described earlier, that provide a living for wretched scavengers, and those, like the East African examples, where even this is too fraught with danger. All are obnoxious, harmful to human beings and the environment, and, with present resources, pose an insoluble problem that can only get worse.

Burying radioactive waste

With the end of dumping radioactive waste at sea, burial in the ground becomes the key issue for the future. The problem in the post-Chernobyl world is that the NIMBY syndrome is activated immediately any proposal is made. By all means bury nuclear waste, but let it be nearer someone else. Hence the attractiveness of using the Sahara (a West German–Sudanese scheme defeated only by the ousting of Nimeiry), the Australian outback (rejected by Canberra) or the Gobi Desert (a West German–China deal that, like the waste, appears at present to have gone underground).[54]

British and European problems

When the British House of Commons Environment Committee issued its Report on Radioactive Waste in 1986 it damned the government approach to waste disposal as 'amateurish, haphazard and complacent'. Others would have used stronger language and had even less influence on the government.

Officially only LLW is disposed of at Drigg, near Sellafield, Cumbria. Drums, boxes and sacks are dumped in trenches excavated in the local clay of the 270,000-acre site, to be buried under a layer of soil 1.5 metres deep. By February 1989 seven trenches, containing some 600,000 cubic metres of waste, were full and being capped. The Commons Committee were disturbed that rainwater was allowed to run through the trenches into the River Irt and so to the Irish Sea. In addition, not all the waste was packaged or labelled and included material outside the LLW category on the dubious principle that it would be diluted and dispersed over a long period if it escaped. The committee concluded that this 'haphazard approach' to what goes into Drigg 'does not inspire confidence' and contrasted it with the careful sorting and labelling of waste which the French placed in concrete, clay-lined trenches at the equivalent dump at Centre de la Manche, near Cherbourg.[55]

The main problem is that, following recent increased use of containers, Drigg will be full by 1999. Attempts by the Nuclear Industry Radioactive Waste Executive (NIREX), the body responsible for waste disposal, to find alternatives, met with no success. Plans to dump long-lived intermediate waste in a disused anhydride mine at Billingham on Teeside aroused so much local opposition that ICI, who owned the mine, was unprepared to sell it for the purpose; and the government did an abrupt policy reversal in May 1987 over four sites for LLW at Elstow, Bradwell, Fulbeck and South Killingholme, which many maintained was not unconnected with the following month's general election and the possible loss of Tory seats. NIREX announced it would henceforth concentrate on prospecting for a deep-burial site, which was unlikely to be ready before 2003. Meanwhile, Drigg would have to be expanded.[56]

So the British Government eventually got round to the 'deep-burial' option already in use, or planned, in West Germany, Sweden, Switzerland, Belgium, Canada and Finland. The House of Commons Environment Committee was impressed by the salt mine depository at Gorlebenn, Lower Saxony, the granite dumps being tried out in the USA, the granite stores planned by Canada, and the huge granite caverns which the Swedes had excavated under the Baltic Sea bed at Forsmark. Even the French maintained that they were only using a surface trench while planning deep disposal. The choice of granite appears to have impressed NIREX. By mid-1990 its options had been reduced to two: Scottish granite at Dounreay in the far north and Cumbrian granite near Sellafield, where BNFL was engaged in brightening its image as a tourist attraction. In February 1989 it opened the first of its new vaults at Drigg, a concrete-based, clay- and earth-capped affair, able to hold 200,000 cubic metres, or a further five years' production, of LLW and in July 1991 NIREX announced its choice of Sellafield as the preferred site for Britain's 800-metre deep underground repository, thereby arousing the opposition of geologists who were less sanguine about the suitability of the rock there.[57]

Of the situation in Eastern Europe, such information as has reached the West on the overall absence of care for the environment is sufficient to make credible the harrowing report of the hairless children of Sillamäe, Estonia. Until 1989 the town was 'closed', its all-Russian population employed in military industries. Nearly 300 children now suffer from alopecia (baldness). The two kindergartens they attended were built on top of what the former director of the Baltiyets factory revealed was a waste dump covered only with a thin layer of sand, where side-products from the enrichment of uranium for military purposes were probably disposed of. A special commission from the Soviet Ministry of Health found radiation near the kindergartens to be higher than 1989 levels at Chernobyl.[58]

The other end of the process can be equally dangerous. A TV documentary team from the British Channel Four, filming in southern East Germany, discovered the village of Lobichau and the Drosen uranium mine, which has been operational almost since the end of the Second World War. Now children play on the edges of waste heaps of uranium tailings scattered around the area and gather mushrooms there to eat or to sell to the smart hotel at Gera, south of Leipzig.[59]

USA, Japan and the Far East

If British MPs were impressed by the granite dumps being tried out in the United States, others found areas for considerable concern. Three examples, those of Hanford, Yucca Mountain and New Mexico, must suffice.

The Hanford Reservation, which extends over 1,350 square kilometres in the south-eastern corner of Washington State and has nine nuclear reactors along with reprocessing plants, was the heart of the US production complex for nuclear weapons during the 1950s and 1960s. Operated for the government by the Westinghouse Corporation and protected from both public view and official bodies such as the EPA and the Occupational Safety and Health Administration, its management operated with the criminal carelessness of military installations whose greatest freedom is from accountability. By 1990 some 190,000 cubic metres of highly radioactive waste filled 160–70 underground tanks, in which the sludge, settled at the bottom, gave off so much heat that it had cracked many of the tanks. At the end of July a panel of experts from the Department of Energy (DOE)'s Advisory Committee on Nuclear Safety was so concerned that it warned of the danger of an explosion that would scatter radioactive waste over a wide area. Already some two million litres of liquid waste may have leaked from the tanks to join the 760 billion litres of less radioactive waste and toxic chemicals dumped or poured into the ground. During the late 1940s Hanford's bomb-makers pumped liquid waste containing more than four million kilograms of plutonium directly into rocks under the reservation that were saturated with water, an action reminiscent of Sellafield's dumping of plutonium into the Irish Sea. When this ceased, the management continued to store radioactive waste in leaky evaporation ponds, seepage basins and burial pits, relying on the size of the reservation for underground water to dilute the waste by the time it reached the borders. Using recently developed techniques, such as incineration by a plasma centrifugal reactor or bacteria to consume underground methane gas, the DOE now proposes to clean up the site in 15–16 years time. But the fact that it will then need 'long-term institutional control' implies that the area will be out of bounds to the public for several centuries.[60]

When, in 1987, Congress designated Yucca Mountain in the Nevada Desert as the sole site for a repository for all types of nuclear waste in what was known as the 'Screw Nevada Bill', the DOE thought it had solved the problem. Congress had already ruled out other sites when it discovered that the NIMBY syndrome was affecting Republican candidates, and Nevada had the advantage of being the state with the fewest elected representatives. Nuclear companies offered to pay a levy towards construction costs, and the DOE signed contracts to start accepting waste from 1998. Its isolation apart, Yucca had the advantages of a hot, dry climate and a deep water table 200–400 metres below the repository, which, if preliminary estimates were correct that it would take 10,000 years for any seepage to reach, offered effective protection. Unfortunately, the site was within 12 miles of a volcano, eight major earthquakes had occurred within 250 miles and the nearest tests at the Nevada nuclear testing site had taken place just 20 kilometres away. Other critics claimed that the site jeopardized some endangered animal species.

After two years of objections, the DOE agreed to take a second look and, finding that it could not satisfy all the geological and legal requirements of a 1982 nuclear waste law, postponed the proposed opening until 2010. In July 1990 a report from the National Academy of Sciences, requested by the DOE, pointed out that the exact prediction of geological processes demanded by the law 'stretches the limits of our understanding of geology, groundwater chemistry and movement'. In plain language, guarantees of safety were impossible under the standards demanded. To add to the confusion geologists at the University of New Mexico and the Yucca Mountain Project Office in Las Vegas produced new estimates on the volcanic aspect. Where previous studies indicated that several volcanic cones last erupted 250,000 years ago, they now concluded that volcanic activity occurred just 20 km from the site as recently as 20,000 years ago. The non-specialist may find the difference academic, but the siting of a depository containing HLW within range of a volcano that might possibly erupt or cause an earthquake can hardly be considered desirable. Meanwhile, the 21,000 tonnes of waste currently stored are increasing at the rate of 2,000 tonnes a year.[61]

Further controversy over safety focuses on the Waste Isolation Pilot Plant (WIPP) built in an underground salt formation near Carlsbad, New Mexico. The plan was to store 25-gallon drums of toxic chemicals and transuranic elements, such as plutonium, 655 metres below the surface. After the vault had been sealed, the salt would slowly surround and seal the wastes. Opening of the plant was delayed when scientists found that more brine was seeping through the salt than expected and that, below the formation, there were underground lakes of brine under high pressure. Brine seeping into the WIPP could thus produce a pressurized slurry of radioactive and toxic waste which, if punctured by drilling, could spurt to the surface. Backing down on the storage of toxic chemicals, the DOE announced that studies into the radioactive aspect would be carried out as it began to fill the vault with drums of plutonium-contaminated waste. Declaring this a ruse to get the waste underground, opponents of the scheme pointed out that, since the tests would yield only unverifiable data, they had no scientific justification. At the end of 1989 the plant was still shut down.[62]

The waste would have come from the Rocky Flats plant in Colorado which produced the plutonium cores of all US nuclear weapons and is thus crucial to the government's military programme. Doubtless this explains the Colorado governor's failure to carry out previous threats to close down the plant for non-acceptance of state regulations. The plant's operators, Rockwell International, have also fallen foul of the Federal Bureau of Investigation (FBI), which used an aeroplane equipped with infra-red detectors for night flights and a team of 70 agents. They charged that Rockwell were using an incinerator at night for which it lacked a permit, that hazardous chemicals were secretly poured into evaporation ponds that were known to leak, and that monitoring of streams flowing through the plant revealed periodic discharges of chemical pollutants which the management had not reported to the EPA. To add to Rockwell's problems, the Governor of Idaho, which had temporarily stored some of the plutonium-contaminated waste, announced that his state would not accept any more shipments after September 1989.[63] With the continued impasse at WIPP and increasing doubts over Yucca, Rocky Flats will have nowhere to send its waste. One is thus forced to conclude that ultimately the US administration has no more permanent solution to the problem of radioactive waste than has the British Government.

Japan also faces problems of disposal. Its LLW is stored on site and its HLW is shortly due for return from Western reprocessing facilities. When a plan to dump up to 300,000 drums of LLW in the Pacific Ocean aroused opposition among the island nations, and the London Dumping Convention suspended dumping at sea, the government announced that a permanent centre for research and for the storage of HLW would be built at Horonobe, a town of 3,700 people, in a farming and fishing district in the far north of the northern island of Hokkaido. A surprise preparatory site inspection by the Power Reactor and Nuclear Fuel Development Corporation, Donen, outraged the local inhabitants, 2,000 of whom occupied the site. Further demonstrations in 1986 were dispersed by riot police.[64]

While retaining the Horonobe option for HLW, the government has now concentrated on constructing a massive nuclear complex at Rokkasho, in Aomori Prefecture at the northern end of the main island, Honshu, that will include a reprocessing plant, a store for HLW and a burial site for three million drums of LLW. Already opposition has caused changes in the design of the site. The original proposal, in April 1988, to store waste in concrete pits on a rock bed and cover them with four metres of soil was amended in October 1989 to storage in pits in rock covered with two metres of clay and four metres of soil. By mid-1990 the construction company was still waiting for government permission to start work on the pits themselves.[65]

The 'Papan controversy' in Malaysia illustrates clearly further problems affecting Third World countries. It dates back to the 1970s when the Japanese multinational, Mitsubishi Chemicals, joined a number of local Chinese and Malay interests to set up the company Asian Rare Earths Sdn Bhd (ARE). Before this Mitsubishi had imported monazite, part of a tin tailing waste, for processing in Japan, but in the mid-1970s the Malaysian Government banned its export and ARE established its own reprocessing factory near Bukit Merah, about six kilometres from Papan. Monazite contains thorium oxide which, in reprocessing, is converted into radioactive thorium hydroxide that forms 14 per cent of the waste, disposal of which had already caused problems in Japan. The government proposed storing this at the predominantly Malay town of Parit, on the Perak River, 15km from the factory, but, when the news leaked out in July 1982, local opposition forced a change of plans. In November 1983 a vegetable farmer discovered three newly dug trenches in a foothill 1.5km from Papan, a largely Chinese town. Not satisfied by discussions with the government and ARE, and alarmed by the poor state of the trenches, an action committee was formed and received widespread publicity through a daily three-week picketing of the site, a rare event in Malaysia. Foreign experts from the British National Radiological Protection Board and the International Atomic Energy Agency were brought in and attention turned to the high levels of radioactivity near the ARE factory.

The outcome was an official decision in January 1985 to site the trenches three kilometres upstream from Papan and a declaration that ARE's operations were safe. But the issue had wider implications in demonstrating the difficulties of opposition in a country where the press was instructed to play down the controversy and Chinese—Malay differences could be exploited, where affluent residents are disinclined to take action and language difficulties hamper communication. At the same time it highlighted the role of multinationals in Third World countries and, as in Japan, provided an opportunity for women to play an important protest role.[66]

The final(?) solution

As for that ultimate in nuclear waste, the reactor itself, Nuclear Electric, the British state-owned power company, has come up with the novel suggestion of '*in situ* decommissioning'. Instead of dumping waste in the earth, let the earth rise to cover the waste. Treat obsolete nuclear power stations as if they were human beings, and bury them, but above ground. According to Nuclear Electric, 'this approach involves mounding over the reactors and other plants *in situ*. Preliminary studies show that, by using pumped sand from the local seabed or river, a stable mound could be engineered covering all the plant'. The great advantage would, of course, be reduced costs.[67]

The proposal evokes a surreal vision of a brave new world by 2030 AD. No one can fail to be impressed by contemporary Sellafield with its panoramic backcloth of Cumbrian mountains. But the new Mount Sellafield will vie with Scafell Pike as it rises while the latter diminishes daily under the depredations of climbers' boots. Approaching Dover through the deepened Channel, the visitor eyes with awe the new Mount Dungeness, towering over a flat and featureless plain. Alas poor Trawsfynydd, set in the midst of granite Snowdonia with no covering sand nearer than the distant beach at Porthmadog!

But why stop at nuclear reactors? Why not mound over *all* waste dumps? Let the earth cover the lot and humanity's latest, perhaps its last, contribution be to create a sand-covered Mount Fresh Kills on Staten Island, an earth-capped Smokey Mountain at Manila, or Mount Makupa at Mombasa, towering above the Indian Ocean, a giant landmark for those at sea.

And if, through failure to control the Greenhouse Effect, the seas rise even higher than predicted, the world of 3030 AD will have a series of new archipelagos, island havens, each with a defunct reactor or the remnants of domestic waste at its core. What could be a more appropriate monument to humanity than a greatly reduced land mass consisting solely of buried waste?

Agricultural waste − through earth to water

There is no need to bury agricultural waste; much of it is already on or in the ground. The snag is that it doesn't stay there. There are three main causes for concern: the disposal of slurry and the use (or misuse) of artificial fertilizers and of pesticides.

It was a long time before the dangers from slurry or silage effluent were recognized. Only in mid-1989, following an earlier outbreak of cryptosporidiosis, an acute form of diarrhoea, in the Oxford−Swindon area from contaminated drinking water, did British scientists begin a thorough investigation of *cryptospiridium*, a parasitic microbe living in the guts of animals, commonly calves and sheep, which is passed on in bodily waste. The parasite is so small that it would take 30,000 to cover the head of the proverbial pin and an infected cow produces some 10,000 million parasites in its faeces every day. Effluents and slurry containing the waste enter the food chain if dumped on land or find their way into the water system, including drinking water, in both the UK and the USA, if the effluent is discharged into or dumped in water. The parasite causes children and babies to become very ill with an acute and often protracted form of gastro-enteritis, and is a serious hazard to those with weak or damaged immune systems, including people with AIDS, for whom it is probably the most common gut infection worldwide.[68]

In July 1990 a government-appointed committee of experts under Sir John Badenoch admitted that British tap water, though almost always safe for drinking, was not entirely without risk. The whole country was affected, with some evidence that livestock areas were more at risk than others. Monitoring under existing methods, by which it took a technician half a day to do one sample, was both technically and economically unfeasible; chlorine, the all-purpose water-purifier, had no effect on the parasite, and the only remedy was to boil the water. The experts placed responsibility on 'modern farming methods'. Outbreaks would thus continue, with typical cases in which 500 people served by the same treatment works would get sick and between 10 and 20 per cent need hospital treatment.[69]

The nitrate problem
In September 1990 an unpublished report by the British Nature Conservancy Council, the government body responsible for overseeing implementation of the 1981 Wildlife and Countryside Act, produced alarming evidence that modern farming methods were turning one of the country's most treasured areas, the Norfolk Broads, into a wildlife desert. The waters of the Broads themselves contained little more than algae and bacteria, while an investigation of the 2,640 dykes connecting the grazing marshes showed that more than half those with the most important plant life had 'become floristically impoverished within the last 17 years'.

Nitrates from fertilizers applied to arable crops over much of East

Norfolk have built up during the last 30 years in the groundwater that feeds many of the dykes, and the polluted water is expected to go on seeping into the dykes for decades, even if all fertilizer use were to be halted.[70]

The WWF report, *Agriculture and Habitat Loss in Europe*, is even more damning of the EC Common Agricultural Policy for its effect on the environment. Continued intensive farming is one of the main causes of the 'threatened' status of many European species of amphibians, fish and reptiles.

In West Germany, 561 species of plants are 'declining', 173 because of drainage of farmland, 89 because of herbicides, and 56 because of excess nutrients in surface water caused by agricultural fertilisers.[71]

Higher subsidies for arable crops such as grain have caused the loss of 40 per cent of France's vineyards, orchards and other sources of permanent crops; over half the wetlands in Holland and West Germany were lost through drainage between 1950 and 1985; and even nature reserves such as the Blankaart wetland in Flanders are under the combined threat of drainage from surrounding farmlands and excess nutrients from artificial fertilizers.[72] From the present viewpoint the only comfort is that waste is not the sole cause of disaster. The whole system is damned as environmentally destructive.

The greatest immediate danger to human beings, however, comes from the presence of nitrates in drinking water. This affects not only Britain and Europe but also North America and even China. Professor William Steward, secretary of the British Agriculture and Food Research Council (AFRC) and chairman of the Royal Society study group on nitrate pollution, has pointed out that, of the 1.6 million tons of nitrogen fertilizer spread by British farmers at a cost of around £600 million in 1987, between 10 and 30 per cent was wasted, lost either to the atmosphere or the water supply. Even more disconcerting is that the problem is not new. AFRC scientists have watched the build-up of nitrate levels since World War II and pointed out that, for the last 20 years, they have increased substantially. Much of the leached nitrate has thus been stored in the lower soil for 40 years or more and shed as new fertilizer is delivered. Professor Steward concludes: 'Even if they stop adding fertilizer nitrogen tomorrow, the nitrate problem is not going to go away for a long time'.[73]

A major difficulty is that nitrate is highly soluble and so either washes off fields where artificial fertilizer has been applied or leaches through the soil to infect underground aquifers supplying drinking water. Nitrate is essential for plant growth and in itself not particularly poisonous to human beings; action by bacteria in the human gut, however, converts it into nitrite which combines with the red blood pigment haemoglobin and prevents the blood from carrying oxygen around the body efficiently. At high levels this produces the condition of methaemoglobinemia, which, though rare in adults, is responsible for the 'blue baby' syndrome. Further reactions lead to the production of nitrosamines, which have been shown to cause stomach cancer in laboratory animals, thus arousing fears that human beings could be similarly affected.[74]

The WHO has recommended a limit of 100 milligrams per litre for nitrates in public water, and the EC the more stringent 50 milligrams.[75] In 1980 the British Government and other EC countries agreed to clean up their water by 17 July 1985 to meet EC limits for some 60 different substances. When the directive came into force, the British Government's first action was to exempt around 50 suppliers exceeding the 50mg limit from their obligations on the grounds that there was no danger to health below the 100 mg/litre (mg/l) level.[76] By 1989, on the government's own admission, there were not 50 but 74 water supplies in England and Wales, serving 1.6 million people, that exceeded these limits, if only marginally, with the highest levels in farming areas such as Norfolk, Cambridgeshire, Lincolnshire, Hereford and Worcestershire.

In July of that year, the then environment secretary, Nicholas Ridley, denounced some of the limits as 'ridiculous, extravagant and unnecessary', while the government reversed a provision added to the water privatization bill by the House of Lords that all drinking water should reach EC standards by 1993. Both minister and the water industry admitted that some supplies would still break safety limits by 1995, ten years after the original deadline.[77]

Not surprisingly, in September 1989, the European Environment Commissioner, Carlo Ripa di Meana, decided to take the British Government to the European Court of Justice for failure to clean up its water supply, the selected nitrate charge being that of Norfolk, where levels reached from 60–100 mg/l.[78] Belgium also was being sued for allowing drinking water containing excess lead, and the West German Government was under observation for pesticide levels.[79]

While the British DoE promoted new regulations that came into force on 1 September 1989, within three months the Ministry of Agriculture had sent documents to farming organizations that either scrapped or diluted measures to limit nitrate pollution. In particular it did away with proposals to set absolute limits for fertilizer used on ten different crops, undermined a requirement that farmers should 'avoid making changes to the farming system that will increase nitrate leaching from the land', and abandoned a requirement that farmers should not plough up land which had grown grass for more than three years. Ploughing land has the effect of releasing nitrates from the soil and the National Rivers Authority warned that 'a single ploughing could negate five years of land use control'.[80] It would almost appear that, where farming interests are concerned, those who aim to protect the environment are in a 'no-win' situation.

The pesticide problem
We saw in Chapter 2 how pesticides, applied through the air, can cause harm and that only a fraction reaches the target, the rest falling to the ground as

waste. Like nitrates, pesticide residues dissolve in water, are washed into adjoining water courses or leach into the soil, and so find their way into the drinking supply.

So much is certain, because pesticide residues have been found in drinking water. What disturbs the non-specialist is our ignorance of the processes taking place in the soil itself. Scientists have established that it may take up to 30 years before the effects are actually revealed and that, in consequence, immediate action to halt the situation cannot be effective. We know also that pesticides themselves are applied by being dissolved in fluids known euphemistically as inerts, many of which are highly toxic, and it is probable that at least some of these breakdown products are lethal. Studies have already shown that the combined effects of mixing different pesticides in the water supply can be 100 times more dangerous to health than that of an individual chemical. But we still do not know what actually takes place in the soil to the extent of being able to predict the long-term effects on human beings who drink even a diluted version of this poisonous cocktail.[81]

Even the authorities' standards appear to be based as much on guesswork as on science. The non-selective herbicide Atrazine, for example, is given a Maximum Acceptable Concentration (MAC) by the EC as 0.1 mg/1. The WHO, however, set a tentative guideline of 2 mg/1 based on an 'acceptable daily intake', a quantity without scientific precision which the WHO admits 'has no sound scientific justification and is based on a more or less arbitrary decision'.[82] The British Government's guideline figure is 30 mg/1, 300 times higher than the EC's MAC. What action, then, should be taken by people using drinking water supplied by the Mid-Southern Water Company of the Thames Region with an Atrazine reading of 4.5 mg/1[83], which is 45 times the EC recommended limit and more than double that of the WHO but well within that prescribed by the DoE?

Atrazine is now on the British Government's Red List of substances 'whose discharge to water should be minimized as far as possible', and even the DoE admits that 'there must be some doubt whether Atrazine should be approved under the standards now prevailing'.[84] The snag is that many pesticides still in use were approved long before current regulations came into existence, and have escaped the net. Under the present system many of the 1,000 pesticide products in use in the UK remain free from criticism, not because they have been tested and passed as safe, but because, thanks on the one hand to the expense of monitoring ('One sample can cost up to £700'), and, on the other, to commercial secrecy, which means that the Water Authorities do not know the actual contents of the pesticides, they have never been put to the test.[85] Between July 1985 and June 1987 there were 298 known breaches of the MAC for a single pesticide in England and Wales, but faced with charges from the EC of failure to clean up its drinking water the government's reaction was a request to 'review the pesticides parameter', in short, to shift the goalposts so that what is now illegal, if viewed by its scientists as safe, is brought within the law.[86]

Pesticides not only enter the earth, they enter, and remain in, its products, which are then passed to the consumer. The dangers of pesticide residues, that is, waste, through the growing or storage of food, previously claimed by the Ministry of Agriculture to be extremely small and harmless, have now been recognized to the extent that, in July 1988, the British Medical Association (BMA) decided to investigate the effect of pesticides on human health. Their concern arose from the whistle-blowing by the former chairman of the Commons Agriculture Select Committee, Sir Richard Body, himself a farmer, whose report on pesticide hazards so angered three other Tories on the Committee that they opposed its publication. The report highlights the problems of pesticide residues in bran, which remain in wholemeal breads and pastas, and in the 'baby' carrots and beetroots often grown in peat blocks impregnated with pesticides.[87]

Illustrative of the dangers of pesticide residues, and of the different approaches by official bodies in the UK and in the USA, are the fungicides maneb, mancozeb and zineb, and the apple growth-boosting chemical, alar. The three fungicides, used by almost every arable farmer in the UK and by many in the USA, are on the list of long-established pesticides now under suspicion because they escaped modern safety analysis before approval. They are sprayed before harvest on wheat, barley, hops, potatoes, onions, leeks, apples, pears, blackcurrants and gooseberries, and manufactured mainly by Rohm and Haas of Pennsylvania. Studies by the EPA early in 1989 suggested that their continued use might cause 125,000 additional cancers among the population of 250 million. The EPA was expected to ban, or at least severely restrict their use, after almost 40 years of their having been sprayed on fruit and vegetables.[88]

Alar (daminozide), developed in the 1960s and thus another older pesticide, was not included in the British Ministry of Agriculture's review list owing to an 'oversight'. Three months after the EPA announced, in February 1989, that it would ban alar by 1990 because of a direct link with 'life-threatening tumours' (the Natural Resources Defence Council put it more bluntly that, thanks to alar residues, 5,500 American children would get cancer in their lifetimes), the British Government's Advisory Committee on Pesticides (ACP) gave alar the all clear. It published no data, gave no explanation, merely issued a bald statement that alar 'did not pose a health risk to consumers'.

The ACP is the government's body of independent experts. It consists of 12 scientists, all men, mostly medical doctors with additional qualifications in toxicology or pharmacology. Their independence is, however, impossible to determine. The agriculture minister chooses them on advice from officials, which is never made public, and each member signs a declaration that he (sic) has 'no financial or commercial interest' likely to 'prejudice the proper discharge of (his) functions as a member'. But 'prejudice' and 'interest' are nowhere defined and there is no obligation to make public any links with the chemical industry. Indeed, the major obligation appears to be not to disclose (without permission) anything learnt during the ACP's deliberations. The committee thus remains a body operating in secret, the interests of its members likewise secret, with one exception. Because his membership of the Medicines Commission forced him to declare his interests, we now know that Professor Anthony Dayan acts as a paid consultant to eight pharmaceutical companies, including Beecham and Celltech. His research department is supported by Glaxo and he holds shares in four drug companies. Obviously Professor Dayan is able to bring considerable experience to the ACP, but his presence there would at times appear to be not without conflicting loyalties. One may assume that some of his colleagues have similar difficulties.

In July 1989 Uniroyal, the manufacturers of alar, received a summary of data on cancers found in rats and mice fed UDMH, the highly dangerous breakdown product of Alar. Particularly disturbing was the 'low dose' result. The final report, submitted in October, was presumably so alarming that, two weeks later, Uniroyal not only ordered an immediate worldwide halt to sales but asked the US authorities to revoke alar's licence for food use. As, following ACP clearance, Uniroyal could not ask to have its licence revoked in the UK, it decided 'not to continue to provide studies requested by the ACP in order to support the continued approval of the product'. This delightful phrasing is worthy of Sir Humphrey at his best. The ACP can now revoke the licence because of the company's failure to provide the data required, while its members can claim that they know of no danger from alar because they have not seen the data.[89]

Human beings are not the only victims of pesticide residues. A 1990 study by the British Trust for Ornithology, which is responsible for keeping a census of all bird species, reveals that organochloride pesticides, used as seed dressings, were reducing the yellowhammer population, while 'the use of pesticides and changes in the farming calendar are probably to blame for the recent decline of several species'. Herbicides destroy seed-bearing weeds, on which skylarks, linnets and corn buntings depend.[90] If this demonstrates the ill-effects of pesticides themselves rather than pesticides as waste, it illustrates clearly the ecological interdependence of the earth's inhabitants.

Wasteful use of pesticides has had disastrous results worldwide. In Italy drinking water is so contaminated with pesticides, notably atrazine, that, were Italy to comply immediately with the 1980 EC directive, more than two million Italians would be without drinking water.[91] In the USA, the San Joaquin Valley, California, the world's richest, most intensively cultivated farm belt, is perhaps the world's prime example of pesticide misuse. About 7 per cent of all pesticides used in the USA is sprayed, injected or sprinkled onto an area that is 1 per cent of the country's crop land. A state task force found that, between February 1979 and January 1983, 'more than 17 tons and 11,000 gallons of pesticides linked to cancer, genetic damage, birth defects and reproductive problems' were used in the McFarland area. Between 1975 and 1988 16 children became victims of cancer, of whom 9 died; half the cases were diagnosed between 1982 and 1985, eight times the number expected in a rural town of 6,000 people. 'Children play in fields sprayed with pesticides, they bounce on the knees of farm worker parents covered by pesticides.' In Fresno County a third of the drinking-water wells were contaminated by a cancer-causing pesticide.[92]

Where rice is the people's basic food, excessive use of pesticides can be disastrous. Among the first examples of environmental glasnost in the USSR was a letter to *Literaturnaya Gazeta* of 24 August 1988 from O. Razmakhin of Krasnodor Kray. The writer complained about excessive use of pesticides in rice fields near Rostov. A 27 per cent overall increase in cancer in the past five years and a rise in birth defects of 55–60 per cent had led him to conclude: 'We feel that chemical warfare has been declared against us and no one will stop it'.[93]

In the Third World pesticides inevitably cause problems. Thailand, now one of the wealthiest countries in South-East Asia from logging its tropical forests, may seem an unlikely example; but the policy of promoting National Parks, 52 since 1961, while allowing people to continue to use them has brought unforeseen hazards. In the Doi Inthanaon park, for example, the government set up a centre for agricultural development so that today's visitor encounters, not wildlife or recreational facilities, but a large, treeless valley cultivated with cabbages, carnations, peaches and strawberries. The results are seen downstream from the neat fields. Few animals live in the watercourses. Despite a ban on the sale of pesticides in nearby towns and instructions against overuse, the farmers apply heavy doses of DDT and other chemicals to their crops. According to one farmer most fruit growers sprayed their crops every few days to guarantee unblemished produce. But the people know better than to eat the fruit. A 1985 survey showed that 24 people died and 2,400 became ill after eating food contaminated with pesticide residues.[94]

In Latin America use of the herbicide Tebuthiuron (Spike) to destroy coca plants as part of the war on drug production has had unfortunate results. In Peru it destroyed more than the coca plants at which it was directed, in Guatemala spray from planes killed honey bees and affected legal crops as well as poppy fields, while in Guatemala and Belize growers of Marijuana whose crops are damaged by herbicide merely leave the degraded land and go on to clear yet another part of the forest.[95] It is also suggested that heavy use of pesticides and fungicides on South American plantations, especially those chemicals banned in the USA, may be severely affecting migrant species of birds.[96]

Perhaps the most tragic incident occurred in Indonesia in 1983, when the government imported rat poison to protect the first rice crop of a new peasant settlement. The makers, ICI, proposed that the pesticide should be put in paraffin tablets attractive to rats but inedible to human beings, but the government decided on the cheaper option of impregnating rice, which would be strewn outside the store. The crop failed and the starving peasants were left with only a few bags of the contaminated rice to eat. Knowing that it was poisoned, for ICI had put warning labels on the rice in their own language, they nevertheless washed the rice repeatedly to rid it of the poison before boiling it and feeding it to a 'volunteer'. When he was still alive the next day, they all ate, only to die within a few days as the slow-acting poison did its work.[97] Three years later Indonesia banned the import of more than 50 pesticides.

At least ICI acted responsibly and the blame must lie with the poverty and indebtedness that causes Third World governments to take the cheaper option. The prize for pesticide mistreatment of Third World peoples by the West must go to the Swiss chemical firm, CIBA-Geigy, which admitted in 1976 that it had used Egyptian children to test a suspected carcinogenic pesticide, Galecron. The children were stood in a field, sprayed by an aeroplane, and their urine was then tested for residues. CIBA claimed that it had acted with the consent of the Egyptian Government.[98]

Notes

1. *Guardian* 3 September 1988
2. *WR 1988−89* p. 47
3. Sheridan 1989
4. Wright 1989
5. Goldsmith and Hildyard 1988 pp. 171−3
6. *Nordwest Zeitung*, Oldenburg 25 March 1986, quoted TWN 1989 pp. 87−8
7. EEB nd p. 111
8. Lean 1988; HoC 1989 paras 61−2
9. Goldsmith and Hildyard 1988 pp. 171−3
10. HoC 1989 para. 56
11. Ibid. para. 46
12. Goldsmith and Holdyard 1988 p. 174; *Newsweek* 2 June 1980; EEB nd2 p. 89
13. TWN 1989 p. 16
14. EEB nd2 p. 89
15. Goldsmith and Hildyard 1988 p. 161
16. Postel 1988 p. 123.
17. Goldsmith and Hildyard 1988 p. 216
18. Quoted Magnusen 1985
19. Ibid.
20. Quoted Ibid.
21. Ibid.
22. Ibid.
23. Ibid.; Goldsmith and Hildyard 1988 p. 216
24. MacKenzie 1989a
25. *Guardian* 11 October 1988
26. EEB nd2 p. 89; Goldsmith and Hildyard 1988 p. 161
27. EEB nd2 pp. 89−90
28. Ibid. p. 90
29. Goldsmith and Hildyard 1990 p. 90
30. Lean and Ghazi 1990
31. HoC 1989 paras 103−4
32. Ibid. paras 5, 6
33. Ibid. para. 108
34. Ibid. para. 118
35. Ibid. para. 124
36. Ibid. para. 110
37. Lean and Ghazi 1990
38. *Guardian* 10 May 1990; *New Scientist* 12 May 1990
39. *Guardian* 31 August 1989, 1 September 1989

40. *Observer* 1 July 1990
41. *New Scientist* 28 July 1990
42. BRRI 1989 pp. 29–30; *Guardian* 6 July 1988
43. Traynor 1990; *Guardian* 19 January 1990
44. *Guardian* 19 January 1990
45. Ibid.
46. *New Scientist* 27 January 1990
47. MacKenzie 1989b
48. Postel 1988 p. 120
49. Ibid.
50. TWN 1989 p. 16
51. Ibid. p. 99
52. *RSRS 8* p. 19
53. Ibid. p. 20
54. *Observer* 5 May 1985, 16 June 1985
55. *Guardian* 13 March 1986; *New Scientist* 4 February 1989
56. *Guardian* 2 May 1987, 7 September 1987
57. Ibid. 13 March 1986, 24 July 1991; *New Scientist* 4 February 1989
58. *Observer* 17 September 1989
59. Thorpe 1990c
60. Charles 1989; *Guardian* 1 August 1990
61. *New Scientist* 15 October 1988, 28 July 1990; *Guardian* 1 December 1989
62. *New Scientist* 10 June 1989; *Guardian* 1 December 1989
63. Charles 1989 ; *New Scientist* 10 June 1989
64. Holliman 1989
65. Cross 1990a, 1990b
66. Singh 1985
67. Milne 1990b
68. Brown, P. 1990a ; Milne 1989c
69. Brown, P. 1990a
70. Lean 1990a
71. MacKenzie 1990a
72. Ibid.
73. Radford 1988b
74. Goldsmith and Hildyard 1990 p. 114
75. Radford 1988b
76. *Guardian* 30 January 1989
77. Lean and Pearce 1989
78. *Guardian* 21 September 1989
79. Ibid. 22 September 1989; *New Scientist* 30 September 1989
80. Lean 1990b
81. Peckham 1989
82. Quoted Ibid.
83. Ardill 1988
84. Quoted Peckham 1989
85. Ibid.
86. Ardill 1988
87. *Guardian* 3 August 1988
88. Erlichman 1989a
89. Erlichman 1989b
90. *New Scientist* 26 May 1990
91. Ibid. 30 September 1989
92. *Guardian* 31 August 1988
93. Perera 1988

94. Ewins and Bazely 1989
95. *WR 1990−91* p. 44 Box 3.3
96. Ibid. p. 136
97. Erlichman 1990
98. Ibid.

5.   Into the Water

As a repository for waste, Water differs from Earth in two elementary but important aspects: 1) unlike the solid rock of the best landfills, it is the natural habitat of numerous living creatures, ranging from microscopic algae to giant whales; 2) it moves; it receives, and eventually carries away, one waste, only to accept another. On a river's journey to the sea, discharges from industry or sewage works mingle with run-off from agricultural land so that it is impossible to separate each type of waste, while the synergistic effects, when pollutants, irrespective of source, interact, produce concoctions that are even less desirable than the sum of their individual components.

All wastes go into the world's waters, and many of the world's waters receive all types of waste. As humanity has extended its exploitation to the most remote areas, so waste has inevitably followed. Even the polar regions are no longer exempt. The highest levels of PCBs recorded in human beings occur, not in the inhabitants of the industrialized regions of Europe or North America that produced and used them, but in the Inuit people of northern Canada who survive the Arctic winter by eating animal products rich in fat, particularly fish in which PCBs have accumulated in the fatty tissue.[1] The world's most aesthetically revolting rubbish dump is not Fresh Kills or Smokey Mountain but at McMurdo Sound, 826 nautical miles from the South Pole, where the huge US base of 700 resident scientists and hundreds of support personnel produces 500 tonnes of solid waste annually and has created an eyesore out of the all-American plastic dream. A Greenpeace protest mission collected effluent from the Sound, claiming that it was raw sewage laced with heavy metals, and hauled seven 40-gallon drums of it, labelled 'Danger! Cadmium!' in front of the National Science Foundation Headquarters. With an international reputation to uphold, the Americans responded by requesting Congress for $30 million for a five-year clean-up programme, and demanded the hitherto unthinkable, namely that supplies be sent in non-plastic wrapping. They also attempted to inculcate new mores to replace those of the throwaway society, beginning with the introduction of separate bins for different sorts of waste, an essential procedure that had become second nature for years on the Antarctic bases of other countries. Not satisfied with the progress made, in October 1990 a US pressure group, the Environmental Defense Fund, threatened to sue to National Science Foundation in order to stop open-pit burning and landfilling of waste.[2]

Inland waters

To what extent have sewage, industrial and agricultural wastes affected the world's major rivers? Research by the Global Environmental Monitoring System (GEMS) concludes that, thanks to run-off from agricultural waste, 10 per cent of the rivers monitored at one or more stations throughout the world had nitrate levels in excess of WHO standards so that the water was unfit to drink without treatment. In Europe 90 per cent of the rivers had some form of nitrate pollution and 5 per cent had concentrations over 200 times those of unpolluted rivers. Pesticides, PCBs and other synthetic organic chemicals are found in many rivers throughout the world. In the USA 42–82 per cent of water and sediment samples from over 150 rivers were contaminated with organochloral insecticides and 2–7 per cent with organophosphate insecticides (see Box 2.2).[3] In general, Third World waters are less contaminated than those of more developed nations but, as the survey that follows shows, they are already 'catching up with the West'.

British rivers and lakes
The DoE sums up the position of water quality in non-tidal rivers and canals in England and Wales as follows:

> Between 1958 and 1980 the proportion of water length classified as poor or grossly polluted... fell from 13 per cent to 7 per cent.... Between 1980 and 1985 over a quarter of the total river length was recorded as having changed quality but it is not possible to say whether the small apparent net deterioration represents a real change.[4]

In plain language, for the 22 years to 1980 things improved; since then, they have got worse. How small or apparent is the change we can judge from the DoE's own statistics. In 1980 75 per cent of non-tidal rivers and canals were classed as 'unpolluted'; in 1985 the combined new categories 'Good 1A' and 'Good 1B' totalled 67 per cent. By 1988 this was down to 65 per cent. At this point, owing to unavailability of 1985 data for some 97km of river, the figures become confusing and the *total length* of 1A and 1B for England and Wales in 1988 somehow *exceeds* that of 1985 by some 48km. This, however, disguises discrepancies between regions. While the Severn, Trent and Welsh Water Authorities increased their 1A rivers by 187, 151 and 166km respectively (though the Welsh lost 238 from 1B, giving an overall loss for both categories of 72km), Anglian lost 83km of 1A, North West 109, South West 81 and Yorkshire 43km of 1A and 52km of 1B. With Wessex's 18km of 1A lost, this makes a total loss of top grade water of 334km.

On the specific question of nitrates in water and their relation to agriculture, the DoE's comments are revealing. Using data for 25 rivers in England, Wales and Scotland with abstraction points for drinking water going back to the 1950s or 1960s, a special study concluded:

> At 15 of the sampling points, mean nitrate concentrations for 1981−5 are below those recorded in the 5-year period 1976−80 but higher than previously. At nine sampling points, mean nitrate concentrations for 1981−5 are *greater than in any previous period. These are primarily in arable farming areas such as East Anglia.*[5] (my stress)

The connection between agricultural waste and polluted water could not be more succintly demonstrated.

The mixture of wastes, and subsequent pollution, reaching a river can be illustrated by a closer look at a particular stream. The River Tyne in the north of England is by no means the worst of rivers. It has a high lead concentration of 16.00 mg/l,[6] yet the NRA class it as the best salmon river in England with half the wild salmon catch for England and Wales, some 45,000, caught off the mouth.

The river itself[7] is formed by the junction of two streams, the South Tyne, which rises in the Pennines near Cross Fell, and the North Tyne, which flows from Kielder Reservoir, one of the largest man-made lakes in Europe. The South Tyne is unfortunate in its source; the North Pennines have some of the highest levels of that product of waste gases, acid rain, which stunts tree growth and kills the heather. On Great Dun Fell, acidity is so high that aluminium leaches from the feldspar granite soils into drinking water supplied to the neighbouring Tees valley, thereby necessitating a 'permanent relaxation' in water standards. Along the banks of the South Tyne and its tributary, the Nent, above the village of Alston are dumps of lead and cadmium waste, the spoils of nearly two centuries of lead mining, which heavy rains wash into the river as slurry. When there are floods, the water is unfit for human beings or animals. An Alston inhabitant claimed that, in summer, the local sewage works also released raw sewage into the water once a week, but was uncertain whether it was Tuesdays or Thursdays! On the hills, the main activity, sheep farming, has about 1,000 sheep-dip baths that are used at least once annually by law and often twice, and from which the waste drains into the river. The build-up of lindane in exported lamb and freshwater fish over the years led to its being replaced by organophosphate pesticides. As a result, since 1981 sheep-dip phenols have been found in Newcastle and Gateshead drinking water, while in 1990 the organophosphate diazinon was measured in the East Allen river which also flows into the South Tyne.

For the North Tyne, the planting of Kielder Forest around the reservoir in the 1950s had unexpected consequences. Deep ploughing caused massive peat erosion that has not only affected the ecology and wildlife but necessitated complex treatment of the water to remove acidity, the result being a residue of aluminium in drinking water. Further downstream a range of forest industries — a chipboard factory, a paper mill, a tissue paper plant and a paper-recycling factory — discharges its waste into the water, and there have reputedly been spillages of phenols, oil, bleach and even dioxins over the last 20 years.

The final stretches of the river at least have improved since the RCEP reported in 1982 'riverside discharges of crude sewage and industrial process water', including what they preferred to call 'sewage solids'.[8] An interceptor sewer running parallel to the main river now carries sewage, domestic waste and industrial effluent to the estuary, where it still has to be disposed of. By this time the sewage is so contaminated with lead and cadmium as to be useless. In consequence 500,000 tonnes of sewage sludge are taken by what the locals call 'Bovril boats' and dumped in the North Sea, while South Shields, at the mouth of the Tyne, houses the depot for North Sea incinerator ships. To ensure that even the estuary does not escape, the company operating these, Velva Liquids, has permission to discharge a wide range of wastes into the water, including toxic chemicals such as toluene, xylene, tetrahydrofuran, trichloroethane, trichlorethylene, chloroform, dichlormethane and oil. Despite the record salmon catch, the local fishermen, in search of lesser fry, are not impressed.

The Tyne's troubles are constant and thus rarely reported; elsewhere it is the isolated incident that reveals hidden dangers or is itself their cause. In October 1989 competitors in a four-mile swimming race in the River Ouse, Norfolk, were warned of the risk of catching disease from the water; the cause — Sewage. Samples of water taken before the race recorded up to 28,000 particles of coliform bacteria per hundred millilitres and, at the end, 12,000. Officially, there are no sewage limits for rivers as swimming in such waters is discouraged, but the corresponding EC guideline for the sea is 2,000.[9]

In June 1990 it was reported that the NRA had successfully prosecuted the East Lancashire Paper Mill company of Radcliffe for polluting the River Irwell on three occasions during the summer of 1989 by discharging waste effluent from paper making,[10] while in February 1990 Shell Oil (UK) was strongly criticized and fined £1 million for allowing 156 tons of crude oil to enter the River Mersey from a fractured pipeline. On 19 August 1989, corrosion, resulting from contact with sea water, caused a 6-inch split in the 16-year old 12-inch pipe at Bromborough, but the situation was made worse when Shell staff, allegedly more concerned to save the pipe than with environmental consequences, twice attempted to flush out the oil and produced a further gush. The spill spread ten miles, killed 300 birds, affected 2,000 others and covered mussel beds. Strong winds and an exceptionally high tide reduced the prospect of further damage.[11] With an estimated content of 43,000 different chemical pollutants and high levels of mercury in sewage sludge,[12] the Mersey may well not have noticed the addition of a few hundred tons of oil any more than Shell noticed the corrosion of the pipe. The official inquiry, published in December 1990, criticized Shell for failure 'to give adequate consideration' to the effects of increasing the oil temperature from 65°C to 80°C and concluded that the methods used were inadequate to detect the resulting corrosion.[13]

It was ironical that the opening of the new Hyde sewage works in the Greater Manchester area on 2 October 1988 by the then environment secretary, Nicholas Ridley, had to be postponed because the waste effluent discharged by the plant into the River Tame, a major tributary of the Mersey, was so bad that the North West Water Authority could have been prosecuted under the 1974 Control of Pollution Act. Of 110 river samples investigated for oxygen depletion, 40 exceeded the limits which the DoE had itself set, while tests for suspended solids scored 47 failures out of 162 samples, with one sample 16 times the limit. Micro-organisms whose function was to break down the sewage sludge had themselves been killed off by excessive toxic levels on several occasions so that virtually untreated waste effluent poured into the river.[14]

A different problem faced the Severn. The Kidderminster carpet industry operates under a legal consent, approved in 1970, by which it flushes into the water residues from washing fleeces imported from Third World countries. Many of these still use, as protection against moths, the pesticide dieldrin, now banned in the UK. As a result, eels in the Severn showed dieldrin concentrations four times higher than the WHO danger level. In 1988 the Pollution Inspectorate decided that the existing consent was unacceptably high and tried to reduce it. The Kidderminster Carpet Manufacturers and Spinners Association, whose members would have had to install new equipment to extract the pesticides if their consents were changed, appealed, and, while the appeal was being considered, the DoE issued more stringent standards for moth-proofing agents than even those requested by the Inspectorate. Two years later, in June 1990, the matter was still unresolved and unwarrantable pesticide waste was still being discharged into the Severn.[15]

As 'still' water, lakes are inevitably affected by waste. Early in 1989 visitors to Lake Windermere, the most popular tourist attraction of the Lake District, might have seen what the North West Water Authority described as 'aesthetically revolting' and 'grossly offensive' — raw sewage dangling from branches above the lake. Apparently a valve had accidentally been left closed and the overflow seeped into Bowness Bay instead of being pumped through mesh screens into deeper waters. The incident may have been more spectacular than serious but it did little to alleviate concern over enriching the lake with algae-producing nutrients, and their eventual effect on the fish.[16]

The appearance of toxic algae in many lakes during the second half of 1989 was attributed by Water Authorities to the long hot summer and by environmentalists to phosphates from sewage and nutrients from fertilizers. The deaths of a number of lambs and eight dogs, which exercised in Rutland Water, Leicestershire, a huge reservoir supplying 700,000 consumers with drinking water, aroused public concern and led to the closure of all reservoirs in the Anglian region, together with ten lakes and pools. By the end of September algae were found in two reservoirs in the south-west and the NRA named 16 other waters throughout the country, advising owners to ban fishing and water sports and to advise animal owners of the danger.[17] The most disconcerting feature was uncertainty over the cause. Was this simply a freak phenomenon, the outcome of freak weather, though, as a potential forerunner of climatic change, the long hot summer might ultimately be traced to the effect of waste gases on the atmosphere, or were the algae the direct result of undesirable waste entering the waters? Among the certainties is that none of the incidents described is ancient history; all took place in the three-year period 1988–90 and show clearly that, despite the actions of regulatory authorities and pressure groups, the problems remain.

Rivers and lakes in Europe and the USSR

The Rhine is notorious for its contents. For its entire length between Switzerland and the sea it is seldom free from the poisoning effects of industrial effluent. Near Basel the giant Ciba-Geigy chemical works discharges unwanted waste into its waters; between the Swiss border and its junction with the Necker, it receives waste from the Hoehst works at Hoehst and Griesheim, BASF at Ludwigshafen and the Waldhof paper mill at Mannheim; the Main river, which passes through Frankfurt, adds its share of effluent at Mainz, while between Mainz and the Dutch border, the cities of Dusseldorf and Cologne make their contributions, the greatest industrial discharge coming from the Bayer works at Burrig. As the Rhine enters the Netherlands, it contains lead, phenols, arsenic, cadmium, mercury and PCBs, supplemented only too often by large-scale releases caused by accidents such as the Sandoz fire in November 1986 and the major pollution incidents that followed.[18]

Throughout the river's course, this industrial waste is augmented by increasing volumes of agricultural runoff, domestic waste (including detergents) and sewage. Where industry is responsible for heavy metals, these add nitrates, phosphates and an organic mixture that eats up the oxygen in the water to produce obnoxious algae. When the Rhine reaches the North Sea it disgorges an annual load of 420,000 tonnes of nitrogen and 37,000 tonnes of phosphorus alongside its 13.8 tonnes of cadmium and 3.9 tonnes of mercury into the comparatively shallow waters.[19] Yet it supplies 20,000,000 Europeans with their drinking water and even the most sophisticated purification processes cannot hope to eliminate every type of pollution. It is even possible that the use of chlorine, chlorine dioxide and ozone as reagents leads to further problems, not excluding increased rates of cancer.[20] On the credit side, despite the setback caused by the Sandoz incident, studies over the period 1900–80 have shown that, while concentrations of heavy metals increased for most of this century, they have decreased during the past 10–15 years as heavy metal wastes have been reduced and treatment improved.[21]

Yet is the Rhine the 'dirtiest river in Europe'? The Seine, with 9.67mg/l of lead, 14.33 of copper and 20.67 of chromium, can hardly be called clean,[22] especially when, just upstream from Paris, concentrations of bacteria have increased from fewer than 10 coliforms per 100 millilitres in the mid-1920s to approximatley 500, as the result of overloading the sewage system.[23] The claim for the Rhine would, however, probably have gone undisputed but for the opening up of Eastern Europe in 1989. Now there are serious challengers in the Elbe and Vistula. As it passes through East Germany, the Elbe receives ten times the mercury and heavy metals West Germany discharges into the Rhine. Polluted by waste from cellulose and pharmaceutical factories, it also collects runoff and seepage from the 50 million tonnes of artificial fertilizer used annually throughout the country.[24]

In Poland a 1988 report by the Academy of Sciences claimed that there was a complete breakdown of the 'state of natural balance', presumably between pollution and renewal, in 27 areas of the country in which more than 12 million people, a third of the population, lived. Some six billion cubic metres of industrial waste effluent, around half the annual total, was discharged untreated into rivers[25] so that a third of them were devoid of life.[26] Between Warsaw and Gdansk the Vistula was reportedly so polluted that it would corrode industrial machinery. The Academy of Sciences claimed that, when it reached the Baltic, it discharged 90,000 tons of nitrogen, 5,000 tons of phosphorus, 130 tons of oil, three tons of phenols and lead, together with unknown quantities of cadmium, mercury and zinc every year.[27] Not surprisingly, bathing in the river in once pleasant stretches near Warsaw was prohibited.[28] Even the upper reaches were affected. Not far from Auschwitz, on the site of the chemical factory that manufactured some of the deadly Cyclon-B, a new, and larger, chemical works poured its steaming waste into the waters.[29]

Other East European rivers have suffered from the excesses of Stalinist industrialization. In Czechoslovakia, as the Vltava enters Prague, it is a second-class river on a scale of one to four; when it leaves, it is a fourth-class stream in which nothing can live.[30] In Romania, waste discharges from industry and agriculture have made 85 per cent of the main rivers unfit for use as drinking water, and the River Tissa, which flows into Hungary, is so polluted as to cause the Hungarians serious concern.[31]

Limited as is our knowledge, every new piece of information adds to a picture of water misused through discharge of waste. In January 1990, the Russian newspaper *Sovetskaya Rossyia* reported carcinogenic and mutagenic substances in the river Volga, while fish in the Kuibyshev reservoir had stopped breeding, 70 per cent of them contaminated with mercury compounds from agricultural waste.[32] At the 60-nation Ramsar Convention meeting in Switzerland in July 1990 on the world's important wetlands, Russian scientists were outspoken in condemning the ecological threats from untreated sewage, industrial waste and fertilizer and pesticide runoff to the country's rivers and lakes. The Volga delta on the northern shores of the Caspian Sea, used by millions of migratory birds as a spring and autumn stopover, was suffering from industrial pollution and water diversion for agriculture; the Dnieper and Dneister areas and the basins of the Baikal, Ob and Amur were either 'on the brink of ecological disaster' or faced serious problems.[33]

In Chapter 2 the Soviets were described as 'considerably more cavalier' than even the Americans in their treatment of nuclear waste, at least in the earliest days. From 1949 onwards liquid waste from nuclear plants in the Sverdlovsk and Chelyabinsk regions of the Urals was simply dumped in the local Techa river. When this became so polluted that it had to be fenced off and people living nearby evacuated, the waste was emptied into Lake Karachai, near Kyshtym. Heat from the radionuclides caused the lake, which covered about 10 square kilometres, to dry out, the presence of about 120 million curies of long-lived isotopes, mostly strontium-90, caesium-137 and residual plutonium, made it necessary to concrete over the whole area.[34]

The greatest concern, however, was for the huge inland lakes — Baikal and the Aral Sea. In 1989 Lake Baikal, the 'sacred lake' and 'pearl of Siberia', renowned until the twentieth century for the magnificence of its scenery and the purity of its waters, received waste effluent from over 100 factories on its shores, all of them without purification facilities. Included in the waste water were the heavy metals mercury, zinc, tungsten and molybdenum. At the same time almost 700 agricultural units on the lake's tributaries added fertilizers, slurry and pesticides. The lake's largest tributary, the Selenga, brought partially treated sewage and effluent from some 50 factories in Ulan-Ude, capital of the Buryat Autonomous Republic, contributing 500 of the 700 tonnes of nitrates entering the lake. The most notorious sources of pollution were two pulp and cellulose mills, one at Baikalsk, the other on the River Selenga at Selenginsk. When it began operations in 1966, the Baikalsk plant discharged almost 400 tonnes of toxic material into the lake in 18 months; 23 years later it had poured more than 1.5bn cubic metres of industrial waste into the water. Not surprisingly fish have been affected, all but one species monitored containing traces of DDT, PCBs or HCH, while the epidemic in which thousands of freshwater seals died since 1987 is known worldwide. Recent legislation has brought improvements, but nothing can restore Lake Baikal to its former purity.[35]

The Aral Sea, once the fourth largest lake in the world, is now the sixth; between 1960 and 1989 its area decreased by 40 per cent, the result of misplaced irrigation schemes that have led to increased salinization and loss of commercial fishing. Lack of foresight rather than waste is responsible, but industrialization and massive use of pesticides, particularly DDT, on the region's cotton crop are blamed for declining health, which in turn is exacerbated by absence of proper sewage and waste-treatment facilities.[36]

Heavy industrialization in the Ukraine, Crimea and the eastern parts of the Black Sea coast has led to increased pollution, beaches are regularly closed.[37] Of the effluent discharged into rivers and the Black Sea in

Bulgaria, 40 per cent is untreated or poorly treated. Soviet scientists maintain that 70 per cent of deadly metallic poisoning entering the Black Sea does so through the Danube.[38]

North America

What the USSR, through concentration on heavy industry and intensive agriculture, has experienced over the last half century had already left its mark on the largest freshwater system of the world, the Great Lakes of North America. Covering 242,000 square kilometres, by mid-Twentieth Century the lakes had become the centre of a massive development area in which 40 million people lived, 80 per cent of them in large conurbations. Until the mid-1960s untreated raw sewage was pumped directly into Lake Erie and Lake Ontario. Together with contamination from agricultural runoff, particularly phosphates, this led to eutrophication and the deaths of many types of fish. By 1983 the International Joint Commission had identified 8,000 alien substances in the water.

Measures to halt eutrophication led to the annual amount of phosphorus introduced into Lake Michigan and Lake Superior falling below the permitted level, while other lakes approached it. Phosphate fertilizers are still, however, being washed into the lake and, while the major harmful pesticides (DDT, aldrin, dieldrin, heptachlor) were banned at the beginning of the 1970s and PCBs at the end of the decade, the time lag in the ultimate removal of highly persistent wastes militates against a quick solution. In 1980 PCB concentrations in sea trout still measured 5.3ppm as opposed to the desired 0.1ppm, a target which it is doubtful can be reached this century.[39]

Nor does the situation of North American rivers offer grounds for complacency. In the north, at the mouth of the St Lawrence river, small Beluga whales, 5,000 of which, at the turn of the century, deserted their Arctic habitat for an area where the Saguenay river meets the St Lawrence, east of Quebec, had been reduced, by the end of the 1980s, to between 300 and 500. It was even claimed, in November 1990, that there were fewer than 100 left and that one dead whale was washed ashore every month.[40] Investigation showed that the whales had problems with their digestive systems, had developed tumours and had suffered damage to their immune systems, most probably from PCBs and DDT reaching the open waters through the atmosphere. But the main cause of death, the carcinogen BAP, which attacks the DNA, was traced up river to the Alcan aluminium works, which over the years had discharged 15 tons of BAP into the river. PCBs also entered the St Lawrence from Massena where, in the years before they were banned, they were dumped. In 1990 land dumps were leaking into the river through outfalls in which the presence of PCBs was four times higher than official state limits. They have been found in birds (330ppm in the brain), in the brains of frogs, and in eels, which are eaten by people and by belugas. Massena itself is the home of the Mowhawk Indians, who are no longer able to eat the fish they once caught and so have turned to farming.

The PCBs were dumped by industrial firms in the days when their use was legal. Among those responsible are General Motors, which dumped PCBs on site, Alcoa Aluminium, Central Foundry and Reynolds Motors, which for 30 years dumped fluorides and PCBs so that the soil is now highly contaminated. Reynolds Motors was actually found guilty of discharging PCBs. Up to 6ppm of the fire-resistant and toxic pesticide, Mirex, banned as a carcinogen in 1976, have been found in whale blubber, transmitted through eels from Lake Ontario, where it lodged in the sediment and was ingested by tiny organisms eaten by the eels. The source was the Armstrong firm, which, 30 years ago, dumped it, quite legally, into the river. Higher upstream, at Niagara Falls, a sewage outlet into the Niagara River discharges more Mirex. The land on which this occurs is now owned by Occidental, but the Mirex was made long ago by Hooker Chemicals. With Hooker the wheel comes full circle; we are back to Love Canal.[41]

One prefers not to think of the situation in New Orleans where drinking water comes from the Mississippi at the end of a long stretch that serves as a sewer for communities and industries from Minnesota to Louisiana, including a line of petrochemical plants. Drinking water is treated to a cocktail of the chemicals chlorine, potassium permanganate, ferrous sulphate and lime, before being given a final dose of chlorine. No one can complain that the resultant liquid is tasteless![42]

Latin America
In South America, the use of mercury in gold mining has affected the rivers of the Amazon system, which, it is estimated, now contain up to 1,800 tonnes of mercury.[43] Recent research into the Madeira River, which flows into the Amazon from the south, shows that for every kilogram of gold at least 1.32 kg of mercury is 'wasted' and 'lost to the environment'. In practice, under rough conditions in which mercury cannot be recovered, the ratio is more likely to be 6:1, or even 10:1. This means that the annual mercury waste entering the Madeira is estimated at 12.6 tons, about a quarter of the amount entering the entire North Sea. Tributaries and small forest streams, flooded by the Madeira for 2–3 months a year, collect more mercury than the main river, where the actual mining takes place, as there is less water movement. The greatest danger comes from the transformation of mercury into the highly toxic methylmercury, which poisoned the Japanese fishermen of Minamata. The result is a 'direct environmental and health threat for local ecosystems and people', with levels of mercury in fish exceeding WHO danger limits.[44] As the mercury enters the food chain and affects the diet of fish-eating peoples, the miners themselves have become contaminated with 20 times the WHO's permitted level.[45]

Elsewhere the major problems are sewage and industrial waste. As little, if any, sewage is treated, twice as many rivers as in other regions have counts of coliform bacteria exceeding 100,000 per millilitre (8 per cent against 4 per cent) compared with the WHO recommended count for drinking water of 0 per 100 ml.[46] In Ecuador, where 90 per cent of Sangay National Park is under threat from concessions for gold mining granted to national and multinational companies, more than half the population lives in urban areas. On the government's own estimates, 400,000 homes lack basic plumbing and water, and the second largest city, Guayaquil, with a population of 1.2 million, is sited on the estuary of two rivers fouled by untreated sewage, domestic rubbish and industrial waste.[47] In Peru, chemical waste from the narcotics industry, that is, kerosene, sulphuric acid, acetone, toluene, carbide and lime, is dumped or poured into rivers by both dealers and the police who confiscate the chemicals, putting at risk people fishing in the rivers; while the herbicide tebuthiuron ('spike'), scattered as pellets to prevent drift into the rainforests, is considered by the EPA as dangerous for use in wetlands, where it can remain in rivers for up to five years.[48] Untreated waste water dumped into rivers, then used to irrigate vegetables grown for urban use, threatens the people of both Mexico City and Bogota, Colombia, where the River Tunjuelito has high levels of cadmium and lead.[49] In Chile the Maipo river receives effluents from chemical, plastic and rubber industries, few of which are treated, while waste from the pulp and paper industry receives no treatment at all.[50]

Elsewhere in the Third World

The rivers of Africa receive similar influxes of waste, especially where there are large urban conurbations. With more than 12 million citizens, a high birthrate and the inevitable influx of villagers from the countryside, Cairo is now the largest city in the Middle East and Africa, but its sewage system dates from the days when the population was a third of what it is now. In the 1970s untreated sewage regularly flooded many areas of the city and, by the end of the eighties, after ten years of reconstruction, less than half the two million cubic metres of sewage entering the system daily was treated for use as fertilizer; the rest flowed into open drains that emptied into the Nile or Lake Manzala on the Mediterranean coast. Sewage from the three million inhabitants not linked to the system accumulated in cesspits or was thrown into canals that others used for washing, cooking or drinking.

In 1977 the government embarked on a grand renovation and development scheme, first with money provided by its rich Arab allies, then, after the Sadat–Begin agreement of 1975, with British and US support. Phase 1, beginning in 1980, planned to overhaul the existing system by removing accumulated grit and solid waste; Phase 2 included the construction of a deep tunnel, stretching the length of the city, through which sewage could be flushed to a new treatment plant. The technological problems were immense. Nevertheless, by the end of the eighties, the project was complete, except for one vital factor — the new treatment plant, north of the city, from which it was originally estimated that treated effluent could irrigate 400 square kilometres of reclaimed desert by the year 2000. As the 1990s opened, money for this had still to be found, and untreated and partially treated sewage continues to drain into the Nile and Lake Manzala.[51]

In Kenya the problem of sewage in rivers is exacerbated by the discharge of commercial and industrial effluent. Overloaded and partially treated sewage and effluent enter River Nairobi at Nairobi, to be carried to the Athi. In the Kiambu district these are joined by waste effluent from slaughterhouses, tanneries, and cement and coffee factories, and by pesticide and insecticide wastes from their extensive use on agricultural land. The river is affected to between 20 and 65km downstream at times of low water.[52] Inland, on the western border, sugar wastes from untreated molasses enter the vast expanse of Lake Victoria to swell the nutrient content and affect, if only locally, the survival of fish.[53]

In Asia, the rivers of the Indian sub-continent are notorious for the quantity of sewage and domestic and industrial detritus they receive. Hence this description of the Ganga in the early 1980s:

> Along every kilometre...in Uttar Pradesh, Bihar and West Bengal, people are pouring their garbage, excreta and muck into what is gradually turning from river to drain...48 class I cities and 66 class II towns dump largely untreated sewage into the water everyday. To this is added the burden of other human activities like bathing, washing of clothes and immersing of ashes or unburnt corpses.... Industries contribute chemical effluent to the Ganga's pollution load. DDT factories, tanneries, paper and pulp mills, petrochemical and fertilizer complexes, rubber factories and a host of others use the river to get rid of their wastes.[54]

Around the sprawling conurbation of Calcutta, beyond which the Indian branch of the Ganga becomes the Hoogly, 150 major factories, including 87 jute mills, 12 textile mills, 150 major tanneries, 5 paper and pulp factories and 4 distilleries choke the estuary with their waste, as raw sewage pours continuously into the river from 361 outfalls.[55]

Deadly in a different way are the uranium tailings from the Jaduguda mill (see Chapter 2), decanted, with fluid, into a ravine; 50 metres downstream the effluent contains radium, manganese and sulphate 'above the desired water concentrations' and, by the time it reaches the Subarnarekha river, both uranium and radium concentrations have increased, the former by 2.5 times to 3.2 mg/cubic metre. To these are then added radioactive tailings from a nearby copper plant. The result? At sites ten kilometres distant, grass and milk samples show that radium has entered the water system.[56]

In the south, the Periyar, largest river of Kerala, has factories on its lower banks making fertilizers, chemicals, metallurgical items and rayon. The 170m litres of waste effluent discharged into the river contain suspended solids, metals, urea, ammonia, fluorides, chlorides and other chemicals, while effluent from India Rare Earths, Ltd. contains mercury and radioactive waste.[57]

Of the 20 well-known high-altitude lakes, all but two are dying, those near large cities killed by lack of oxygen. Within the next 80 years the most famous of all, the Dal Lake at Srinagar, Kashmir, already reduced in surface from over 25 sq km in 1955 to 12 in 1985, will become a small lake surrounded by vegetable farms and swamps, as floating gardens, runoff from artificial fertilizer, substantial quantities of silt and raw sewage, and waste water from tourists' houseboats increase the nitrates and phosphates in the water, and noxious weed takes over large areas, making life in the lake impossible.[58]

The dangers of pesticide use and subsequent runoff are illustrated by Malaysia where dieldrin in concentrations of over 1,000 nanograms per litre is found in fresh water, while the same levels of PCBs occur in Indonesia as the result of rapid and unregulated industrialization.[59]

Attempted improvements are often frustrated by the sheer magnitude of the task. A European visitor to China in 1989, describing the West Lake at Hangzhou at the southern end of the 1,800 km Grand Canal from Beijing, reported that 15 million Chinese holidaymakers visited the lake's picturesque islands annually, but until recently the lake itself, deprived of water from the Qiantang river, was so rich in phosphates and nitrates from domestic and industrial effluent that it was disfigured with dense algal blooms. The Chinese have now built a ring sewer round the lake to intercept waste waters, and the sewage from visitors to the islands is brought ashore for disposal.

Conversely, the Grand Canal itself, which carries 10 per cent of Hangzhou's freight traffic is an open sewer receiving 50,000 tonnes of waste water daily. In the black evil-smelling section that runs through the city fish cannot survive; when the canal overflows after torrential rains, it contaminates rivers and ponds, killing the fish. The Dutch Government have promised nearly £1 million in aid to clean up the southern section, and the optimistic Chinese aim to have fish in the canal by the year 2000.[60]

So far success has eluded the Philippines, where the Comprehensive Water Quality Management Project, set up in the early 1970s to deal with the largest freshwater lake in Southeast Asia, Laguna de Bay, has yet to overcome the acute eutrophication of the waters caused by excess nitrogen from agricultural and urban runoff and the effects of industrial discharges of toxic waste and heavy metals. The lake itself is fed by 21 tributaries and has a catchment area of 3,822 sq km, which includes 50 towns, several industrial areas, intensive farming and the prospect of supplying Manila with water. The Laguna Lake Authority took all appropriate action. It measured water quality, set interim standards, inventoried sources of pollution and monitored discharges, concluding that 80 per cent of the nitrogen load came from farm and domestic wastes and that, left unchecked, the extent of nitrogen pollution would double by the year 2000. Despite plans for low-cost sewage treatment facilities, proposed changes in farming practice, and environmental impact statements to monitor progress, the programme has found itself hampered by what are described as 'competing interests and a lack of authority for the entire river basin'. The result? Pollution in the lake has not been reduced as planned.[61]

The coastal zone

The coastal zone is the stretch of shallow water between the shore and the edge of the continental shelf, where the seabed makes a sudden dip to the ocean depths. Although only 10 per cent of the surface area of the world's oceans and 0.5 per cent of its volume, its nearness to land ensures its domination by human activities. Seventy per cent of the world's people live on its coastal plains; most of the remainder visit the sea as tourists or choose it for retirement. Traditionally the home of the fishing industry, the coastal zone is now mined for fossil fuels. And, as the largest stretch of water conveniently available, it receives all forms of waste, through direct outflows, from rivers and estuaries, or through runoff from the land. Surveying the sea from the shore, one is so impressed by its sheer size that one can appreciate why our grandparents regarded it as a bottomless dustbin in which the waters would 'dilute and disperse' even the most obnoxious poisons.

So far the sea has obliged. But there are signs that continued abuse is outstripping absorptive capacity. The appearance of toxic algae along the coasts of Norway, Denmark and Sweden in 1988 and the seal deaths that followed, the deaths of large numbers of dolphins along the east coast of the USA the same year, the appearance of a stinking green slime that caused tourists to flee the beaches of the Adriatic in 1989 and the more frequent appearance throughout the world of red tides, glutinous green slimes and filthy froths of yellow foam suggest some deeper cause than the increased temperatures and dry summers of government apologists.

Algal blooms result from increasing eutrophication caused by large additions of nutrients, and the largest additions are those from waste in the form of agricultural and industrial runoff and human sewage. Were this all, the situation would arouse concern, but the additional influx of heavy metals and chemical effluent, from which many toxic substances accumulate in sediments to lie undetected for years, are cause for alarm. Particularly disconcerting is the incompleteness of our knowledge of the processes taking place in this highly volatile area of the sea. Some chemicals produce immediate and identifiable effects; with others we simply do not know, even when we know what the chemicals are! The ultimate danger is that, as we add more and more waste regardless of consequences, the system will reach the point of no return. Carried to excess, eutrophication can lead to a 'flip' into a new state, anoxia, that is, a complete absence of oxygen or a diminution so great that the water can no longer support the forms of life that previously existed. The living seas become dead oceans.[62]

Britain and the northern seas
What, then, goes into coastal waters? And, equally important, since much of it remains in sediment, what has already gone in?

If we take Britain as an example of an 'advanced industrial society', even a cursory overview is disconcerting. Starting with the shore itself, how clean are Britain's beaches? In June 1990, in presenting 29 British beaches with Blue Flag Awards, the highest European accolade for water quality, cleanliness, litter and toilet facilities, Environment Minister David Trippier pointed out that 76 per cent of UK-designated bathing waters met European standards compared with 67 per cent in 1988. He did not mention that Britain was fifth from the bottom of the list of European countries awarded flags, or that Denmark won 128, Spain 137, Portugal 101 and Greece 83; nor did he recall that two weeks previously the EC had announced that it would prosecute Britain over three of its most polluted beaches, including the country's most popular resort, Blackpool. Neither did he refer to a Department of Health warning then in operation against eating shellfish or crustaceans caught between the Humber and Montrose, north of Dundee, because of contamination by potentially fatal toxins caused by blue-green algae.[63] Even the Blue Flag designation has been queried. According to Dr David Wheeler of the University of Surrey, on a strict interpretation of EC law, water samples should be free of viruses, but since this is impossible to abide by, it was ignored in favour of a bacteria test. Were the law to be strictly applied, most of the cleanest Blue Flag beaches would probably fail the test.[64] This assessment corroborated the results of research by Professor Alisdair MacIntyre of Aberdeen University for the United Nations Environment Programme (UNEP), which suggested that it was necessary to revise the concept that seawater killed off viruses in a very short time. In an 'extreme example' a harmful virus had survived for 17 months in sewage-polluted sediments![65] The example may be extreme and the odds against resulting infection so high that, for practical purposes, they can be ignored. Nevertheless, the fact is there, undiscovered until early 1990. How many more revisions do we have to make to present understanding before we can say with certainty that the waters are safe?

As for discharging sewage into the sea, in March 1990 Britain was still using more than 500 pipelines through which raw, that is, untreated, sewage passed to the waters. To meet EC objections it proposed to replace many of these with long outfall pipes, discharging a mile of so out at sea, where, it was claimed, the combined effects of sun, sea and microbes would bring about speedy and effective breakdown. In short, faced with the visible problem of turds on bathing beaches, the answer was to turn it into a less visible problem which seaside visitors were unlikely to notice. In the event, on the eve of the March 1990 North Sea Conference, the proposal was withdrawn; new outfalls will now have sewage works attached and the estimated cost of between £2.5bn and £7bn be passed to the consumer.[66]

More controversial than the discharge of sewage directly into the sea is the dumping of some 10 million tons of sewage sludge annually at licensed points around the coast — the Thames estuary, off Humberside and Tyneside, in the Clyde, Forth and Mersey estuaries, the Bristol Channel and the English Channel between Cornwall and Portsmouth. While other members of the EC banned the dumping of sewage sludge, Britain continued to argue that it was the cheapest option and that there was no scientific evidence of damage to marine life apart from 'smothering' in the immediate area. Where common sense suggests that the sewage should be spread on land as fertilizer, this is ruled out by the lack of farmland within reasonable distance of sewage works and, more importantly, contamination of the sludge by heavy metals from industry.[67]

Industrial waste follows the dual pattern of sewage: direct discharges or dumping, both under licence from the Ministry of Agriculture. The greater part of dumping goes into the Thames estuary or into the sea off the north-east coast. In 1986 the North Sea states agreed a 50 per cent reduction in dangerous chemical dumping by 1995, but the British Red List of 23 chemicals is one of the shortest in Europe.[68] In January 1990 Britain overrode objections from five of the other seven North Sea countries by announcing its intention to start an annual dumping of 51,000 tonnes of toxic chemicals. Fisons Ltd wished to dump 6,000 tonnes, Orsynthetics Ltd 42,000 tonnes and Sterling Organics 3,000 tonnes. A further nine licences had been applied for; the government was, however, still 'committed' to phasing out dumping as quickly as possible and had cut licences by 50 per cent since 1987.[69]

The approaching North Sea Conference and the prospect of Britain again being labelled the 'dirty man of Europe' concentrated minds sharply. Ten days before the conference, Agriculture Minister John Gummer announced that licensing would cease 'after the end of 1992'. In practice this meant that dumping would continue until early 1993, and there were two exceptions. ICI and Sterling Organics Ltd, both in the north-east, might not be able to find alternative land disposal until mid-1993, though the minister hoped that dumping at sea would cease in the first few months of that year[70]. As part of Britain's largest chemical company, the ICI plant at Billingham, near the Tees estuary, manufactures the plastic methylmethacrylate, discharging 300,000 tonnes of acidic ammonium sulphate into waterways each year and dumping up to 165,000 tonnes of slurry into the North Sea and a further 60,000 tonnes into the Tees estuary. In July 1989 the company announced a £35 million clean-up programme by which it would phase out both dumping operations and build a plant for converting the acid waste into sulphuric acid for use in manufacturing acrylic products, resins and paints.[71] ICI's end to dumping in 1993 presumably depends on the plant being operational by that time. Hopes of further enhancing Britain's image swiftly followed with the announcement by the then Environment Secretary, Chris Patten, that the dumping of sewage sludge would end in 1998.[72]

The Gummer announcement also promised an early-1993 end to the annual dumping of 550,000 tons of 'fly-ash' from burnt pulverized coal used by the CEGB in power stations. For a number of years two ships had left Blyth daily for a 20-mile square dumping area 3 miles offshore, where the ash was deposited at depths of 90 to 140 feet. While the CEGB claimed that the tonnage was only 1.5 per cent of the total produced in British power stations (the remainder went for land reclamation, covering landfill sites and making building blocks, an argument whose relevance to the issue is elusive) the local North Shields Fishing Association, representing 380 men and 70 vessels, maintained that the dumping had created a 'marine desert' where the ash 'set solid like concrete', so that only weeds could live and the fish had moved away. The issue gained publicity in January 1990 when Greenpeace activists chained themselves to the dumping ship, the *MVA*, in an attempt to stop the practice.[73]

It is a measure of the complacency with which the inhabitants of the British Isles have accepted this situation that only when something untoward occurs with either sewage or industrial waste does the public actually hear of it. In August 1989, for example, a vast blanket of toxic orange algae, at one stage up to four miles long, covered the sea in the tourist area of Mount's Bay, Cornwall, where a large number of short outfalls pour an extra weight of sewage into the sea at the height of the season. High temperatures, bright sunlight and several months of calm seas provided ideal conditions for an algal bloom. Local skippers, waiting to take visitors out fishing, were less scientific in their observations: 'This is brown, yellow shit...you can see the neat sewage coming out, the paper floating around. It does tourism a world of good'.[74]

In May 1990 Scottish fishermen in the Clyde estuary became extremely perturbed when some of them discovered explosives in their nets. Over 100 tonnes of explosive waste from ICI's factory at Ardeer, Ayrshire, had been legally dumped, at an approved site, in hessian sacks, designed to rot away and allow sea water to break down the explosives and render them safer. Although aware of the actual dumping grounds, the fishermen had made their 'catches' at three sites to the south of the approved area after ICI had given up use of the dump the previous year.[75]

Pride of place in the discharge stakes must, however, go to the multinational firm of Albright and Wilson, whose Marchon works, Cumbria, produces a range of chemicals for detergents and toiletries, and is licensed to discharge 11 million gallons of effluent daily into the Irish Sea. In the first private prosecution of a company for illegal waste discharges that exceeded limits authorized under the 1989 Water Act, Greenpeace claimed that a sample taken on 29 June 1990 included discharges of uranium, aluminium, beryllium, boron, titanium and other metals in addition to those for which the works had a licence. The company admitted that its discharges may have been above the limit. Its excuse was that at the request of the local water authority it had been trying to save water and might, therefore, have failed to dilute the discharges sufficiently![76] Thus, the hot, dry summer was not only the cause of obnoxious algae but had driven virtuous chemical companies into sinful action! The problem, as the Ministry of Agriculture admits, is simply that it is impossible to monitor every licensed discharge to ensure that it conforms to what is authorized. In the first place, there is the question of discovering the actual contents of the discharge; in the second, with dumping, there is the additional problem of ascertaining that it takes place at the authorized site. The dumping vessel sets out with its cargo; hours later it returns; but where it actually deposited its waste is known only to those involved, who, being human and unobserved, may not be above taking advantage of their situation.

Sewage and industrial waste are not the only forms of unwanted matter entering the waters around the British Isles. Each of the UK's 14 coastal nuclear power stations uses its position to discharge radioactive effluent into the waiting waters. Despite recent attempts to clean up the 'nuclear image', nothing can undo what has already been done. Thanks to Sellafield, the Irish Sea remains, as the Commons Environment Committee found it, 'the most radioactive sea in the world'.[77]

The problem with radioactivity is that it refuses to go away. In February 1990, following freak storms and high seas, the little town of Towyn on the north Welsh coast was flooded by sea water, which eventually retreated, leaving a highly unpleasant trail of silt. The silt was even less desirable than expected. Eight out of 14 samples taken from streets, houses and gardens turned out to be radioactive, with concentrations of americium ten times higher than the NRPB's 'generalized derived limits'. As the sediment dried there was the further radiation hazard of inhaling radioactive dust containing isotopes of americium and plutonium. Inevitably the danger from such a 'one-off dosage' was played down as offering only a very small risk to the public, as it may have done. Nevertheless, the fact remains that it was there, and the reprocessing plant at Sellafield was suspected as its source.[78] And in July 1990 holidaymakers were advised not to go along a 15-mile stretch of beach on the West Cumbrian coast. Items contaminated by the 1983 Sellafield discharges and since buried in the sand had been disturbed by recent storms, still contaminated with caesium-137, plutonium, or americium, and some had now surfaced.[79]

More specialized, and limited in extent, is the dumping of colliery spoil and washery slurry on the beaches adjoining Seaham harbour, County Durham. The Commons Environment Committee was 'appalled by the impact of dumping on the Durham beaches' but apparently accepted that 'the economics of production' of the coalfields were such that to end the dumping of spoil on the beaches would make the pits unprofitable. The committee concluded that the situation had developed only because the agencies which had originally allowed this method of disposal 'had no particular commitment to environmental protection'.[80] Less charitable observers might delete the 'particular' and wonder whether, in practice, they were any less committed than their present-day counterparts. Their crime is that they were unable to hide the results of their activities, which stand as a hideous memorial to times when economic forces seemed unchallengeable.

Nutrients from agricultural waste, hazardous chemical effluent, radioactive waste, colliery spoil, fly ash and the omnipresent sewage — the list of wastes deposited in British coastal waters is all-inclusive. Except that we have still to add the toxic excess pesticides and inevitable faecal matter from Scottish fish farming described in Chapter 2, the residue and airborne contaminants from incineration at sea (see Chapter 6), and the hydrocarbon-polluted mud churned out by oil rigs during operations, which, in its blanketing effect on the seabed, is probably more dangerous than floating oil slicks from tankers illegally discharging their wastes by washing out tanks at sea.

Common sense suggests that this superabundance of waste entering the waters must, despite the dilute and disperse syndrome, have some impact on their inhabitants, a topic that leads from the narrow aspects of British coastal waters to those of northern Europe as a whole. Scientists at the Federal Research Institute for Fisheries at Cuxhaven, West Germany, for example, noted a high incidence of abnormalities in the embryos of certain North Sea fish. Half the whiting embryos tested over the three years to 1990 and 5–20 per cent of the embryos of sole, cod, flounder and plaice were fatally deformed, with the highest rates occurring in the centre of the German Bight, where waste from the titanium dioxide industry was dumped for over 20 years.[81] PCBs have been found in cod, whiting, dab, flounder and sole, all of which are sold commercially in Britain and so, presumably, eaten. The Ministry of Agriculture, Food and Fisheries (MAFF) admitted as much but maintained that the levels were low and mainly concentrated in fish liver, which was not normally eaten. Besides, we all have PCBs in our bodies from a variety of other sources.[82]

The incident arousing greatest public concern, however, was the 1988 epidemic that killed some 17,000 common seals in European and British waters. In mid-April 1988 nearly 100 common seal pups were born prematurely near the Danish island of Anholt; and shortly afterwards sick adults were reported on both sides of the Kattegat. By mid-May hundreds of dead seals appeared in the Kattegat and bodies were washed ashore on the German island of Sylt off the north-east coast. This coincided with an unusual algal bloom that moved westward from the Baltic along the north shore of the Kattegat and with the failure of some seabirds in Scotland to breed. Not surprisingly pollution was cited as the cause of all three events, though some scientists were later to reject this hypothesis.

By the end of June observers had reported 3,800 dead seals in the Skaggerak and Kattegat and a further 2,700 in the Wadden Sea to the south. In mid-August it was obvious that the epidemic had reached Britain; by September dead seals were reported from Scotland and Northern Ireland. By October the death toll was decreasing in the Kattegat but rising in the Wadden Sea, where 7,800 bodies were recovered, and in Britain, where it was approaching 2,000. More importantly, after a number of false starts and some highly improbable suggestions, scientists had at last pinned down the cause of the disease to a phocine distemper virus (PDV), closely related to the canine distemper virus from the morbilli family. In the 1989 season there were further deaths but on nothing like the same scale as the previous epidemic.

The question remains of how far were waste pollutants discharged into offshore waters and the North Sea responsible for the seal deaths? Dr John Harwood, Director of the Sea Mammal Research Unit in Cambridge, and

Peter Reijnders of the Research Institute for Nature Management, Texel, the Netherlands, confirm that seals, as top of the marine food chain and thus liable to receive the full effects of biological accumulation of toxins, are particularly vulnerable to pollution and that PCBs in particular are responsible both for widespread infertility and, as suppressors of the immune system, increasing the susceptibility of mammals to disease. As, however, the greatest number of deaths did not occur in the most polluted areas of the Wadden Sea and the Baltic, while dead seals analysed had not shown unusual levels of pesticides or PCBs, they were inclined to conclude that 'pollution may have played only a small role'. Conversely, Dr Albert Osterhaus of the National Institute of Public Health and Environmental Hygiene in the Netherlands, pointing out that the average daily intake of PCBs by seals in the North Sea was 1.5 milligrams compared with 0.22 milligrams in the cleaner North Atlantic, was more inclined to assert that PCBs and other persistent chemicals had undermined the seals' resistance and made them more vulnerable to viruses.[83]

Even more at risk, because they are so few, are the bottlenosed dolphins once found in abundance in the waters of Cardigan Bay, Wales, and the Moray Firth, Scotland. The Welsh waters suffer from the regular discharge of macerated solids by the sewage outfall at Llanina Point, Newquay, and from the offloading of stinking animal wastes, while, further north, the sea off Barmouth has some of the highest lindane levels in the country. In 1988 a baby dolphin found floating dead in the bay was discovered to have died from toxic hepatitis with 320 ppm of PCBs in its blubber, according to MAFF investigators, while a harbour porpoise that also died, along with 32 dolphins, had 93 ppm. The Moray Firth, whose inlet at Dornoch was once described as 'the last undisturbed natural sanctuary in this area of the bottlenosed dolphin', is also threatened by raw sewage from the rapidly growing town of Inverness. The Longman outfall pipeline is completely exposed at low tide and the shore covered with sewage, while at the adjoining Cromarty Firth an oil rig service industry is responsible for regular spills of oil and diesel fuel. Not surprisingly a once thriving fishing industry has found its stocks depleted.[84]

Waste in the Mediterranean

Seals of the northern waters were not the only creatures affected by a morbillivirus. In September and October 1990 over 400 dead dolphins were found on beaches in Spain, France and Italy, the cause of their deaths unknown until it was traced to infection by a morbillivirus similar to that which destroyed the seals. Morbilliviral epidemics, such as the rinderpest outbreak that slaughtered whole herds of African cattle, are especially devastating in their wholesale destruction, spreading rapidly and killing every creature not previously exposed to the virus. Of particular concern were the rare monk seals, one of the world's most endangered species with, in one estimate, as few as 190 still in existence off the coasts of Morocco, Mauritania and the eastern Aegean. By the beginning of November five monk seals had been washed up in North Africa and south-west Spain, too badly decomposed for full analysis.[85] Again, some scientists suggested that PCBs could have weakened the immune system, especially as the quantity found in their bodies was ten times the accepted level.[86]

Seals and dolphins were not the only poisoned creatures. In March 1990 it was reported that Italian environmentalists had uncovered a potentially lethal load of swordfish, containing 1.5 mg/kilo of mercury, more than twice the maximum permitted level. The fish were supplied by Transfish of Catania, Sicily, and caught in response to the growing demand from London smart-set restaurants.[87]

What, then, has gone wrong with the Mediterranean that it has become a sick sea? The answer is simply that humanity has subjected this stretch of water to greater stress than it can bear. Because it is almost landlocked, water exchange between the sea and ocean is slow and limited, while the nature of the coasts, particularly the rocky bays, concentrates pollution. Pressure on the environment is increased by overpopulation and the annual influx of a hundred million tourists, mostly during the summer, who, between them, eat 45 million tonnes of meat and 250 million tonnes of cereals. Their arrival induces farmers to apply artificial fertilizers in order to supply food requirements; their presence puts an impossible strain on the local sewage systems. The result is an excess of nutrients, nitrogen and phosphorus, entering the waters and subsequent algal blooms, like the strinking green slime of the northern Adriatic in 1989, which drove more than 12,000 tourists to cancel their holidays as news spread of the 1,000 km of affected coastline,[88] from Trieste south to Pescara. Fishermen complained that the algae clogged their engines and tore their nets.[89] The Gulf of Lyons, the Lake of Tunis and the Bay of Izmir often show similar forms of eutrophication.[90]

The underlying causes became clear when, at the start of the Conference on Security and Co-operation in Europe (CSCE) in October 1990, 34 European countries, together with the USA and Canada, discussed the continued decline of the Mediterranean. Despite designation as one of the world's 'special seas' under the 1973 MARPOL Convention, and implementation of the Barcelona Convention in 1976 with its protocols to curb pollution from land, dumping at sea, and pollution by oil and other harmful substances, every year 2.5 million tonnes of fossil fuels and heavy metals and 300,000 tonnes of phosphates reach the waters, while 90 per cent of human waste, and its nitrogen content, is still dumped untreated into the sea. The conference even failed to agree to an Italian proposal to ban driftnet fishing, largely as the result of surprise British opposition. Although Britain did not use driftnets, its representative argued that such a ban might be extended to the North Sea and the Atlantic and so affect future British practice. The upshot was to 'suggest' that Mediterranean nations should not use driftnets, a linguistic device echoed by the use of 'appeal' and 'recommend', usually preceded by 'should', in the final document, which basically committed the signatories to nothing. There was a North-South divide which Hentati Adel of the National Tunisian Agency for the Protection of the Environment exposed:

> Many developing nations would be more than willing to adopt Western standards of environmental control. But when they try to implement them, the Western multinationals threaten to withdraw their factories because, as they rightly point out, if they were going to abide by the rules of their nations of origin, they would have stayed at home.[91]

Ultimately, at least part of the Mediterranean problem of waste is the result of an outworn neo-colonialism.

Two places that at least have mainly themselves to blame are Venice and Gibraltar. In Venice the question of how to save the city from sinking is now less important than the quality of the water into which it will sink. Every year 4,900 tonnes of nitrates and 500 tonnes of phosphates, 40 per cent of them from agriculture, 30 per cent each from industry and domestic users, collect in the lagoon, generating the inevitable putrifying and noxious algal blooms.[92] In March 1990 Venice had a further and more immediate problem. After a winter drought and weeks of low tides, many of the 176 small canals were reduced to unnavigable, muddy streams. For 30 years the authorities had failed to dredge the city's only sewage system. 'The normal tidal changes...flush out to sea what 79,000 Venetian and 20,000 to 100,000 tourists flush out by pulling their lavatory chains. But the canals cannot function properly unless they are dredged every five to seven years. The beds of the small canals are now covered with about four feet of sewer mud'.[93]

For Gilbraltar, with a population of 30,000 and reportedly the fourth most crowded place on earth, the problem was how to dispose of domestic waste. Refuse was collected daily, including Sundays, and burned in a 40-tonne capacity incinerator, which, unfortunately, had to be taken out of service for six weeks every year and, according to locals, usually broke down for a further six weeks. While it was out of action, rubbish, including worn-out cars, was sent down a chute into the Mediterranean. The cars became breeding grounds for fish and much of the other waste burnt itself out through combustion.

In February 1985, however, following agreement between the UK and Spain, the frontier was opened, the annual number of visitors rose from under 600,000 to almost three million, and the amount of waste increased accordingly. The effect of pollution on the water was equalled only by the squalor of the chute and its contents, which British TV viewers were able to see in all its unaesthetic splendour on 14 December 1989. By that time a series of protests had forced the authorities to spend £180,000 on a self-propelled barge with a range of 12 miles, enough to reach international waters before dumping its unsavoury load. The Mediterranean itself is, of course, so polluted that the ingestion of 45 tonnes of Gibraltar's surplus domestic waste may appear a comparatively minor matter.[94] Unfortunately, much of the waste consists of plastic litter. This may in part explain why up to 70 per cent of the debris found floating in the Mediterranean is plastic.[95]

A glance at the rest of the world

We could extend the analysis to America and the Third World were it not that the law of diminishing returns would blunt the effect. The fact with which this chapter started — that water moves — means that the waste going into rivers, described in the previous section, eventually finds its way to the sea to join that entering coastal waters directly. Throughout the world of waste the only differences are in emphasis. Industrialized countries discharge more industrial effluent than those of the Third World but in general have fewer people and more advanced techniques for coping with the waste they themselves produce. Third World countries, with larger and more rapidly increasing populations, have fewer restrictions and lack the technology. Hence it is not surprising to find sewage disposal dominating Third World coastal areas and effluent or seepage from agro-industry those of more developed nations. Hence the prevalence of faecal coliform bacteria at levels above national standards in shellfish beds in the Straits of Malacca, contamination of oysters and mussels by sewage in the Gulf of Thailand, the presence of pathogens in fish and shellfish in the waters of Jakarta, while sewage is 'the greatest single pollutant of coastal waters in the wider Caribbean'.[96] In Hong Kong the 1988 epidemic of hepatitis, with nearly 1,400 cases reported, was associated with eating shellfish.[97] Sewage again causes problems in places as disparate as Jeddah on the Red Sea,[98] Goa on the west coast of India,[99] Karachi in Pakistan[100] and, in Latin America, in Havana, Caracas, Panama and Cartagena, where large conurbations lack adequate means of disposal.[101]

Not that the First World is without similar problems. Despite improvements since the days when Tom Lehrer satirized its pollution in song, San Francisco Bay has still to recover from the sewage poured into it, especially the copper content, which accumulates in clams. But the bay suffered a further poisoning, from industrial waste, so that it still receives more selenium than any other estuary in the world, while concentrations of mercury in striped bass are high enough to produce health warnings for children and pregnant women.[102] And, on the opposite side of the globe, Sydney, Australia, is notorious for its discharges into offshore waters. The three main outfalls, at Malabar and Bondi beaches and North Head, discharge respectively 640 million, 165 million and 325 million litres of sewage daily in dry weather (with storm water in addition after heavy rains), most of it untreated or with only 10−15 per cent of the solids extracted. Moreover, at least 40 per cent of the sewage consists of industrial waste so that concentrations of organochlorines, namely, benzene hexachloride, heptachlor epoxide and DDT, have been found in the liver and muscles of fish. More immediately dangerous to users of Bondi Beach are the discarded syringes of drug users, which are either flushed down lavatories or dumped on the beach. In 1989 the situation was not improved by the illegal dumping of chemical waste into the sewage system through a manhole and a 5,000 litre oilspill off the coast which forced the closure of a number of beaches.[103]

The outcome of dumping waste at sea, death to the local inhabitants, is the same wherever it occurs. The bottlenose dolphins of Europe were in good company in 1987 when 3,000 of their number were killed in the Gulf of Mexico by what a scientific investigatory group afterwards diagnosed as a 'red tide' of poisonous algae containing 'naturally occurring toxins'. Others attributed the 'tide' to the dumping of toxic waste or oil. The incident was repeated on a lesser scale between January and May 1990, when over 300 dead or dying dolphins were washed up in states bordering the Gulf, most of them in such an advanced state of decay that it was impossible to ascertain the cause of death.[104] Feelings were not pacified when, in June, a Norwegian supertanker, the *Mega Borg*, caught fire in the Gulf and threatened the Texas coastline, 57 miles away, with massive oil pollution.[105] The discovery of DDT and DDE in grouper fish in the Gulf of Mexico[106] pointed in yet another direction, that of runoff of pesticides used in agriculture. Whatever the final decision, if one is ever reached, one cause of the deaths is certain, if only as a contributory factor — waste.

If any waste-producing activity may be considered the prerogative of the Third World it is the mining of those minerals which pose the greatest threat to the environment. In South America mining tailings from the extraction of copper have polluted the coastal waters off Chile, causing high mortality among marine organisms, hindering harbour and recreational activities and affecting geomorphological aspects of the coast.[107] In South-east Asia, copper mining in the Philippines, as seen in Chapter 2, has led to the discharging of toxic tailings into Calancan Bay. The waste has spread over an area 5 kilometres long and half a kilometre in width, burying coral reefs, poisoning the water, and killing or driving away the fish, thus reducing the catch by 90 per cent. During the dry season strong winds carry fine tailings particles inland, destroying plant life, contaminating water supplies and causing the local people to suffer respiratory, stomach and skin disorders.[108] And in Papua New Guinea, operations at Bougainville copper mine (see Chapter 3) before its closure resulted in half the 3,663 tonnes of waste tailings dumped in the Jaba Valley being carried downstream into Empress Augusta Bay.

The outcome was a rise of 30 metres in the river bed near the outflow and a continuing rise of 3.5 metres per year. The entire valley is covered by sediment up to 60 metres deep and 1 kilometre wide in basins, and all aquatic life has been killed. Deposition caused a 7,000 hectare delta to form at the mouth of the Jaba river and some 8,000 hectares (23 per cent) of the bay to be covered by tailings with a copper concentration of more than 500ppm, while lower levels now cover all or most of the bay, depleting considerably, if not entirely killing off, all forms of life at the bottom of the sea.[109]

Although further from the sea, the OK Tedi gold and copper mine on the Upper Fly River may yet prove even more deadly to sea life. In late 1989 villagers along the lower reaches of the river claimed that it was being poisoned by mine waste, and Australian tour-boat operators reported seeing large numbers of dead crocodiles and dead fish. But the hard evidence came in November when researchers from the Ocean Sciences Institute at the University of Sydney reported 'higher than acceptable levels' of cadmium and copper in prawns, not in the river itself, but in the Torres Strait between Papua New Guinea and Australia's Cape York Peninsula. At 22 ppm the levels of copper were more than double those set as acceptable by the Australian National and Medical Research Council, while the cadmium levels, though 'moderate', were 'perhaps sufficient to affect reproduction and growth of prawns', the major fishing industry of the 20,000 island inhabitants of the strait. Without further monitoring it was impossible to tell to what extent the seafood diet of the islanders was contaminated. Inevitably the mining company disputed the scientists' claims.[110]

The open ocean

In their 1982 survey, *The Review of the Health of the Oceans*, the UN Group of Experts on the Scientific Aspects of Marine Pollution (GESAMP) concluded that, apart from several 'hot spots', contamination of the seas was 'local' and restricted to the coastal zone, with the open ocean given a clear bill of health. In their 1990 update, more neutrally, and perhaps significantly, entitled *The State of the Marine Environment*, their overall assessment is less optimistic: 'Most of the world's coastal areas are polluted. The open ocean, however, is relatively clean except for floating tar and plastic debris, found mainly in shipping lanes and drift lines where currents converge'.[111] Inevitably one asks how 'clean' is 'relatively'? In relation to what? Especially as GESAMP itself points out that 'chemical contamination and litter can be observed from the poles to the tropics and from beaches to abyssal depths',[112] in short, throughout the whole length, breadth and depth of the world ocean.

The floating tar results from the 1.47 million tonnes of petroleum discharged into the seas annually during transportation, almost half the total entering the oceans. The main causes are tanker operations, tanker accidents and washing out bilge and fuel oils whilst at sea. In consequence, floating tar tends to concentrate on the main tanker routes, which are also the scene of major oil spills.[113]

Of the litter reaching the open seas, washed out from the coastal zone or discarded by ships, plastics are the most deadly ingredients. Supplemented by lost or discarded plastic fishing nets, especially monofilament driftnets (see pp. 53–54), and other equipment — the annual loss in fishing gear is estimated at 150,000 tonnes — they not only last for up to 50 years but float or drift beneath the surface. Sections of netting entangle fish, birds and marine mammals; plastic bands encircle them, tightening as they grow; when particles are swallowed as food, they cause death:

Up to 70 per cent of the debris examined in the Mediterranean and more than 80 per cent of it in the Pacific was plastic. A three-hour survey of 563 kilometres of Oregon beaches in 1984 yielded more than 26 metric tons of plastic materials, mostly pieces of polystyrene, food utensils, bags and sheet material, and bottles,[114] all waiting to be swept out to sea.

A study by marine biologists from the University of Newcastle upon Tyne revealed that, during a 44-day voyage, the ship's crew threw overboard 320 cardboard and paper boxes, 370 plastic beer-can holders, 162 crisps packets, 19 plastic bags, two plastic drums, 240 bottles, 5,176 cans and two large metal drums.[115] A second survey of a comparatively small area of the German Bight estimated that the minimum amount of rubbish drifting annually between Heligoland and the Elbe estuary was approximately 8.5 million pieces and weighed 1,000 tons.[116]

The coming into force of Annex V of the International Convention for the Prevention of Pollution from Ships (MARPOL) in December 1988 now makes it illegal for vessels of the 31 ratifying nations to dispose 'into the sea...all plastics, including but not limited to synthetic ropes, synthetic fishing nets, and plastic garbage bags'.[117] Yet, even if all United Nations members were to ratify Annex V, and guarantee its enforcement, much of the plastic already in the sea will still be drifting around over the next 50 years.

Where will it drift? The North Atlantic is a basin in which the water flows clockwise. Plastic from the UK is carried south-west to the bulge of Africa, whence it passes west to the Caribbean; here it turns northwards to join the Gulf Stream and so back to Britain at the rate of 12 miles a day. The British Isles divides the stream so that part of it goes to the north to reach the long fiords of the Russian island of Novaya Zemlya. Robert Fannin's personal experience gives added meaning to GESAMP's scientific conclusions. Becalmed on a schooner in mid-Atlantic, he was 'surprised at the amount of plastic floating by'; three months later, in an Arctic fiord on the west coast of Novaya Zemlya, he

watched reflections of snow-capped mountains in waters that had not been disturbed by bow or propeller since the trappers had moved off in the 1930s.... Along the shore the shingled beaches were awash with the bright and brazen colours of plastic. It was here that the Atlantic finally dumped its unwanted waste.

He 'picked up a washing-up liquid container and could still make out the print. It had been produced in Newcastle upon Tyne.'[118]

To the deaths of Dall's porpoises in the North Pacific, of fur seals in the eastern Aleutian islands, of Hawaiian monk seals, of turtles, whales and countless unknown fish, and to the infecting of 25 per cent of the world's seabird species with plastic particles in their digestive tracts[119] must be added a crime of a different order — aesthetic desecration — its perpetrators

— thoughtless humanity. The presence of a plastic washing-up liquid container among the pristine Arctic ice is no longer pollution. 'Pollution' is too weak a word. It is an obscenity.

The open spaces of the sea have also been the scene for the dumping of matter that is longer lived than even plastic: the high-level radioactive nuclear waste of the world's nuclear industry. Between 1946 and 1982, when, despite British opposition, a moratorium on dumping was agreed in 1983, at 11 sites in the north-west Atlantic, 15 in the north-east, 16 in the north-east Pacific and 5 in the West Pacific, an estimated 46 petabecquerels (1 PBq = one billion million becquerels) of packaged, unpackaged or liquid waste was dumped into the waters. Most of it was packaged in metal containers lined with concrete or bitumen. At the 1990 meeting of the signatories of the 1972 London Dumping Convention (LDC), the USA, the UK, France and Japan were still opposing moves to turn the temporary ban into a permanent one. Britain was responsible for 77.5 per cent of the waste dumped in the North Atlantic, the USA for 97.1 per cent of that dumped in the Pacific. In keeping with the usual secrecy in nuclear matters, these figures were not made public until the 1990 meeting.[120]

And, while the politicians continue to deliberate, we are left with a race against time. Will the decaying radioactive waste break down into less harmful forms before the containers themselves disintegrate? Or will the containers break up before this happens, spilling their contents into the waters? The answer, of course, depends on the type of waste and the radioactive half-lives of its components; but the scientific consensus would appear to be that, hopefully in a much less lethal form, it will outlive its containers, to be 'diluted and dispersed' in the ocean depths. One can only hope that this prognosis is well founded.

Notes

1. Parker 1989 pp. 18−19
2. Brown, P. 1989a, 1989b; *New Scientist* 6 October 1990
3. *WR 1990-91* pp. 164−5
4. DoE 1989a p.4
5. Ibid. pp. 27−30; Table 3.4, Figs. 1.4, 1.5
6. *WR 1988−89* Table 21.2
7. Data that follow are taken from Clouston 1990 and Routledge 1990
8. *RCEP 10* p. 71
9. *Guardian* 13 October 1989
10. *Green Magazine* June 1990 p. 11
11. *Guardian* 24 February 1990
12. See Gourlay 1988 p. 125
13. Brown, P. 1990b
14. *Guardian* 15 September 1988
15. Ibid. 14 July 1990
16. Turner 1989
17. *Guardian* 11, 15 and 23 September 1989
18. Maywald *et al.* 1988; Goldsmith and Hildyard 1988 pp. 206−7
19. *Guardian* 26 November 1987

20. Goldsmith and Hildyard 1988 p. 207
21. *WR 1990−91* p. 164
22. *WR 1988−89* Table 21.2
23. *WR 1990−91* p. 162
24. Thorpe 1990c
25. Traynor 1990
26. Buerk 1989
27. *Guardian* 1 December 1988
28. Ibid. 28 December 1988
29. Buerk 1989
30. Thorpe 1990a
31. *Guardian* 19 January 1990
32. *Green Magazine* February 1990 p. 8
33. *Guardian* 8 July 1990
34. Medvedev 1990 p. 25
35. Stewart 1990
36. Medvedev 1990
37. *Guardian* 19 January 1990
38. *New Scientist* 26 November 1988; *Guardian* 26 November 1988
39. Maywald *et al.* 1988 pp. 85−6
40. Triona Holden, BBC *Nature* 19 November 1990
41. Ibid.; *Guardian* 24 August 1988
42. Powledge 1982 pp. 359−60
43. Goldsmith and Hildyard 1990 p. 108
44. Malm *et al.* 1990 pp. 12−14
45. Nicholson 1990
46. *WR 1990−91* pp. 162−3
47. Ibid. p. 37
48. Ibid. p. 44
49. Ibid. p. 41
50. Ibid. p. 163
51. Bedding 1989
52. Pathmarajah and Meith 1985 pp. 174, 176−8, 207−8
53. *RSRS 13* p. 69
54. Agarwal *et al.* 1982 p. 23
55. Ibid. p. 25
56. Agarwal and Narain 1985 p. 288
57. Agarwal *et al.* 1982 p. 22
58. Agarwal and Narain 1985 p. 42
59. *WR 1990−91* p. 165 and Table 10.1
60. Silvertown 1989
61. *WR 1988−89* p. 138
62. Pain 1990a
63. *Guardian* 6 June 1990
64. Ibid. 12 September 1990
65. Ibid. 20 March 1990
66. Ibid. 6 March 1990
67. Ibid. 3 March 1990; *New Scientist* 17 March 1990
68. *Observer* 4 March 1990
69. *Guardian* 12 January 1990
70. Ibid. 23 February 1990
71. *New Scientist* 8 July 1989
72. *Guardian* 8 March 1990
73. Ibid. 17 January 1990
74. Bowcott 1989
75. *Guardian* 7 May 1990

76. Ibid. 24 October 1990
77. HoC 1986 para. 116
78. *Guardian* 27 March 1990
79. Ibid. 10 July 1990
80. HoC 1989 para. 88
81. *New Scientist* 27 January 1990
82. *Green Magazine* October 1989 p. 20
83. Goldsmith and Hildyard 1990 p. 145; Harwood and Reijnders 1988; *Guardian* 30 August 1989
84. Brown, P. 1989c
85. Pain 1990b; *Guardian* 11 November 1990
86. *New Scientist* 15 September 1990
87. *Green Magazine* March 1990 p. 12
88. Stansell 1990; *New Scientist* 11 August 1990
89. *WR 1990—91* p. 197
90. Ibid. p. 182
91. Lake 1990; *New Scientist* 27 October 1990
92. O'Neill, Bill 1990
93. *Guardian* 10 March 1990
94. BBC *Nature*: 'Dying for a holiday', 14 December 1989
95. *WR 1990—91* p. 185
96. Ibid. p. 183
97. Ibid.
98. *TAO* 1983 p. 173
99. Pathmarajah and Meith 1985 p. 186
100. Ibid.
101. *WR 1990—91* p. 190
102. MacQuitty 1988
103. Beder 1990; *Guardian* 14 January 1989
104. *Guardian* 12 May 1990
105. Ibid. 12, 13 June 1990
106. *WR 1990—91* p. 190
107. *TAO* 1983 p. 172
108. Manz 1989
109. *Parting Company* June 1987, based on Powell 1982
110. *New Scientist* 18 November 1989
111. GESAMP 1990 quoted *WR 1990—91* p. 181
112. Ibid. p. 179
113. *WR 1990—91* p. 186 and Box 11.1
114. Ibid. pp. 185—6
115. *Green Magazine* November 1989 p. 23
116. Ibid.
117. *WR 1988—89* p. 159
118. Fannin 1990
119. *WR 1990—91* p. 185
120. *New Scientist* 3 November 1990

6. Into (and Out of) the Fire

The pros and cons of combustion

Not all waste can be burnt, and there are distinct types of waste suitable for burning. The British House of Commons Environment Committee distinguished between 1) 'volatile toxic organic wastes, mainly from the chemical industry', 2) 'domestic refuse and commercial wastes', and 3) 'hospital and other clinical wastes,[1] each of which required different treatment. In practice, excluding those used at sea, there are four main types of incinerators:

- high-temperature incinerators, purpose-built for destroying hazardous waste. A distinguishing feature is that they include 'scrubbers' for removing toxic gases from the chimneys;
- industrial boilers, furnaces or kilns, which burn waste as cheap and efficient fuel;
- municipal incinerators; and
- hospital incinerators (see Chapter 2).

The basic essential is efficient operation, without which there can be no success. The combustion chamber must always be kept at the correct temperature, the waste must remain in it for the right length of time, and there must be adequate turbulence to ensure that the waste is well mixed with oxygen.[2] Even when these conditions are fulfilled, incineration does not lead to final disposal. During combustion the chimneys emit gases and fly ash; and, when the process is complete, even if the volume of waste is reduced, up to 40 per cent of it remains as ash and non-combustible material that can only be disposed of by landfill.[3]

The great dangers of incineration are thus that 1) not all hazardous substances are destroyed, and 2) in the burning process new products are formed, namely, the euphemistically named PICs, products of incomplete combustion, that may be even more dangerous than the original waste. These products either escape into the atmosphere during burning or remain in the ash to contaminate landfill sites.

High-temperature (UK) and mass-burn incineration (USA)

The Commons Environment Committee was emphatic that 'high-tempera-ture incineration is a safe and effective way of disposing of combustible organic wastes' unsuitable for landfill (because of its toxicity) and had 'proved particularly effective for the destruction of PCBs and other noxious organic materials'. To ensure this it was necessary for the waste to be burnt 'at temperatures in excess of 1,050°C in the presence of excess air in purpose-engineered plant'. Under these conditions the incinerator would produce 'inert ash and filter cake...suitable for landfill'.[4] Against this, the US Science Advisory Board maintained that some 24 organic compounds had been found in emissions from high-temperature incinerators, many of which had still to be identified chemically before they could be assessed for their effects on human health or the environment.[5] To this the British group would doubtless reply that it did not invalidate their argument but merely showed how necessary it was that the plant was operated efficiently.

In practice, high-temperature incinerators have aroused the greatest controversy, both in Europe and North America, especially where mismanagement is suspected, or found, and the local population are victims of operational incompetence.

In the UK overcapacity at the beginning of the 1970s led to a reduction in the number of incinerators from eight to four by the mid-1980s, with an estimated capacity of 82,000 tonnes of waste per annum. Rechem had plants at Pontypool in Wales, Fawley in England and Bonnybridge in Scotland, though the latter closed at the end of 1984, allegedly for commercial reasons, after it had been the centre of a number of protests. Cleanaway owned the only other surviving plant at Ellesmere Port on the Mersey. By the end of the 1980s, the boom in the UK hazardous waste market led to a belief that there was room for a further incinerator to bring total capacity up to 110,000 tonnes. Rechem planned to spend £8m in replacing the old Fawley plant, Cleanaway £20m in updating Ellesmere Port, but Leigh Environmental were unsuccessful in their application to build an incinerator at Doncaster, and Ocean Environmental failed to get permission for one on Teeside.[6]

Meanwhile, opposition to high-temperature incineration had increased. In 1989 Rechem came into direct conflict with Torfaen District Council, the local authority for Pontypool, which, urged on by a local pressure group, called for an inquiry into the plant after a study of foliage in fields and close to houses during February showed PCB levels of between 500 and 1,200ppb, as opposed to between 30 and 250ppb the previous August and the official 13.5ppb level of the pollution inspectorate in 1986. Relations did not improve when, at the end of July, the government announced that it had agreed to the importation of 1,500 tonnes of toxic waste from Canada to be disposed of by the Rechem incinerator, despite the outcry over the *Karin B* the previous year and the fact that a letter from the Canadian Environment Ministry, dated 31 January 1989, to the leader of the protesting group, promised that PCB-contamintaed remains from the St Basil le Grand warehouse, Montreal, would not be exported. In the event, the waste was returned to Canada (see Chapter 3). By September Rechem had obtained an injunction from the High Court preventing the local authority from distributing its report, claiming *inter alia*, that it was unfair that its business should be commercially damaged on the basis of inaccurate information and that the report was part of a wider campaign to force the plant to close. A month later the two sides reached an out of court agreement to set up a community liaison committee, part of whose task would be to exchange samples for monitoring. The action may have been partly prompted by the Ministry of Agriculture issuing a warning against eating both ducks and their eggs from a smallholding close to the incinerator after tests showed levels of up to 600ppb of PCBs in both. The company's standing was not improved when it was revealed in December that, while the pollution inspectorate visited the plant about once a month, it was Rechem, not HMIP, that did the actual testing for emissions of PCBs and dioxins. In February 1990 the EC agreed to investigate fears of toxic waste contamination by sending Dr Ludwig Kramer of the Environment Commissioner's office to conduct interviews and to test the surrounding area.[7] Nothing, however, will convince many of the local inhabitants that, as long as the plant exists, their health will not be in danger.

In the USA, according to Greenpeace,

> State and federal environmental agencies have very limited control over the process of hazardous waste incineration. There are no federal limits on the quantities of heavy metals and toxics that incinerators are allowed to emit. No one knows what's coming out of the stacks because no one tests for all the poisonous compounds released by incineration.[8]

Loopholes in the Resource Conservation and Recovery Act (RCRA), the federal law regulating hazardous waste, enabled the largest commercial firm concerned, Marine Shale Processers of Amelia, Louisiana, to operate without a permit to burn hazardous waste. The company simply followed Charles Nugent's example (see Chapter 3) and claimed that it was not operating an incinerator but a recycling plant to produce an allegedly safe material called aggregate. In May 1989 the Louisiana authorities suspended all Marine Shale Processers' permits but, because the firm contested the action, it was allowed to continue, and was still operating three months later.[9] Chicago's Chemical Waste Management, which operates a large modern incinerator for burning toxic waste, including PCBs, was less fortunate. The EPA fined it $4.5 million when, in a joint investigation with the State of Illinois, it discovered 'disconnected air monitors, improper record keeping, incorrect scrubber water'. But it was not the regulatory bodies that initiated the action; 'the violations were discovered by employees and citizens, not the government.'[10]

Municipal incinerators

In 1989 there were 35 local authority incinerators in England and Wales, mainly in large urban areas, responsible for burning about 10 per cent of domestic and commercial waste. High operating costs, which are at least twice those of landfill, and poor operating standards by plants built in the 1960s and 1970s had brought the method into disfavour, except for more enterprising authorities, such as Newcastle, Sheffield and Coventry, where the waste or steam produced was used to provide heat or to generate electricity. An EC directive on emission standards, then in draft, would further add to the decline as, with the necessary retrofitting at a cost of £1 million for each plant, probably more than half will eventually close.[11]

In contrast, the USA has 70 waste-to-energy plants where incineration is used productively. In Columbus, Ohio, there is a $200 million incinerator that consumes 2,000 tons of rubbish daily, generating in the process 50,000kW of electricity per hour. The city's mayor boasts that 'a 30 pound bag of garbage will keep two 100W street lamps alight for 24 hours'.[12]

The most advanced technology is still, however, subject to human fallibility. In the autumn of 1988 the Maine Energy Recovery Company (MERC) 'trash-to-energy' incinerator at Biddeford suffered three 'catastrophic failures' during which an ash-like substance was released over the town. Analysis of the ash by the Department of Environment Protection (DEP) concluded that 'certain sub-groups of the population may have been exposed to unacceptable levels of lead and, to a lesser extent, dioxin', mainly through eating home-grown vegetables. On 31 March 1989 the company reported that the failures occurred in the baghouse, where exhaust gases are filtered, and that they had taken steps to ensure that, should a pressure build-up occur, a computerized system would either redirect the gases or cause a complete shutdown. Despite this, at the end of April, there was a further release of ash from the plant. While the manager maintained that it had not come from the smokestacks but escaped from a bin when workers attempted to fix something that was clogged inside it, a security guard claimed to have seen billows of black smoke coming from the chimneys between 7 and 9 pm. Unfortunately, the air-monitoring equipment was temporarily out of action and the computer records did not show that a fallout had occurred. Unimpressed by this explanation, on 15 May the City Council unanimously approved an ordinance that would fine the company up to $25,000 a day for noise, odour and ash problems it created, and the following week sent letters to the state DEP and the Attorney General's office calling for more air and soil tests and the installation of monitoring stations to check emissions from the plant's chimney. Incineration may be technologically sound, but the people of Biddeford, Maine, found its actual implementation a different matter. As the local *Journal Tribune* put it: 'If we could make the choice all over again, we might not be so quick to choose incineration'.[13]

The people of Red Wing, Minnesota, would probably agree. The municipal incinerator, operating since 1982 to produce steam, was required by the Minnesota Pollution Control Agency (MPCA) in January 1985 to install an 'electrostatic precipitator' to trap particulates. The following year the plant was still emitting high levels of dioxins owing to what the MPCA described as 'seriously corroded equipment' and 'poor operating practices'. By February 1989, despite some improvement, emissions were still not low enough, and at 23.8 nanograms (ng) per dry standard cubic metre (dscm) were at least 230 times greater than Swedish dioxin guidelines for new incinerators. Fish from the Mississippi could be a potential source of contagion for local inhabitants.[14]

Even the new Blount mass-burn incinerator in Warren County, New Jersey, installed in 1988 as the 'model' for all others, came under severe criticism for its first year's operation. The plant is surrounded by 87 dairy farms and 3 fish hatcheries; half the forage eaten by the cows is locally produced. Residents' photographs showed the stack plume reaching the ground a short distance from the plant, which adjoins the farmland. Of particular concern were mercury emissions, which, while satisfying the New Jersey standard of 0.5 pounds per hour per 200 ton unit, would have failed the more stringent Minnesota standard of 0.16 per hour. Mercury is also a problem at the Ogden Martin plant in Stanislaus County, California, which a new scrubber system and operation at 140°C (below which mercury is supposed to condense out) have failed to solve, while out of 22 mercury hot spots in the Great Lakes area, 18 contain rubbish or sewage sludge incinerators. Scientists have suggested that, in their efforts to destroy organic waste by using higher temperatures, operators push more metals into the vapour phase, with sub-micron particles then eluding the equipment intended to trap them.[15]

The other waste, ash, is also a problem. It was, we recall, the attempt to dispose of toxic ash from the Philadelphia municipal incinerator that led to the ill-fated voyage of the *Khian Sea* and, when it first operated, the New Jersey plant failed almost half the toxicity tests for levels of cadmium and lead in the ash produced. The addition of lime apparently led to satisfactory results, though sceptics, noting that acidity (pH) was increased to a range at which lead and cadmium were less soluble, suggested that the new figures were not due to the ash being less toxic but to the lime interfering with the test results.[16]

At the Jackson County, Michigan, incinerator, situated on property of the Southern Michigan State prison for which it supplied steam, levels of lead in the ash, ranging from 5.8 to 94ppm, were so high that the Department of Natural Resources (DNR) declared the ash a hazardous waste, disposal of which would cost the county more than $1 million a year. On 5 November 1988 the County Board of Commissioners decided they had no alternative but to close the plant indefinitely.[17]

The dangers of toxic ash are taken a stage nearer the general public when it is used as de-icing grit for roads or as aggregate in building or concrete blocks. An analytical comparison by Dr Richard Denison of the heavy metal content of coal ashes and ashes from Municipal Solid Waste (MSW) incinerators reveals that, while the highest total level of lead in coal ash was 140ppm, the corresponding figure for ash from an MSW economizer was 28,300ppm. For cadmium the comparison is 15ppm for coal and 835ppm for MSW ash; and for chromium 23ppm against 413ppm. These figures are reinforced by a further comparison between levels of heavy metals in ordinary cement blocks and those made using MSW combined or fly ash. A cement block has a lead level of 4 ppm (Portland cement 1ppm), a combined ash block 5,137ppm and a fly ash block 7,278ppm. For cadmium the corresponding figures are 0.26 for cement (0.04 for Portland cement), but 44 and 731 for MSW ash blocks. For chromium they are 31 for cement (38 for Portland) but 146 and 190 for incinerator ash. To the non-scientist a cement block appears solid enough but Dr Denison is concerned both with the persistence of heavy metals and with exposure to utilized ash, especially the questions of weathering and of dust from such blocks. His conclusion is little short of alarming: 'For many of these [routes and time frames] the tools needed for such an evaluation are not yet developed...there is no procedure for measuring — let alone any data on — the rate of erosion or dusting from a cement surface under various conditions'. And while this may be 'of little concern for ordinary cement, which does not have an appreciable toxic metals content, it is of major concern for cement formed using ash as a substitute aggregate'.[18]

Denison sums up the situation for both fly ash (from the chimney) and bottom ash (the residue) as follows:

> MSW incinerator ash, especially from facilities achieving less than optimal combustion efficiency, may contain significant levels of toxic organic contaminants, including dioxins. Dioxins and PCBs tend to concentrate almost exclusively in fly ash...certain polycyclic aromatic hydrocarbons (PAHs)...preferentially in bottom ash.[19]

In less scientific language, when operators are not doing their job properly, incineration poses a double danger, from both chimney emissions and in the resulting ash. That dioxins and PCBs have been found is itself evidence that this inefficiency is by no means exceptional.

Events in the Netherlands in mid-1989 demonstrated clearly this link between ineffective incineration and dioxins in milk. Researchers at the National Institute for Public Health and Environmental Protection, Bilthoven, engaged in plotting the paths of dioxins carried from chimneys by fly ash, had their predictions confirmed at several hot spots. Taking samples of milk from the whole of the Lickebaert area, they found that background levels ranged from 0.8 to 2.5 picograms per gram of milk fat, that the levels were higher, at around 4 picograms, in the hot spots, and that there was one really outstanding example of 8 picograms in the predicted spot near Rotterdam. This pointed to Rotterdam's Rijnmond Waste Disposal Centre, which burns 950,000 tonnes of domestic waste and 75,000 tonnes of toxic waste annually. In August 1989 the Dutch authorities announced that they were considering holding the plant's operators responsible for losses to dairy farmers. At the end of June they had found it necessary to ban the sale of milk from 1,000 cows as a result of the contamination. The problem had been to prove the connection, especially when it was estimated that only 30 per cent of the background dioxins in the Netherlands are Dutch; the rest drift in from incinerators in other countries. The national institute's work provided the necessary evidence.[20]

Fire at sea

While land incinerators have tall chimneys with scrubbers so that, in theory at least, the filtered plume has the chance to disperse (even if it eventually descends in someone else's backyard), the ships specially designed for incineration at sea have no scrubbers and discharge their plumes near the surface in order to use the sea's alkaline capacity and its ability to act as a sink for acids and other materials.[21] Supporters of the process, such as the US Chemical Waste Management with its highly sophisticated vessel *Vulcanus II*, maintain that research shows a 99.999 per cent destruction efficiency.

Against this there are four main objections. Even if Chemical Waste Management's figure is correct, this still leaves 1 tonne of unburned waste to enter the atmosphere for every 10,000 tonnes burned. The dangers are that this residue will affect the thin surface layer of the sea or be concentrated in marine organisms and so enter the food chain, a highly undesirable prospect when the contents include PCBs and heavy metals.

A second danger is the risk of a major accident to the incinerator vessel, followed by a leak, and, while Chemical Waste Management assess this as likely only once in 24,000 years, similar calculations in the nuclear and chemical industries hardly inspire confidence that the accident will occur in the last decade rather than the first. Should it happen, the outcome would be a major catastophe. A 1983 EPA study calculated that a discharge of 500,000 US gallons of liquid PCBs, less than half a ship's cargo, would contaminate the 'upper foot of the entire Gulf of Mexico...with 2.5ppb of PCB', sufficient to 'deteriorate all life' over an area of some 1,507,000 square kilometres.[22]

Third, there is the difficulty of policing the actual burn, that is, of ensuring that it occurs at the licensed site, that incineration is fully carried out and that potentially poisonous matter is not just dumped overboard. Finally, as the British DoE Chief Scientist pointed out to the Commons Environment Committee, there is 'the difficulty of monitoring the impact... on the marine ecosystem'.[23]

Nevertheless, with pressure increasing on landfill sites, incineration at sea was considered a viable alternative and had the further advantage of being cheaper than incineration on land. The result was that, between 1981 and

1984, in the North Sea area alone, Belgium incinerated over 290,000 tonnes of chemical waste at sea, almost half the total, West Germany 200,000 tonnes, France almost 31,000 tonnes, Norway 19,600, Sweden 14,500, Switzerland 10,000 and the United Kingdom 6,168.[24] In 1986 the UK was responsible for sending 3,754 tonnes, or 3.2 per cent of the total, and in 1987 4,050 tonnes.[25] Across the Atlantic, the EPA considered the possibility of marine incineration but never finally gave approval, though some 5,678,000 litres (1.5m US gallons) were burnt in 1981–82.[26]

Joint protest action by Greenpeace and fishing trawlers from Denmark, Britain, Belgium and Holland against the *Vesta* and *Vulcanus II* in 1987 and against the *Vulcanus II* in 1988 ensured that incineration at the licensed North Sea burn site, 100 miles off Scarborough, received widespread publicity.[27] But it was hard scientific evidence and action by the EC and the Oslo commission, which is responsible *inter alia* for monitoring the extent of pollution in the North Sea, that eventually led the North Sea states to ban incineration by 1994.

A team of West German scientists from the University of Hamburg, led by Joachim Lohse, claimed to have found partially burned chemicals in seabed sediments over a 20-mile diameter area coinciding with the burn zone. The chemicals, hexachlorobenzene (HCB) and octachlorostyrene, produced by incomplete burning of chlorinated hydrocarbons at high temperatures, are both highly toxic. Lohse argued that impure gases, escaping from the short stacks, drifted out to the nearby ocean surface, where they bonded themselves to faecal particles from marine creatures and so sank to the bottom and into the sediment. Far from solving the problem, ocean incineration was thus itself the cause of further hazardous waste pollution.[28]

Theoretically, the technique may be (almost) infallible; the human beings who operate it are not. And governments in their wisdom decided not to risk relying on those who had already demonstrated their irresponsibility.

Incineration, whether on land or at sea, despite its initial attractions, remains a highly dubious business. We should do well to avoid it.

Notes

1. HoC 1989 para. 68
2. Goldsmith and Hildyard 1988 p. 165
3. HoC 1989 para. 78
4. Ibid. para. 69
5. Goldsmith and Hildyard 1988 p. 165
6. Gabb 1989 pp. 60–61
7. *Guardian* 7 March 1989, 29 July 1989, 2 September 1989, 14 December 1989; *Observer* 6 August 1989, 6 October 1989, 4 February 1990
8. *Waste Not* No. 65, 27 July 1989
9. Ibid.
10. Ibid
11. HoC 1989 paras. 78–80
12. *Newsweek* 27 June 1987
13. *Waste Not* No. 59, 15 June 1989

14.   *Waste Not* No. 45, 7 March 1989
15.   *Waste Not* No. 68, 7 September 1989
16.   Ibid.
17.   *Waste Not* No. 32, 29 November 1988
18.   Denison 1989
19.   Ibid.
20.   MacKenzie 1989d
21.   HoC 1989 para. 77
22.   Goldsmith and Hildyard 1988 p. 192
23.   HoC 1989 para. 77
24.   *WR 1988—89* p. 330, Table 22.3
25.   HoC 1989 para. 76
26.   *WR 1988—89* Table 22.3
27.   *Greenpeace News* Autumn 1988
28.   *New Scientist* 29 September 1988; *Guardian* 25 April 1988

7. Into the Air

The waste gases described in Chapter 2 are better known by their effects:

- increased tropospheric ozone, the familiar 'smog' of the world's major cities;
- acid rain;
- depletion of the ozone layer, and
- climatic change,

It is impossible to give full accounts of each of these here. Nor is it necessary. Thanks to personal experience and environmental publicity, there is now widespread awareness, at least in Western Europe and North America, of actual and potential dangers. Our concern here is to view these dangers in a wider context, to see them as arising from a familiar cause, the production of waste, which, except where modern technology is used to prevent it, goes directly 'into the air'.

The perils of smog

A Worldwatch Institute Report,[1] published early in 1990, maintains that, while efforts in the West to combat air pollution, which, since the 1950s (when London's notorious 'black fogs' made headline news, now usurped by global warming) have been 'marginally successful', in Eastern Europe, the Soviet Union and much of the developing world, the problem of urban smog is only beginning to be recognized. Yet the Global Health Threat is in many places a more immediate danger than the prospect of global climatic change:

> In the United States some 150 million people breathe air considered unhealthy by the Environmental Protection Agency (EPA). In greater Athens, the number of deaths is six times higher on heavily polluted days than on those when the air is relatively clear. In Hungary, a recent report by the National Institute of Public Health concluded that every twenty-fourth disability and every seventeenth death in Hungary is caused by air pollution. In India, breathing the air in Bombay is equivalent to smoking

10 cigarettes a day. And in Mexico, the capital city is considered a hardship post for diplomats because of its unhealthy air, and some governments advise women not to plan having children while posted there.[2]

This report goes on to point out that gains made in the industrialized West in reducing emissions of SO_2 and particulates are now threatened by the introduction of diesel-powered vehicles. In Eastern Europe rapid industrialization and the dependence on high-sulphur lignite for energy made such gains impossible, and the Third World's rush to industrialize is inevitably a rush to poison the urban air. A UNEP–WHO report maintained that, for sulphur dioxide, 27 out of 54 cities with data available had average annual concentrations in the 1980–84 period in excess of or on the borderline of WHO standards. Foremost among these were Shenyang (146 days per annum above standard), Tehran (104), and Seoul (87), but Milan (66), Paris (46) and Madrid (35) were also included. For particulates, 37 out of 41 cities monitored were in the excessive or borderline category, with New Delhi (294), Xian (273), Beijing (272), Shenyang (219) and Tehran (174) heading the list. And while natural dust is in part responsible, diesel-powered vehicles and two-stroke motor scooters are also blamed. The UNEP–WHO report concludes that: 'Nearly 625 million people around the world are exposed to unhealthy levels of sulphur dioxide and more than a billion — one in five people in the world — to excessive levels of suspended particulates'.[3] The hot, dry summers of 1988 and 1989 in many parts of the world, themselves precursors of anticipated global warming, have exacerbated these effects. In New York City in 1988 the air violated the federal health standard on 34 days, that is, two or three times a week throughout the summer. In Washington the standard was, on average, exceeded every third day, and in Los Angeles ozone levels exceeded the federal standard on 172 days, though this was almost doubled in Mexico City with over 300 days a year. All told 15–20 per cent of urban residents of North America and Europe are exposed to unacceptable levels of nitrogen dioxide and 50 per cent to carbon monoxide.[4]

Press reports suggest an inverse pride in claiming the title of 'most polluted city'. In Athens, for example, where the population has risen to four million over the last 20 years and 700,000 cars belch waste exhaust fumes into the atmosphere to join emissions from half of Greece's industry, now concentrated in the Attica basin, nitrogen dioxide levels reached 581 micrograms per cubic metre in September 1988, more than twice the danger level of 200. In response, the government banned half the cars from circulating in the city's outer ring road for 12 hours daily and ordered industry to cut production by 30 per cent.[5]

In June 1987, according to a leaked internal bulletin of the Czechoslovak Communist Party, 20 times the permissible amount of sulphur dioxide was being released into the atmosphere over Prague, which, compared with the industrial towns of Bohemia, was usually considered a non-danger zone. The bulletin claimed the smog as responsible for cardiovascular diseases, tubercular illness and respiratory disorders among schoolchildren.[6]

Towards the end of 1986 it was claimed that 'the air in Rome now has the highest concentration of carbon dioxide in the world', the result of 35 years of accumulation during which the number of vehicles rose from 30,000 to 1.5m, or one for every two residents. Traffic police appeared wearing masks, which they were ordered to remove as they were violating anti-terrorism laws, but were unwilling to do so when a medical check-up revealed that 30 per cent of their members had chronic bronchitis.[7]

In November 1989 local experts claimed that the 'rat-coloured pall of filth' rising over and engulfing Santiago gave Chile's capital 'the most toxic urban smog anywhere on the planet'. Some 45,000 tons of particulates and gases enter the air that is breathed by the city's four million inhabitants. When pollution reaches the danger level, the authorities order a 50 per cent cut in bus transport, but only a 20 per cent ban on private cars, and temporary closure of the 50 most polluting factories. Monitoring, however, is inadequate for scientific comparison, though studies reveal the presence of 20 times more carcinogenic particles than in other industrial cities, while children suffer between three and eight times more bronchial and lung disease than in a nearby, unpolluted town.[8]

London lost its 1950s undisputed claim to be leader in smog production when the authorities carried out a systematic clean-up. But there are signs that the city is making a comeback. In November 1989 it was claimed that, at certain points, among them Victoria, High Holborn, Whitehall and the Royal Free Hospital, the EC legal limit for nitrogen dioxide of 200 micrograms per cubic metre was exceeded. Elsewhere a lower 'guide value' of 135 micrograms per cubic metre, above which public health *might* be endangered, was exceeded in Maidstone, Farnham, Coventry, Cambridge, Wirral, Bicester and Cheltenham. The government was in no position to refute these charges; the extent of its concern is demonstrated by the fact that it had only six monitoring stations for nitrogen dioxide throughout the country, compared with 89 in the Netherlands.[9]

When we extol the merits of civilization, we would do well to remember also the air human beings are forced to breathe in Athens, Prague, Rome, Santiago and, of course, London and New York.

Acid rain

As the product of waste sulphur and nitrogen emissions into the air, acid rain has been with us since the Industrial Revolution, when the English chemist, Robert Angus Smith, first used the phrase in 1853, but it is only in the second half of the twentieth century that its effects have become widespread and its link with environmental destruction (after considerable controversy) scientifically established.

Rainfall is naturally acid with a pH of around 5.6. The pH scale of 0—14 is used for measuring acidity, with 7 as the neutral figure for distilled water, anything below being acidic, anything above alkaline. But since it is a logarithmic scale, a change of one unit implies a tenfold increase or decrease; a pH of 6 is ten times the acidity of a pH of 7 and a pH of 5 a hundred times. Any precipitation with a pH value of 5 or less (some scientists use the figure of 5.6) is considered as acid rain. On this basis almost the whole of Western Europe north of Spain, northern Italy and Yugoslavia and the eastern seaboard of North America from Florida to Newfoundland are major areas of acid rain.[10] The phenomenon, however, is not limited to these parts of the world but occurs wherever industry, power stations and motor vehicles discharge their waste products into the air.

Acid rain affects, not necessarily directly, inland waters, trees, the soil and even railway tracks and buildings. In Scandinavia 20,000 of the 90,000 lakes in Sweden are acidified and 4,000 devoid of fish, while 80 per cent of the lakes in southern Norway are either dead or on the critical list. Across the Atlantic, nine rivers of Nova Scotia no longer support trout or salmon reproduction, in Ontario 300 lakes are estimated to have a pH of less than 5, as have 10 per cent of the lakes in the Adirondack region of the USA.

Waldsterben, or tree death, affects 52 per cent or 38,000 square kilometres of forest in West Germany, 43 per cent of the conifers in the Alpine region of Switzerland, up to 10 per cent of the conifers in southern Sweden, 59.7 per cent of forests in the Netherlands, 49.2 per cent in Czechoslovakia, and 67 per cent in the UK, the highest figure for damaged trees in Europe. In North America Canadian sugar maples are dying out over wide areas as the soil becomes more and more acidified, and airborne acids have been implicated in the deterioration of higher elevation coniferous forests throughout the length of the Appalachian Mountains from Georgia to New England.

Among the well-known buildings affected are the Parthenon in Athens, Cologne cathedral, which is literally falling apart, Westminster Abbey, Beverley Minster and St Paul's Cathedral in Britain, Parliament Building in Ottawa, which is covered by a black blight, the Statue of Liberty in New York harbour, where millions of dollars have been spent on repairs, and the Taj Mahal in India, attacked by airborne acid from a local oil refinery. Even older objects of human creativity are under attack. The ancient Mayan remains on the Yucatan peninsula of southern Mexico are threatened with widespread deposition of a 'black, tarry-like substance' or the flaking off of colourful murals and surfaces as the result of emissions from government-owned uncapped oil wells in the Gulf of Mexico and exhaust fumes from cars and buses that stand for hours with their engines running in front of the ancient structures.

Nor have transport and food production escaped. In the industrial area of Upper Silesia, Poland, railway tracks have become so eroded that trains are restricted to a speed of 40kph, while near the Chinese town of Chongging, rain with a pH of under 4.5 turned paddy rice yellow. Rainfall itself can be permanently acidic. In the Chinese city of Guiyang it now has an annual average pH of 4.02 and in Sao Paulo state of Brazil it is less than 4.5.[11]

The processes involved are too complex to be described here. We may note, however, that, while acid rain affects rivers and lakes directly, its impingement on trees is both through direct precipitation, when it is absorbed by the needles of conifers, or, more importantly, through the leaching of pollutants, particularly aluminium, from the soil, which contaminate the roots. Similarly, it is not the acid rain in lakes that directly kills fish but its effect in so lowering the pH as to produce high concentrations of heavy metals, with toxic aluminium giving the final blow. Neither soils nor lakes are homogeneous; greater alkaline soils offer more resistance to acid rain, and lakes with limestone beds are less vulnerable than those in granite. Hence both variations in effects within the same region and the practice of liming, adding lime to water to neutralize the acid effect.[12]

Inevitably the sickness or death of waters and trees affects those who depend on them. In central Wales the River Twyi, once noted for its salmon and trout, is now so acidified that it contains only half the insects and water life of nearby healthier rivers, while trout placed in it died within ten days; in Scotland, Loch Enoch and Loch Fleet, two inland waters of the southern uplands, can support no fish life; and in the Lake District, the rivers Esk and Duddon suffered massive fish deaths in the 1980s, while upland tarns, such as Levers Water and Seathwaite Tarn, are as acid as the most seriously affected Scandinavian lakes. Wild plants, particularly lichens and mosses, have suffered in affected areas. By 1988 154 species (54 per cent of the total) had become extinct in Leicestershire, lungwort had disappeared from oak trees in a Northumberland wood over a 15-year period as the bark became more acidified, and it is estimated that, in the once highly polluted air of what is now the Peak District National Park, 13 out of 18 sphagnum moss species have disappeared over the last 150 years. Birds that depend on fresh-water streams and lakes suffer from food depletion. The dipper, that attractive eater of fresh-water invertebrates, which it catches by swimming upstream and walking on the bed, has declined in numbers in mid-Wales and south-west Scotland, as has the fish-eating osprey in Scandinavia, where the release of aluminium has damaged breeding of the reed bunting, bluethroat and willow warbler by reducing the quality of eggshells. In Czechoslovakia, city levels of sulphur dioxide are so high that the numbers of house martins are declining.

Among amphibians, in 1973 dead frog spawn was found floating on the surface of Lake Tranevatten in southern Sweden; by 1980 frogs were extinct and common toads failed to breed successfully. In North America there has been a decline in the numbers of salamanders, and in Surrey, England, the rare natterjack toad has disappeared from two heathland breeding pools where water has become inexplicably acidic. Even mammals are eventually affected. European surveys report a decline in otters as fish disappear, and groups not previously thought to be at risk, such as the tree-climbing turret snail, or butterflies, including the ringlet and Apollo in Sweden, are caught up in a widening ecological decline.[13] Acid rain may even be at least in part responsible for algal blooms; Swedish scientists at the Kristineberg marine station at Lysekil have suggested that cobalt, released from soils by acid rain, enabled one type of algae to thrive at the expense of others.[14]

Unfortunately, with the solving of many problems, the imposition of regulatory controls on the waste gases concerned, and the emergence of more dramatic and potentially disastrous environmental issues, there is a tendency in the 1990s to regard acid rain as yesterday's problem. The British Government and the electricity industry, which supplied much of the money for research — admittedly in the hope of showing that it was not the guilty party — have withdrawn research funds or diverted them elsewhere. The problem, however, refuses to go away and, under controls at present agreed, will continue to affect the environment for years to come. Giving the results of five years joint British – Scandinavian research in March 1990, the Royal Society Surface Water Acidification Programme showed that trout and salmon in up to a third of the rivers in Scotland and large areas of the Lake District, Wales and the Pennines had been wiped out or badly affected and that the promised 60 per cent reduction of sulphur dioxide within 13 years would be inadequate to reverse the process.[15]

Their conclusions were reinforced, in August 1990, by the independent forecasting organization based in Austria, IIASA, which, after five years' research, produced an even gloomier scenario. Acid rain would cost Europe 118m cubic metres of wood, valued at £16bn, every year for the next century. Only by reducing waste emissions of sulphur, nitrogen oxides and ammonia (from farm animals) well beyond present agreed restrictions will Western Europe be saved the loss of 48 million cubic metres of timber annually, Eastern Europe 35 and the European part of the USSR a further 35 million. In estimating the chances of forest survival, it should not be forgotten that neither the British Government nor the Forestry Commission, responsible for much of Britain's woodlands, accepts that acid rain is responsible for killing trees in Britain. The government, obsessed with possible consequences for its electricity privatization programme, has already gone back on a decision to spend £2bn to fit sulphur-removing scrubbers to power stations; only the Drax power station in Yorkshire will have this equipment.[16]

The problem, however, may take a different form from reducing waste emissions of sulphur dioxide. Reports from southern Norway indicate that a reduced fallout of sulphuric acid in rainfall has been counterbalanced by an increase in nitric acid, which is now the dominant form of acid rain in Europe, if not yet in Britain. Its main source is the iniquitous car exhausts, the numbers of which, far from declining, are destined to rise well into the next century.[17]

Holes in the sky

A public opinion survey carried out by the Planning for Social Change Unit at the Henley Centre, England, in October 1989 revealed that the 'biggest worry' for people in Britain was no longer the 'threat of nuclear war' (which came fourth) but 'destruction of the ozone layer'.[18] Even if Mrs Thatcher's weekend conversion to greenery after studying CFC data was in part responsible for the 70 per cent figure for Conservative voters most worried about environmental issues, the result is still remarkable. One can only wonder how much respondents actually knew about depletion of ozone, or whether theirs was a gut feeling, rising from what they did not know.

Events had moved swiftly in the field of research. Not only was the Antarctic ozone hole established as an annual phenomenon, with a depletion of up to 95 per cent at one point, and CFC waste gases confirmed as the main cause, but airborne experiments in January and February 1989 concluded that a similar hole existed over the Arctic. There was even worse news for the industrialized West when, in March 1988, it was found that the ozone layer had weakened between the poles. In the Northern Hemisphere between 30 and 64 degrees, that is, the temperate zone covering Europe, the populated parts of North America, the USSR, northern China, Korea and Japan, the ozone layer had decreased on average by one per cent in summer and 4 per cent in winter between 1969 and 1986, almost twice the rate predicted by computer models. By April 1991 further analysis of the data suggested the ozone layer in this region was actually thinning between two and five times as fast as anticipated so that, instead of the 0.5 million skin cancers and 9,000 deaths predicted, there would be 12 million cancers and 200,000 deaths.[19]

Public awareness was further fuelled by diversions in the technological and political fields. The twin chemical giants, Dupont and ICI, who had been responsible for inflicting the greater proportion of CFCs on the world — and the ozone layer — now vied with each other in their claims to have produced less harmful substitutes, and in legal attempts to secure international agreement on reducing the use of CFCs (see also Chapter 9), the industrialized West, which had already benefited from their use, now found itself on the side of the angels against the environmentally destructive policies of developing countries such as India and China, which had not, and which failed to see why they, too, should not have fridges like everyone else.

Among this furore there was a tendency to lose sight of the basic issue, namely, the effect that depletion of the ozone layer would have on the world as we know it. As far back as 1987 articles quoted the US EPA estimates that, if CFC emissions continued to grow at present rates, there would be 40 million more skin cancers and 12 million extra eye cataracts in the US alone over the next 90 years, as well as increases in hepatitis, herpes and the 'viral leishmaniasis diseases' (whatever they were).[20] At the Toronto Conference on the Changing Atmosphere in June 1988, the figures were expressed as an annual increase in the incidence of skin cancers by up to 350,000 and that a 5 per cent decrease in the ozone layer could produce an annual increase of up to 33 per cent for some skin cancers. Indirect effects included a general suppression of the immune system, making human beings more susceptible to schistosomiasis and leprosy.[21]

But it was not until the UNEP's International Committee on the Effects of Ozone Depletion produced its draft report in February 1990 that the wider impact of holes in the ozone layer became inescapable. Cautiously the report stresses the need for further research but confirms and extends the impact of ozone depletion on human beings. Suppression of the immune system will not only lead to more widespread and more severe outbreaks of infectious diseases, for example, measles (too often forgotten as a killer disease in the tropics), herpes, tuberculosis and leprosy, but reduce considerably the effectiveness of vaccination when antigens are injected through skin previously exposed to ultraviolet 'B' radiation. On eye cataracts, the report estimates that, for every 1 per cent depletion, an extra 100,000 people may go blind.

Among other effects noted by the report are a significant increase in levels of tropospheric ozone, or smog, and faster degradability of materials such as plastics, rubber, wood, textiles and paints! The worst consequences, however, may well be the effect on phytoplankton in the world ocean, which lack the protective outer layer of higher plants and animals. A decrease in numbers of phytoplankton could have a double effect. In the first place, they are responsible for fixing more than half the carbon dioxide produced globally each year. 'A 10 per cent decrease in carbon dioxide uptake by the oceans would leave about the same amount of carbon dioxide in the atmosphere as is produced by fossil fuel burning,' thus increasing the Greenhouse Effect and causing sea levels to rise even more than predicted. Second, as the base of the marine food chain, any decrease in phytoplankton will affect the entire marine population, while extra ultraviolet radiation will severely damage or kill off young fish, crabs and shrimps.

On land many types of plants will not grow as well as they should, 'germination and flowering rates will be inhibited, and crop yields will drop'. Particularly endangered is the production of rice, the result of nitrogen deficiencies in rice paddies as the organisms responsible for fixing it, which, even at current levels of ultraviolet radiation, are extremely sensitive, succumb to the increase.[22]

So the world's population, both human and non-human, faces dangers on all sides: increased incidence of disease, declining supplies of basic food and enhanced climatic change. And all because inhabitants of the civilized West find it more convenient to use an aerosol when shaving than to lather their faces with harmless soap as did their grandfathers!

Climatic change[23]

There is one certainty and one almost certainty about the results of discharging waste greenhouse gases into the atmosphere (see Chapter 2). The certainty is that the world will become warmer; the almost certainty that the change has already started.

Controversy over the eventual outcome was settled when, in May 1990,

300 scientific experts of the UN Intergovernmental Panel on Climatic Change (IPCC) reported that they were 'certain that man-made emissions are substantially increasing the atmospheric concentrations of the main greenhouse gases' and that 'these increases will lead to a warming of the earth's surface'.[24] Evidence that the 1980s were the hottest decade ever recorded, with the six warmest years since measurements began, and that, over the last century the world has become between 0.3°C and 0.6°C warmer, though consistent with their conclusions on overall warming, were not universally accepted as proof that the Greenhouse Effect had already started. While some were certain that we had now entered the greenhouse era, others attributed the results to normal climatic fluctuations. Whatever the truth, no one can escape the fact that, thanks to waste gases in the atmosphere, the temperature of the earth's surface will rise, on the best estimate, on average 1.3°C by the year 2020 and by 3°C by the year 2070. To the non-scientist this appears small indeed, but the first rise would make the world hotter than it has been for over 120,000 years, the second than it has been for the last two million. The importance of these predictions is in the speed of the change and the sheer impossibility of plants, animals and human beings adapting in 30 years to what had previously taken place in a timespan 4,000 times as long.

What, then, can we expect? Predictions have concentrated on the one aspect that can be measured with scientific certainty, namely the rise in sea levels as increased heat melts the ice in glaciers and at the poles, and the volume of water in the oceans expands. Estimates of the extent of the rise vary from a conservative 15−30c by the year 2030 to the probability of a metre or more within the next century. Whatever the eventual figure, the results will be disastrous for low-lying areas of the world and the people, animals and plants found there, especially when combined with other natural changes and the continuing effects of human activity.

The comparatively shallow waters of the Mediterranean, which have had a more or less constant level for several thousand years, may be expected to rise by 13−55cm before the year 2025 and by up to two metres within a century. In the Ebro delta of the Spanish Mediterranean coast, parts of which are already retreating, rising seas and potential storms will breach sand dunes and ultimately endanger the very existence of the delta itself; in southern France, the wetlands of the Camargue could be swamped; in northern Italy, Venice and the nearby islands would be flooded more frequently and the coastal towns of the Po delta face destruction. The worst effects are, however, reserved for Egypt, where the Nile delta is already retreating since the Aswan dam stopped the transfer of silt, and where much of Alexandria, with a population of 3.5 millions, is less than a metre above present sea level. By 2050 up to 19 per cent of the cultivable land, the home of 16 per cent of the population, could disappear, and by 2100 a quarter of both.

In Britain, according to a Natural Environment Research Council (NERC) report, many sandy beaches, salt marshes and mud flats will disappear, particularly in such low-lying areas as the Fens, and the marshes of Essex and Kent, while salt water would enter the Norfolk Broads before they disappeared completely into the sea, and inland rivers swell and flood low-lying land more frequently as the seas force them to back up. Coastal towns may survive with the aid of strong, and expensive, sea walls, but loss of salt marshes will disrupt Europe's migrating wader birds, more than half of which winter in Britain.

In the USA preliminary estimates for holding back the sea from the 30,000km (19,000 miles) of coastline at risk range from $32bn to $309bn for a one-and-a-half to two-metre rise. The areas affected include Long Island, North Carolina's Outer Banks, most of Florida, the Bayous of Louisiana, the Texas coast, San Francisco Bay and the Maryland, Massachusetts and New Jersey shores. Much of Manhattan island is less then two metres above present high-tide levels and it is estimated that the relative sea level in Massachusetts has been rising three millimetres annually since 1950.[25]

While the rich industrialized countries of the West have the resources and skills needed to meet the challenge, it is inevitably the poorer countries of the world that will suffer most. Four-fifths of Bangladesh consists of the Ganges–Brahmaputra delta, half of which is less than 4.5 metres above sea level and already sinking from the 120,000 wells drilled to obtain drinking water. By the year 2050 18 per cent of the country could be under water; by 2100 34 per cent, affecting 35 per cent of the population.

In addition to Egypt and Bangladesh, a UNEP report identifies eight other countries as most vulnerable to a rise in sea level — Indonesia, Pakistan, Thailand, The Gambia, Mozambique, Senegal, Surinam and the Maldives. Surprisingly the list does not include the coral atolls of the Pacific, where the Marshall Islands, Tokelau, Tuvalu, Kiribati and the Line Islands are threatened with complete inundation. The main atoll of Tuvalu, Funfani, covers just 2.5 sq km but has 54 km of coastline so that any possible sea defences on one side would be protecting the back of sea defences on the other. Not surprisingly, many of Tuvalu's 8,500 inhabitants would prefer to head for Australia or New Zealand. The Maldives consist of a double chain of 26 atolls with some 1,300 tiny islands, averaging only one to two square kilometres in extent and lying between 1 and 1.5 metres above mean sea level. The population, however, is growing by 3.1 per cent annually and at this rate will double every 22 years. In the capital, Male, there are already 53,000 people crowded into an area of two square kilometres.[26]

The effects of climatic change extend far beyond such readily quantifiable aspects. In higher latitudes, that is, between 60° and 90°, winter temperatures are expected to warm up more than twice as fast as the global average, while the tropics will be less affected. As the rain falls at different times and in different places and wind patterns change, with storms increasing in extent and frequency, the world's agriculture will take on new patterns. The American midwest may see its harvests reduced by a third, and, while still able to support the USA, it will find food supplies available for the rest of the world reduced by 70 per cent. New lands opened up in

Canada will not be able to make up for the loss as the soils are too poor. The Arctic tundra may disappear. The USSR is more fortunate in that losses in the Ukraine may be compensated by developments in Siberia (though political change could nullify this). Mediterranean countries will be hit hard, and the already drying-out countries of Africa and Asia even harder. The present droughts of the Sahel only foreshadow worse to come.

The speed of the change is perhaps most harmful for plants and animals. For every one degree rise in temperature they must move about 90 kilometres northward in order to survive. We can expect many to disappear, animal species dying out with their habitats. As humanity strives to use new areas for growing food, the world's wildernesses will shrink even further and the species that live there with them. The first signs of damage are likely to be in the Arctic where the sea ice is vital to the walruses, seals and polar bears that live there, while the algae growing on the undersurface of the ice are the basis of food chains supporting fish, birds and sea mammals. In the tropics most species are less tolerant of changes in temperature than those in higher latitudes. Corals, which grow slowly near the surface, may fail to keep pace with the rising waters and so be unable to provide habitats for the millions of tropical fish that depend on them. Even biological diversity could be affected. Some turtles, for example, which produce female young at warmer temperatures and males at cooler, will suffer sexual imbalance, and eventual extinction, while changes in rainfall could affect elephants, who gather in large herds during good rains, so providing the dominant bull with a chance to mate with many females. Under drier conditions the females scatter, giving subordinate bulls the chance to pass on inferior genes.[27]

To many forecasters, however, the greatest danger is from 'eco-refugees', those peoples who, either through rising seas or global warming that makes their present living area uninhabitable, are forced to move elsewhere. Previous climatic change was sufficiently gradual to enable a considerably lower global population to migrate over a period with a fair chance of success. But in today's overpopulated world, as national states, obsessed with their own survival, raise their barriers, the new migrants will have nowhere to go. Their frustration can result only in strife and anarchy, a situation paralleled in the animal world under similar constraints.

Such forecasts, whatever their basis in scientific knowledge, may turn out to be wrong. Conversely, they could prove an underestimate of the dangers now facing the planet, with an ultimate vision of the loss of many plants, animals and human beings. Whatever the future, no one can dispute that it will be vastly different from the world we know.

Waste gases are more pervasive in their effects than any other form of waste, a measure less of man's inhumanity to man than of the injustice of rich, industrialized countries towards the less fortunate, whose lot, it would appear, is not to share the material benefits of technologically advanced countries but to see their meagre fields and farms destroyed by drought as the world gets warmer or lost beneath the inundation of rising waters.

Notes

1. French 1990
2. Ibid, p. 98
3. Ibid. p. 100 and Table 6.1
4. Ibid. pp. 102−3
5. *Guardian* 1 September 1988
6. Ibid. 18 June 1987
7. Ibid. 14 November 1986
8. Ibid. 17 November 1989
9. Ibid. 7 November 1989
10. Lean, Hinrichsen and Markham 1990 pp. 86−7
11. Hinrichsen 1988 pp. 66−73; *New Scientist* 29 October 1989
12. Hinrichsen 1988 pp. 70−71; but see also Woodin and Skiba 1990
13. Dudley 1988
14. *New Scientist* 23 June 1988
15. *Guardian* 20 March 1990; *New Scientist* 31 March 1990
16. Bown 1990
17. Pearce 1990
18. *Guardian* 25 October 1989
19. Lean, Hinrichsen and Markham 1990 pp. 99−100; *New Scientist* 13 April 1991
20. *Observer* 15 March 1987
21. *Guardian* 29 June 1988
22. Sinclair 1990
23. This section is based on the excellent summary given in Lean, Hinrichsen and Markham 1990, supplemented by other sources cited and by reports in the *New Scientist* of 8 October 1988, 25 March 1989 and the *Guardian* of 9 October 1988 and 1 July 1989
24. Quoted Lean, Hinrichsen and Markham 1990 p. 93
25. Jacobson 1990 pp. 92−5
26. Wells and Edwards 1989
27. Pain 1988

Part III:

Eliminating Waste: Dilemmas of Development

8. The challenge: responses from science and industry

Where do we go from here?

Despite their limitations, and those of research, the previous chapters show clearly the interconnectedness of problems now facing our planet and the potential consequences of failing to take effective action, and to take it now. Whether it is a question of:

- mountainous rubbish dumps
- sewage or plastics in the sea
- nitrates in drinking water or pesticide residues in food
- various shades of toxic algae
- heavy metals or poisonous chemicals threatening lakes, streams and shores, killing the plant and animal life they support
- radioactivity in coastal waters and sediments
- smog clouding the streets of the world's largest cities
- acid rain maiming forests or destroying lakes
- the growing hole in the ozone layer with its threat to human health
- the now certain global warming with its menace of rising seas and over-rapid climatic change

— all are the results of waste and arise, not from its disposal, but from failure to dispose of it. The challenge facing humanity is simply — what are we prepared to do about it before the World of Waste we have created reaches the stage when it is too late to reverse the process of global destruction?

The response has been an amazing outbreak of common sense, amazing, that is, by comparison with recent human history. Environmentalists have joined scientists and the more responsible sectors of industry and agriculture not merely to find better ways for disposing of waste but to seek its reduction and eventual elimination. Even Mrs Thatcher eventually joined the green crusade, and, if little action followed, at least her rhetoric increased public awareness.

The attack on waste included:

- waste reduction through improved industrial/technological processes;
- waste reduction through conservation of energy;
- recycling of waste, particularly of domestic waste;
- conversion of waste into a useful function, for example, gas production;
- the discovery and clean-up of contaminated sites and land; and
- the substitution of harmless for harmful techniques where waste was produced by failure to use a product for its proper purpose, for example, overuse of artificial fertilizers and pesticides in agriculture.

What happens now depends primarily on three groups of people: the scientists responsible for technological innovations to be used in industry; the willingness of industrialists to accept them; and the politicians and power-brokers who make decisions on policy either with or without the consent of the world's peoples. Scientists and industrialists are considered in this chapter; the contribution of politicians and policymakers in the next. The question of waste cannot, however, be separated from that of energy, which, in industrialized societies, is responsible for it. This, in turn, leads to considerations of growth and development and the final chapter examines the dilemmas of development that arise when humanity is brought face to face with the waste that development inevitably produces.

The marvels of science and technology

The need to identify and clean up contaminated lands, to restore acid lakes and ensure the purity of drinking water, to destroy toxic waste and to eliminate the production of harmful solids or gases has provided scientists with enough research to last them well into the greenhouse era, especially when funds are limited or it is government policy, as in Britain, that industry, as the major cause of waste, should provide most of the cash. The results have varied in aims and scope, from the Thames Bubbler, a £3.5 million vessel developed by the Thames Water Authority to inject up to 30 tonnes of oxygen a day into the river when pollution threatens aquatic life,[1] to a proposal at the 1989 British Association for the Advancement of Science conference that waste carbon dioxide emissions, as the main cause of global warming, could be 'captured' by cooling the gas down into a liquid and then burying or storing it in containers beneath the sea.[2]

Space permits only a brief mention of some of the more potentially useful examples developed during the last few years. One of the most urgent problems is to locate past landfill dumps of toxic waste that have been covered over and long forgotten. Because such waste emits heat, German scientists based in Berlin have been able to develop an infra-red scanner with wide temperature range and spatial coverage to pinpoint ground areas of unexpected or unexplained increases in temperature. It is not an easy task as the users must differentiate between places that are naturally hot, for which they require previous information, and potentially dangerous, if hidden, sites. Although only tested in November 1990, the device would appear to be a useful contribution to the immense task of clean-up.[3]

Once located, the waste must be removed safely. In California engineers have developed a form of steam cleaning that removes petro-chemicals from contaminated soil. The steam is injected into the soil, causing the pollutant to vaporize; the resultant toxic vapours, a mixture of water and pollutants, are forced up to the surface through a recovery well, to be captured and condensed, with the chemicals separated for recycling. Working in the notorious Silicon Valley, the team succeeded in removing 14 different organic compounds from the soil, including trichloroethylene, acetone and xylene.[4]

Even more fascinating (to the non-specialist) is the potential use of solar energy to destroy toxic waste. Researchers from the Solar Energy Research Institute (SERI) at Golden, Colorado, have shown experimentally that sunlight, concentrated 1,000 times above its normal intensity by means of a solar reflector, thus creating temperatures of 1,000°C, can destroy 99.9999 per cent of a sample of dioxin, ten milligrams of it in ten minutes. Other research on solar power at the Sandia National Laboratories in Albuquerque, New Mexico, uses catalysts, such as titanium dioxide, and the ultraviolet part of sunlight to destroy concentrated organic liquids and organic compounds in water. The experiment took five minutes to reduce a trichloroethylene concentration from 1.2ppm to less than 50ppb. The researchers claim that the process is effective for solvents, PCBs, dioxins, pesticides, dyes and cyanide compounds.[5]

A more conventional technology (in that it uses incineration) is the plasma centrifugal reactor, in which a powerful electric arc turns air into superheated plasma at over 9000°C. The result, in the American version developed for cleaning up Hanford waste, is to weld contaminated dirt into a glass-like slag, while hazardous organic chemicals, oxidized in the heat, emerge as water vapour, carbon dioxide and hydrogen chloride, and radioactive elements are trapped in the slag, which is then buried as low-level nuclear waste.[6] While the non-specialist is still pondering the merits of destroying contaminated dirt only to produce carbon dioxide (of which we have too much already) and adding to the pile of nuclear waste, s/he learns that, in Melbourne, Australia, scientists have developed a plasma arc furnace that, it is claimed, destroys even PCBs and dioxins almost instantaneously in temperatures four times as hot as the surface of the sun. What is more, a team at the CSIRO, an Australian Government research organization, is developing a compact plasma arc furnace that can be installed at any plant generating waste, and much of the energy from exhaust gases recovered and recycled as heat or electricity which in turn could be used to power the plasma arc.[7] Yet a third version has turned up in Britain, where a London company, Dunston Ceramics, offers to turn contaminated soil into glass by heating it in a furnace at temperatures allegedly exceeding 16,000°C. The process can cope with heavy metals, asbestos and organic pollutants, and the resulting 'glass' (or 'frit') used for aggregates, tiles or even what the company referred to as 'toilets'.[8]

Also from the USA comes the 'natural' method of waste destruction — using bacteria to break down poisonous organic compounds. When microbiologists found previously unknown types of bacteria in deep aquifers contaminated with chlorinated hydrocarbons, they also found that the bacteria consumed methane and that the enzyme that broke it down would break down trichloroethylene. If large concentrations of these obliging microbes are isolated in a 'bioreactor', and contamined water pumped through it, the microbes are able to attack the trichloroethylene and turn it into what is described as 'harmless carbon dioxide and chlorine'. The project aims to have a bioreactor in place within two years that will handle up to 40 million litres of liquid daily. Unfortunately the report of this gives no data on the quantities of carbon dioxide produced — or what will happen to it — or what it is proposed to do with the chlorine![9]

Bacteria also appear in a technique developed by scientists at the Agricultural University of Wageningen in the Netherlands for extracting nitrates from groundwater. The process uses a double technique of first extracting nitrate ions from the water and replacing them with bicarbonate ions, generated by bacteria that feed on methanol, then using the same bacteria to 'eat' the nitrate and turn it into nitrogen gas. Keeping the processes separate apparently avoids the risk of contaminating the water with either the bacteria or methanol and is an improvement on the simple ion exchange method, used in the USA, which produces very salty water with a high chlorine content. Unfortunately, with apparatus to purify 75 cubic metres of groundwater an hour costing £100,000, Dutch consumers will have to pay dearly for the privilege of not being poisoned.[10] How much simpler it would have been not to let the nitrates get into the water in the first place!

In Britain, researchers at the BNF Metals Technology Centre at Wantage, Oxfordshire, working for Thames Water, have devised a quicker, and allegedly cheaper process, using an electric current to change nitrates into nitrogen gas or ammonia without stopping the water-pumping flow.[11] Of course, one will then have to dispose of the waste nitrogen (as will the Dutch) or ammonia, but at least Londoners will be able to drink the water that comes out of their taps.

Not to be outdone by advances in biology, chemists in the USA have found a method of cleaning up water polluted by toxic metals such as lead, mercury, cadmium and zinc. The process involves what are known as crown ethers, — circular molecules made up of carbon, hydrogen, oxygen and sometimes nitrogen atoms and shaped in the form of a crown, which enables them to 'bind' metal ions inside the central cavity. By discovering a way of attaching crown ethers to sand, chemists at the Brigham Young University in Provo, Utah, have found that, when a solution then passes through the sand, metal ions are extracted by the crown ethers. A practical use is in removing lead from the thousands of litres of sulphuric acid used in processing old car batteries, a waste effluent that would otherwise be discharged into the nearest running water. The chemists claim that the process could be used to decontaminate radioactive material in ground water or even to refine and separate gold![12]

Chemists are even on their way to eliminating one of the great sources of agricultural waste — the use of artificial fertilizers. At the end of 1990 a group from China and Australia claimed to have found a way to make wheat seedlings manufacture their own supplies of nitrogen. Research to introduce nitrogen fixation into non-legume crops such as rice has been going on for years, so far without success. By using the bacterium *Azospirillum* on wheat seedlings to which the herbicide 2,4-D has been applied, chemists at Shandung University, China, and the University of Sidney, Australia, found a possible solution.[13] While other scientists remain sceptical and environmentalists, recalling the association of 2,4-D with Agent Orange in Vietnam, recoil in horror, the possiblity of dispensing with nitrogen fertilizers, and the waste they produce, must be welcomed. A simpler solution is, of course, not to use artificial fertilizers at all.

If 2,4-D can be made to serve a good purpose, another scientific proposal, still to be put into practice, suggests that those major polluters of the world's waters — nutrients — could yet be useful in restoring acid lakes. In 1987 Dr William Davidson of the Freshwater Biological Association Laboratory at Windermere, suggested that, instead of adding lime to streams to 'alkalize' the water, the nutrients in acidified but nutrient-lean upland water systems should be *increased* to develop a substantial basic biomass that would act as a buffer against acidity. This has already been shown to work on a small scale but not on the large one necessary to demonstrate its feasibility. By *controlled* application of nutrients, mainly phosphates, it is estimated that, through several seasonal cycles, there could be an improvement from a pH of just below 4 to something below 5. Any danger of eutrophication could be avoided by adjusting nutrient supplies and allowing the waters — the great lakes of Scandinavia, those of Eastern Canada and the Scottish Highlands are suggested for experimental purposes — to 'revert' to their natural nutrient-lean status. To the non-specialist the idea is so simple, at least in theory, that one can only wonder why it has not been tried. The short answer is that there is no structure capable of bringing the interested parties together so that they can contribute.[14] Even when scientists come up with a possible answer, the will to apply it has still to be found.

In one field at least, that of combatting the waste emissions of road vehicles, industry and governments are more receptive towards scientific and technological innovations. Today everyone in the West knows the advantages, not to say moral uplift, derived from using lead-free petrol or having a catalytic converter fitted to one's car. Both, like the driver, are 'environment friendly'. It is less well known that, while in European countries and the USA a non-toxic additive called MRBE is widely used to replace lead, British oil companies use the easier (and cheaper) method of substituting benzene additives. The petrol is certainly lead-free but, since benzene is an aromatic hydrocarbon[15] and thus both toxic and carcinogenic, one fails to see where the advantage lies, except of course, to the oil companies. In contrast, the Californian Energy Commission introduced a project in 1978 by which cars would use methanol instead of petrol as the former contributed fewer chemicals to the production of urban smog. By 1990 both Ford and General Motors were manufacturing variable-fuelled engines that could run on petrol, methanol or a mixture of the two. As there were only 15 methanol-selling filling stations in California by March 1990, this had the advantage that drivers were not forced to stay within range of one of them, as with a methanol-only vehicle. The mixture, moreover, was better for a cold start than methanol alone. There were technical snags to be overcome. Methanol is highly corrosive, so fuel tanks were made of stainless steel, and conducts electricity, so electrical devices in the engine needed to be well insulated. More importantly, cars using methanol produced far more emissions of formaldehyde than those using petrol; but doubtless catalysts will be developed to remove it.[16]

Parallel with these developments was the announcement by Volvo, the Swedish car manufacturer, that it would follow its addition of 'cats' to cars by fitting 200 diesel-powered vehicles with a device called the Cityfilter that would reduce the soot and other harmful particles expelled from exhausts by at least 80 per cent. The filter uses a platinum catalyst to trap the soot (which is burnt when the vehicle is stationary) and to reduce emissions of hydrocarbons by about 60 per cent and those of carbon monoxide by 50 per cent.[17] So the juggernaut will be able to continue throbbing down our streets, confident that its clean technology raises it above suspicion.

There have even been developments in the uninspiring field of sewage sludge. In 1989 officials in Houston, Texas, announced that they hoped to dispose of their sewage sludge the following year by pumping it into a well 1,500 metres deep, then compressing it. Oxygen pumped down another pipe speeds up the chemical reactions by raising the temperature so that all volatile chemicals are removed and micro-organisms killed off. This wet oxidation process reduces solids in the sludge by about 95 per cent to leave inert ash resembling sand that can be used as an aggregate for concrete or asphalt paving. What happens to heavy metals is apparently uncertain but if they persist and the ash has to be buried, at least there will be considerably less of it.[18]

Not all innovations are as fortunate in their residues. The Drax power station in Yorkshire, England, for example, which, according to some sources, emits more sulphur dioxide waste gas than Norway and Sweden combined, had plans to cut emissions by 90 per cent by installing a flue gas desuphurization (FGD) plant, a 'scrubber'. Unfortunately the method used needs 500,000 tonnes of limestone a year, which has to be quarried, then transported to the site, and produces 800,000 tonnes of gypsum, half of which cannot be sold. The net result, therefore, is 400,000 tonnes of gypsum to be carted away and disposed of.[19] Thus reducing one form of waste leads merely to the creation of another. Again technology comes to the rescue. Researchers at the Department of Oceanography, University of

Southampton, have mixed gypsum and pulverized fuel ash (PFA) from power stations with cement to form blocks which, when laid on the seabed, form an artificial reef that marine life will colonise![20] So waste from power stations is ultimately of benefit to fish!

Other technological innovations are more fittingly discussed as an aspect of industry. The illustrations given here, all of them from the three years 1988–90, are sufficient to indicate the general trend. At their best, as with the highly ambitious 'self-fertilization' scheme for non-leguminous crops or the still-to-be-tried plan for de-acidifying lakes, they may be able to eliminate or reverse the worst effects of waste and thus bring about fundamental change. The majority, however, are little more than palliatives, designed to clear up the mess or prevent further immediate danger. This is not to belittle the achievements of those responsible. But in a finance-dominated world scientists can solve only those problems with which they are presented. Here it is industry, and governments, that determine which research will be undertaken and which projects are considered less urgent. Before reaching a conclusion on the contribution of science and technology to solving the problem of waste, it is necessary to examine what industry proposes to do to put its house in order.

The greening of industry?

The Valdez principles
In 1988 the US Social Investment Forum, which had been working for what is known as Socially Responsible Investment (SRI) in the USA ('Ethical Investment' in the UK) joined leading environmental organizations to form the Coalition for Environmentally Responsible Economies (CERES), with the aim of drawing up a set of guidelines for industrial operations. When the *Exxon Valdez* disaster in March 1989 alerted public opinion to environmental dangers, CERES seized the opportunity to put across a number of agreed ideas to which firms were asked to subscribe, under the topical title of the Valdez Principles.

The first four principles are directly relevant to the question of waste and provide a useful summary of the minimum necessary for the greening of industry:

1. *Protection of the biosphere*
We will minimize and strive to eliminate the release of any pollutant that may cause environmental damage to air, water, or earth, or its inhabitants. We will safeguard habitats in rivers, lakes, wetlands, coastal zones and oceans, and will minimize contributing to global warming, depletion of the ozone layer, acid rain or smog.
2. *Sustainable use of natural resources*
We will make sustainable use of renewable natural resources, such as water, soils and forests. We will conserve non-renewable natural resources through efficient use and careful planning . . . .

3. *Reduction and disposal of waste*

We will minimize the creation of waste, especially hazardous waste, and wherever possible recycle materials. We will dispose of all wastes through safe and responsible methods.

4. *Wise use of energy*

We will make every effort to use environmentally safe and sustainable energy sources to meet our needs. We will invest in improved energy efficiency and conservation in our operations. We will maximize the energy efficiency of the products we produce or sell.[21]

Principles are framed in general terms and any agreement between the world's polluters and those opposed to pollution must be a compromise. One notes immediately that there is no commitment to eliminate waste, only to 'minimize' it, just as those accepting the principles agree to minimize 'contributing to global warming, depletion of the ozone layer, acid rain or smog', though the potential release of any environmentally damaging pollutant is taken a stage further in that signatories promise not only to minimize but to 'strive to eliminate' it. Inevitably, faced with industry's past record, sceptics cannot avoid asking how much 'minimalization' or 'striving' will occur and, more importantly, whether it will have the necessary effect, or whether this is industry donning green clothes in an attempt to dupe the 'green' public and to forestall criticism from the environmental lobby.

Optimists dismiss such criticisms as carping, and stress the positive aspects of the principles — where the signatories make a definite undertaking to do something beneficial, for example, 'we will safeguard habitats', etc., 'we will make sustainable use of renewable natural resources', 'we will invest in improved energy efficiency and conservation in our operations', etc. Indeed, on balance, one should welcome the Valdez Principles as a step in the right direction and offer a muted two cheers that we have come so far. The questions now at issue are: will those industries accepting these guidelines stick to them in today's highly competitive world, how will the general public know that they are not reneging on their pledges, and will their actions be adequate to cope with the problem of waste outlined in Part II?

Before investigating industry in more detail, we may note the 'third force' involved in the project, the investing public. Underlying the principles themselves is the idea that investors, able to distinguish between firms that have accepted and are applying them and those that have not, will withdraw financial support from the latter and 'invest ethically' in the former. Faced with this threat, non-complying companies will have the choice of going green or going out of business. The threat can certainly be effective where large investors, such as state governments in the USA with large pension funds and control over purchasing supplies, are concerned, if not in Britain where Trust Laws oblige fund managers to seek out the highest level of returns on investments, irrespective of source, and local authorities are barred from using social criteria in their purchasing.[22] In short, legislative changes are necessary in the UK if the principles are to be effective.

This applies also to the problem of monitoring the activities of firms to establish the level of compliance. Already the USA has greater freedom of information in this respect, while in Britain commercial secrecy is enshrined as one of the Tablets of the Law, and Principle 8, by which companies undertake to disclose to their employees and the public operational incidents causing environmental harm or affecting health and safety and to refrain from action against employees reporting conditions likely to cause dangers, is hardly one to appeal to the nuclear industry.

Industry is undoubtedly under pressure, from governments anxious to reduce toxic waste or noxious emissions and from the 'green' consumer who is prepared to spend more on environmentally friendly commodities. There are, moreover, new opportunities for the enterprising in the field of eco-technology, the new equipment which, it is claimed, will enable those in the West to maintian their present lifestyles without creating waste and its ensuing pollution. Recycling, energy conservation and waste reduction offer opportunities for the forward-looking entrepreneur to combine continued profit-making with moral uplift.

How far is industry prepared to go? In this respect the CFC story is revealing. It begins with the two giant producers, Du Pont and ICI (see Chapter 2) undergoing an overnight conversion when they could no longer escape the fact that their products were both damaging the ozone layer and increasing the Greenhouse Effect, continues with a highly competitive search for substitutes, in which each of the rivals claimed to be ahead of the other and, for the moment, ends with the two ganging up together when their innovatory hydrochlorofluorocarbons (HCFCs), in developing which both had spent millions of dollars/pounds, turned out to be not so harmless after all. When the West German Government proposed that HCFCs should be banned by the year 2000, and the US Congress proposed to phase them out by 2015, both ICI and Du Pont became finance conscious, claiming that they needed at least a 30-year life cycle to recoup a 'fair' profit from their manufacture! Moreover, they had not been able to develop the newer chlorine-free hydrofluorocarbons (HFCs) to replace all current uses of HCFCs.

Amazingly, so far as refrigerators are concerned, there would appear to be simpler, and cheaper, alternatives. By June 1990 a refrigerator at the South Bank Polytechnic, London, had been running for six months without CFCs. It used propane as a coolant, while in a Munich laboratory another refrigerator was working on water. Early refrigerators used large quantities (up to 11 litres) of propane, which, because of its flammability, made them extremely dangerous. Modern versions need only ten millilitres of coolant, the same about as in a table-top cigarette lighter, which is sealed into the system so that only the fiercest of house fires would rupture it. As to costs: CFC refrigerant is £5 per kilogramme, HFC 134a, its proposed replacement, £30 per kilogramme, propane a mere 50p for the same amount.[23]

The solution for Third World countries such as China and India is obvious — they can tell Du Pont and ICI what to do with their HCFCs and HFCs.

Why, then, if this is the obvious answer did both Du Pont and ICI waste so much money in research? It has been suggested that their scientists were experts on chemicals, not on refrigeration. One might also suggest that it is the *raison d'être* of both firms to produce, and sell, chemicals and that they prefer not to know, and that others should not know, about cheaper substitutes. In short, business takes precedence over the environment. ICI, however, continued to promote its green image, announcing in November 1990 that it was to spend £200 million a year for five years on cleaning up its operations with the aim of cutting waste emissions by 50 per cent, while all new plant would be built to the highest standards operating in any country; in short, no more sub-standard equipment for use in Third World countries. It would also, partly from environmental considerations, pull out of the fertilizer business completely so that the new owner would either clean up the factories or shut them down.[24] The implications are staggering. If it costs £1bn to clean up the industry's operations and still only reduce emissions to half of what they were, what quantities of waste and pollution it must, on its own admission, have been producing!

ICI may be congratulated on its honesty. With others the consumer-friendly, vote-catching green ethic has only brought out a rash of eco-hypocrisy. In the USA, Earth Day 1990 was described at the ecological fair, Earth Tech 90, in Washington DC, as 'an opportunity for corporations to express their concern for the environment and their commitment to working on its behalf'. The speaker was John Cooper, director of environmental affairs at Du Pont, whose commitment, while not as radical as that of ICI's restructuring, included the dedication of a 7,000-acre wildlife habitat park in North Carolina. Also present were Waste Management Inc. (see 'Uncompleted Missions' in the *Prologue*, then facing a £2.7m fine claimed against one of its affiliates by the EPA for burning dangerous waste, and another waste disposal firm, Browning Ferris Industries, which had been fined £900,000 the previous month for 1,400 breaches of the regulations on hazardous waste disposal. This did not prevent them from being proud of the 25 wood duck nesting boxes and 25 bluebird boxes they had placed at their North Shelby landfill site in Tennessee, not to mention the 300 blight-resistant elm seedlings to be planted there by boy scouts.[25] Mini-conservation presumably equals concern for the environment.

Union Carbide, hero of Bhopal, was less fortunate in accepting an invitation to speak about corporate responsibility and the environment at a conference on environmental excellence in London in November 1990. Despite the claim in the firm's annual report that the company was finding ways to reduce the amount of wastes from its production operations, accusations of hypocrisy from British MPs and pressure groups forced the company to withdraw from the conference. It was unfortunate that the meeting coincided both with the start of new hearings in the Indian Supreme Court on behalf of Bhopal victims and the release of a highly critical report that made use of the US 'right to know' law to show that Union Carbide had actually *increased* the amount of toxic waste it generated annually by 32,000 tonnes to 136,400 tonnes, while, during 1988, emissions of methyl isocyanate from the company's West Virginia plant increased by almost two tonnes. Methyl isocyanate, it will be recalled, was the gas that poisoned the people of Bhopal.[26]

The snag is that industry is universally suspect. No matter how well-intentioned or how progressively reformed a corporation may now be, it will be many years before it can live down its previous reputation. Take, for example, another large chemical company, Bayer AG. In December 1990 the UK branch of the firm embarked on a well-funded advertising campaign to demonstrate its green credentials, taking full-page slots in the national press and offering 'further information' to anyone interested. This included a copy of their 'Policy guidelines for environmental protection and safety', in which they claimed that: 'Not only does Bayer comply with legal and official requirements relating to environmental protection, but it also takes additional measures on its own initiative and out of its own sense of responsibility', developing 'environmentally acceptable technology for new production processes', saving energy, conserving waste heat and training its employees in the safe, 'environmentally acceptable handling of its products'. The most remarkable feature is that this is nothing new; the document outlining policy is dated September *1986*. It is perhaps unfortunate that, following the Sandoz fire at Basel, Switzerland, on 1 November 1986, when the resultant pollution of the Rhine allowed others to dump their waste into the water in the hope that it would pass undetected, environmental groups in West Germany forced the Bayer works at Burrig to admit, on 27 November, that they had discharged up to 200 kilogrammes of a chloride disinfectant into the Rhine through defective filters on the 25th and 800 kilogrammes of methanol alcohol into the river on the 26th. Admittedly they were in the excellent company of Ciba-Geigy, Hoehst and Lonza, but these had not issued statements of their environmental policy less than two months previously.[27]

It would be unfair, however, to continue outlining industry's iniquities without some account of positive achievements. After all, it is on industry that people must rely to clear up the present mess and, aided by scientists, evolve the clean technology of the future, especially if it can be shown that good works may actually mean increased profits. Space does not allow more than an outline of three potential fields of activity: 1) reducing the production of waste; 2) recycling and re-using existing waste; 3) tackling the waste from agro-industry.

Waste reduction

By focusing on the production process itself, examining where wastes are generated and exploring how they can be reduced, even simple measures, such as separating wastes so that they can more easily be re-used, using different raw materials or replacing hazardous products with safer substitutes can result in surprisingly large waste reductions. The US-based Worldwatch Institute lists a number of encouraging examples. The Swedish pharmaceuticals firm, Astra, by improving in-plant recycling and replacing solvents with water, cut its toxic wastes by half. Borden Chemicals of California, makers of resins and adhesives, altered their rinsing and operating procedures to cut organic chemicals in waste water by 93 per cent, thereby reducing the costs of sludge disposal by $49,000 a year. By substituting a water-based for a solvent-based ink, Cleo Wrap of Tennessee, makers of gift-wrapping paper, virtually eliminated hazardous waste, and saved themselves $35,000 a year. Du Pont's plant at Valencia, Venezuela, responsible for paints and finishes went even better and, by means of a new solvent recovery unit, eliminated the need to dispose of solvent wastes, thus saving $200,000 a year.[28]

The best known and probably longest running scheme for waste reduction is the 'Pollution Prevention Pays' programme of the Minnesota Mining and Manufacturing Company (3M), launched in 1975. By 1984 the company claimed to have eliminated 10,000 tonnes of water pollutants, 90,000 tonnes of air pollutants and 140,000 tonnes of sludge.[29] Over a 12-year period it maintained that it had halved the creation of waste, and saved itself a total of $300m. 3M attributed its success to equating waste with inefficiency and, while top management made it a priority, employees were encouraged, through award ceremonies, to develop innovative projects. USS Chemicals even gives employees who develop waste-cutting ideas a share of the money saved and, by 1986, had distributed $70,000 in rewards for projects saving a total of $500,000.[30] Against this, a study of 29 US organic chemical plants by the New York environmental research group INFORM, concluded that the waste reductions achieved, while impressive, were only a fraction of the total waste generated. The EPA estimates that, by expanding existing techniques, US-produced industrial waste could be cut by 15−30 per cent.[31] Inevitably the question arises: is this enough?

Recycling, waste exchange and other uses
It is ironical that, in industrialized countries, more than half the domestic waste consists of paper, glass, metal and plastics (see Chapter 2), all of which are, or could be, useful, if not to their present owner or in their present form, but with a little treatment, to another (or even the same) member of society. Hence the move towards recycling, turning 'waste' into something 'wanted'.

The advantages are obvious. A 1987 Worldwatch Institute study found that every time an aluminium can was recycled, the energy equivalent of half a can of petrol was saved. In addition, 'one ton of remelted aluminium eliminates the need [in the original process] for four tonnes of bauxite and 700 kilogrammes of petroleum coke and pitch, while reducing emissions of air polluting aluminium fluoride by 35 kilogrammes'. The report concluded that, by doubling worldwide aluminium recovery rates, 'over a million tonnes of air pollutants — including toxic fluoride — would be eliminated'.[32]

Despite the common sense and practical arguments in its favour, recycling has met with a varied response. Habits of the throwaway culture die hard, especially when backed by ideological views opposing any form of regulation. While, at the end of the 1980s, Denmark recycled 90 per cent of its domestic waste, Japan 65 per cent and West Germany 50 per cent, in Britain the figure was less than 15 per cent. In the USA the states of New Jersey, Oregon and Rhode Island had introduced mandatory recycling, but the prospect of 11 separate containers for domestic rubbish instead of one dustbin appalled the British Councillor, Paul Warrick, Chairman of the Works Committee of the Royal Borough of Kensington: 'I am dead against any form of domestic collection of glass or paper, as I believe it will be very costly and will also result in dumps being left on the street for collection'. This attitude is reflected at the national level, or perhaps reflects that of the government. When the EC issued its 1985 Beverage Containers Directive by which members were to encourage less environmentally damaging drinks packaging, a survey revealed that the British Government 'favoured a voluntary approach .... Other EC countries ... used the directive to introduce restrictive legislation'.[33] The 'voluntary approach' meant simply that the government did not intend to ensure that the directive was carried out.

The results were reflected in each of the main recyclable components of domestic waste, that is, glass, scrap metal, paper and plastics. Between 1979 and 1984 the amount of glass recovered in Europe doubled from 1.3 million tonnes a year to nearly 2.7 million. In the Netherlands more than half the glass used each year was made from recycled material; in Austria, Belgium, France, West Germany and Switzerland it was more than 25 per cent. The Austrian effort resulted in the recovery of about 70,000 tonnes of glass in 1986, or nearly 40 per cent of the jars and bottles used, and reduced the amount of solid waste to be disposed of by 254,000 cubic metres. In 1983 West Germany recycled 580,000 tonnes of bottles and containers collected from households.[34]

According to the Worldwatch survey, the 'European' average of 30 per cent for glass jars or bottles recycled conceals wide disparities. While the Netherlands recycled some 62 per cent of its waste glass, Denmark, West Germany and Switzerland almost half and Italy 35 per cent, the UK congratulated itself on increasing its percentage from 14 in 1987 to 16 in 1988. In contrast, the poor relations of the EC, Spain and Turkey, reached figures of 22 per cent and 27 per cent respectively. The British Glass Manufacturers Confederation's figures for 1988 of 175,000 tonnes of glass collected from 3,850 bottle banks may sound impressive until one realizes that this represents one bank for every 10,000 people, compared with the Netherlands, where there is a bank for every 1,300, and that Canada, which recycles 65 per cent of its glass, is ahead of even the Dutch.[35]

There is a further irony in glass recycling. Why, in Britain, do we take glass bottles to a bottle bank, only to smash them on other bottles so that they have to be transported, melted down and re-made, when the bottle itself is re-usable? What has happened to the returnable bottle on which we used to pay a deposit that was returned when we took the bottle back? If we take into consideration the comparative distances of bottling plant and recycling plant from their collecting points, the number of times a returnable bottle can be used, and the cost of sterilization, re-using bottles still has the economic advantage of requiring less energy than re-making them from broken fragments. Yet in Britain today 're-usables' are limited largely to milk floats and public houses.

It has been suggested that the villains are those lighter, and cheaper substitutes, plastic bottles, and the supermarkets that promoted them. Yet there are few plastics recycling plants, recycled plastic bottles cannot be used for food or drink and it is impossible to re-use them because of the temperature needed for sterilization. Their success is due to the supermarket boom, which, as it increased its proportion of the drinks' manufacturers' output, came to dictate the type of container used and had no time for glass or returnables. Yet supermarkets in Germany stock re-usable glass bottles, as do those of France and Spain.[36] Perhaps it is time for a consumer revolution in Britain.

Metal recycling shows similar disparities. According to the World Bank, recycling aluminium results in a 96 per cent energy saving over the manufacture of a new product, a lesson that is slow in being learned in parts of the industrialized world. While the USA recycles 55 per cent of its waste aluminium, and Japan 42 per cent, the European average is only 13 per cent. Again Britain distinguishes itself; while Denmark introduced a regulation that all beers and soft drinks should be sold in refillable containers, a proviso upheld in the European court, despite a challenge from the EC that it restricted trade, Britain managed to recycle a mere 5 per cent of its waste aluminium.[37] Yet a walk round London's suburbs reveals streets strewn with discarded lager cans; well-known beauty spots are disfigured by mounds of castaway metal cans; and it is not uncommon, while driving around the countryside, to see empty cans hurled from speeding cars. Perhaps rivalry between makers of the steel can, with the advantage of magnetic extraction from mixed rubbish, and of the aluminium can, with its greater energy saving, will lead to increased recycling of both.

Paper is less homogeneous than glass or metal. With newspapers there is the problem of removing the printing ink, with the 'glossies' the China-clay coating that produces the shiny appearance. There is also the psychological barrier by which recycled paper is perceived as 'dirty' or inferior so that paper mills have at times used harmful bleaches to produce a whiteness to satisfy customers. And, by the end of the 1980s there was an unexpected problem — marketing. Between 1975 and 1980 the amount collected in the USA for recycling doubled. Even in Britain 27–30 per cent of paper (20 per cent of newspapers) was recycled by 1989 so that, according to the Department of Trade and Industry (DTI), UK mills supplied about 30 per cent of the total paper consumption, which, it was anticipated, would reach 55 per cent by 1993. The problem was selling it. While the market for cardboard remained steady and that for letter paper excellent, the US, having exhausted its home market, proceeded to flood those of Europe, India and South-east Asia with recycled newsprint, thereby bringing down the price so that British paper mills were unable to compete. If, as a result, recycling plants are driven out of business or forced to reduce their output, the greening of the environment would hardly appear assured if left to market forces.[38]

Plastics proved more difficult. By the end of the 1980s West Germany had got no further than discouraging people from throwing them away by placing the equivalent of a 15p deposit on all plastic drinking containers except those for milk. Denmark, Austria, Sweden and Switzerland were considering banning or restricting the use of polyvinyl chloride (PVC). In Britain recycling was non-existent except for a few pilot schemes.[39] But it was Italy that produced a real soap opera assault on the plastic scourge. As Europe's largest producer, 35 per cent of the plastic manufactured, some three million tonnes, went into packaging — plastic bottles, plastic padding, plastic wrappers, above all, the ubiquitous blue plastic shopping bag — all of which was not only thrown away but was virtually indestructable. As only half the towns had well-organized rubbish collection and there was minimal supervision of rubbish dumps, the results were everywhere visible, choking the dry stream beds of Tuscany in summer or turning the Bay of Naples blue with discarded bags washed up on the incoming tides. Where, previously, hundreds of dolphins and sea-turtles had choked to death on plastic shopping bags, presumable mistaking them for fish, in 1988 environmental organizations launched an 'Open Sea Plastic Bag Fishing Day' along the coast and collected three tons in a matter of hours.

At that point Mayor Elio Armano of Cadoneghe, fed up with the plastic sea that threatened to engulf his plot of countryside, decided to act. In a bundle of old regulations he discovered Article 153, dated 1915, which empowered mayors to take 'emergency action' during 'crises' endangering public health and hygiene. He posted an edict on the town hall notice board imposing an immediate ban on the use of plastic bags, bottles and packaging. The 'Shopping Bag War' was taken up by the media, and the mayors of Venice, Florence, Genoa and a dozen smaller towns followed Cadoneghe's lead by insisting on the use of brown paper, or placing mandatory charges on plastic bags. By the time a regional court ruled that Mayor Armano had no right to his private ban since there was no real and immediate threat to public health, housewives were refusing expensive *plastico* at local supermarkets and even industry had discovered that waste plastic could be burned to produce energy; it could also produce dioxins if the temperature was not high enough, but for the moment that was less important. Bergamo's £9 million recycling plant provided enough power to run the city's sewage purifier and light some streets.[40]

In October 1989 the Italian chemical firm, Feruzzi, claimed to have produced the first truly biodegradable plastic. Maintaining that existing 'biodegradable' plastic carriers, made from webs of polyethylene with starch in the gaps, did not live up to their name — while microbes in soil degraded the starch, the polyethylene remained — Feruzzi claimed that their new plastic, which contained a higher proportion of starch, was, unlike previous varieties, not a mixture of substances, but a genuine alloy. Feruzzi's 20 billion lire (£10m) research programme anticipated the Italian Government's ruling that all non-biodegradable packaging material, including shopping bags, must be phased out by the end of the century.

By the end of 1989 Sweden also had outlawed packaging material made from non-biodegradable PVC. In Britain ICI Biological Products at Cleveland, Teeside, was also working on the production of a truly biodegradable plastic, but as 1990 began, neither it nor Feruzzi had overcome the immediate snag that the new plastic bags were more expensive than the old and thus commercially unattractive.[41] December 1989, however, saw the appearance in 1,800 health shops in Britain of the Bio-Sak, a refuse bag made from recycled plastic which the makers, Multipak Plastics of Madley, Herefordshire, claimed would degrade over a period of between six months and five years, thus allowing the contents to degrade and so overcoming the major weakness of existing dustbin bags, which prevent decomposition.[42] Following the announcement, in February 1990, by the US chemical company, Warner Lambert, that they had developed a biodegradable (if not yet usable) plastic from starch, at the end of April ICI launched Biopol, a totally degradable plastic that had taken 15 years to develop. The international hair-care company, Wella, planned to begin packaging its shampoos in bottles made from the new substance. Alas for Britain and the USA, the bottles would be available only in Germany![43]

Industrial waste, especially when toxic, offers fewer opportunities for recycling than the finished articles of domestic waste. Nevertheless, there remains the possibility that what one company does not want may be of use to another. Hence the promotion of exchanges, clearing-houses listing 'waste available' and 'waste wanted'. In North America 16 non-profit exchanges were operating by 1986, while in Japan, such exchanges have found markets for materials such as sludges, slags and waste plastics that would otherwise have had to be disposed of. Indeed Japan, with its limited space for landfill, would appear to lead the world in its management of industrial waste. In 1983 more than half the waste produced (51 per cent) was either sent for re-use elsewhere (36 per cent) or re-used on site (15 per cent).[44] Without detailed knowledge, on-site re-usage makes precise calculations of waste produced more difficult, but if industry spares us the waste, humanity can survive without the statistics.

Domestic waste has a further, non-recyclable component in its organic or putrescible contents, which in discussing landfill (see chapter 4) we noted as a potential danger through the production of highly explosive landfill gas. In practice such gas can be useful. The British House of Commons Environment Committee 'saw good use made of landfill gas to drive an electricity generator producing 3.7mW which are fed into the grid system'. Ironically, this action was frowned on by the CEGB which took advantage of its monopoly position to ensure that the enterprise remained unprofitable.[45] Keith Richards, who manages the programme of landfill gas research at the Energy Technology Support Unit, Harwell, takes an optimistic view. If the theoretical calculation that one tonne of refuse should produce 400 cubic metres of gas and thus generate 7,500 megajoules of heat is unlikely to be realized in practice, in 1986 the Department of Energy identified over 300 possible sites in England and Wales alone, which together could produce energy equivalent to that of 1.3 million tonnes of coal, a figure that could be increased substantially if toxic materials were excluded from the original waste and sewage sludge added.

Commercial exploitation of landfill gas is comparatively new. The USA began it in the mid-1970s with the world's first project at Palos Verdes, southern California; Britain and West Germany did not start until the beginning of the 1980s. By 1989 there were over 70 sites in the USA, West Germany had listed 500 potential sites of which 50 were operating, and Britain had 24 commercial schemes drawing biogas from 18 sites, so that savings in conventional fuels rose from around £3.5m in 1986 to £6m in 1988; estimates of £12 million were given for 1989 — equivalent to 250,000 tonnes of coal — a figure that could double by 1992. The most profitable use of the gas is as direct fuel for kilns, furnaces or boilers, but as few of these are close to landfill sites, it is mainly used to generate electricity, while some of it is cleaned to replace higher-grade fuels. Although the USA, Britain and West Germany lead the way in this enterprise, smaller schemes are operating in other European nations and in Canada and Australia, as well as in Third World countries such as Brazil, India and Chile.[46] In Shanghai organic wastes are shipped to rural areas around the city to generate biogas for use in 60,000 households and 1,200 village plants.[47] With their high proportion of 'vegetative and putrescent matter' in domestic refuse, Third World countries would appear to have an excellent opportunity for a future biogas industry.

Finally, in the course of ten-year research into the possibilities of turning cellulose materials into liquids, scientists at Batelle Laboratories in Richmond, Washington State, discovered that, by concentrating raw, untreated sewage, digesting it with alkali, and heating the mixture under pressure, they could produce a crude form of oil. Aid from industry in the form of the American Fuel and Power Corporation enabled the production of a usable fuel oil with almost the same heating value as diesel fuel. It is estimated that sewage works using the process could generate the energy needed for disposal, in many cases with a saleable surplus, while reducing waste by 80 per cent the volume and, through the hot alkali, both neutralizing the insecticide lindane and the herbicide 2,4,5-T, and separating heavy metals, which remain in the liquid residue where they can be cleaned out.[48] Faced with this modern scientific–industrial miracle, the old Biblical riddle 'Out of the eater came forth meat, and out of the strong came forth sweetness' must now be extended by 'Out of the excrement came forth oil'.

Tackling agricultural waste[49]

Chapters 2 and 4 revealed how modern intensive farming inevitably led to ever greater dependence on artificial fertilizers and pesticides, residues from which posed increasing threats to human beings and the environment. Integrated Pest Management (IPM) aims at minimizing such dependence by substituting biological 'natural' methods of pest control, improving farming techniques and, above all, changing the farmer's attitude to view crop management as concerned with an ecosystem in which many natural forces affecting pests and weeds interact. It aims, not at eliminating insects and pests but keeping them below the level of damaging economic loss. Farmers continue to use chemicals, but selectively, and to use new pest-resistant crop varieties, but only as part of an integrated policy. The farmer must know more about a pest's life cycle, behaviour and natural enemies, and of the effect of cropping patterns on both pest and predator populations. In China, for the last three decades, a nationwide pest forecasting system from hundreds of data collection centres transmitted information on pest populations, the abundance of their natural enemies, and the weather conditions, to some 500 agricultural units. The result was that, in Jiangsu Province, pesticide use on the cotton crop decreased by 90 per cent and control costs by 84 per cent, while yields increased. Inevitably the amount of waste from pesticides decreased in proportion. In Brazil, where soya beans are plagued by several insect pests, following trials in the 1970s 30 per cent of the growers adopted an IPM so that, by 1982, insecticide use was 80–90 per cent below the 1975 level, the year before the programme started, and likewise the waste. Nor is IPM limited to Third World countries. In southern Texas, USA, application of IPM led to a decrease of 88 per cent in the use of insecticide, while the average net gain by farmers was $77 per hectare.

It is claimed that, with biological control, selective introduction of beneficial organisms into a pest-ridden area leads to their becoming part of the ecosystem and establishing a balance that keeps pest damage below danger level. The African cassava crop, for example, suffered the depredations of mealybugs and green spider mites with no natural enemies in sight, reducing yields by 10–60 per cent and causing losses of up to US$2 billion annually. Research in Latin America, the original home of cassava, led to the introduction of tiny wasps, which effectively controlled the mealybug, over 65 million hectares of the cassava belt in 13 countries.

Altering cropping patterns also helps control weeds, for example, growing nitrogen-fixing legumes between rows of wheat or planting cover crops that inhibit the growth of weeds .... At which point in researching the benefits of IPM, the reader who was at school before, or even during, World War II, experiences an 'I-have-been-here-before' feeling. The wholesale introduction of new organisms into an ecosystem may actually work, as with cassava, but are there not also dangers? 'Ancient' history recalls the introduction of rabbits into Australia, only to produce a population explosion that not even myxomatosis could eradicate. As for this use of alternating legumes and cereals, did not history lessons in British schools once explain the workings of the three-field system in medieval Europe and the principle of rotation of crops? And any anthropologist who has worked among African rural peoples still using traditional methods is familiar with the practice of crop varieties as used, in their ages-old wisdom, by those traditional agriculturists, the women, at least until the Green Revolution handed their task to men not versed in the old ways, and monoculture for export ousted centuries' old practices. IPM's management of the ecosystem as a whole would, in fact, appear to be no more than the use of methods familiar to any primitive people, methods which are novel only by contrast with conventional Green Revolution techniques.

But why stop at this point?

It has always seemed ironical that Western consumers who now wish to buy food not grown with the assistance of chemicals have at present to pay more for it than for the same food grown artificially. Have artificial fertilizers and pesticides a negative cost? Such obvious nonsense is paralleled only by the subsidy system in which farmers who rotate corn with legumes, for example, receive decreased subsidies because they cut the acreage devoted to the product on which subsidies are paid. With price support farmers are encouraged to grow crops for which there is no market and the food mountains increase in size.

In September 1989 the US National Academy of Sciences published a report, *Alternative Agriculture*, that effectively undermined Green Revolution philosophy and caused the Department of Agriculture, long a supporter of crops-at-any-price, to proclaim that there had been a 'strategic shift'. The report maintained that:

> Well-managed alternative farms use less [sic] synthetic chemicals, fertilizers, pesticides and antibiotics, without necessarily decreasing — and in some cases increasing — per-acre crop yields and the productivity of livestock systems ....
>
> Wider adoption of proven alternative systems would result in even greater economic benefits to farmers and environmental gains for the nation.

But, the report concludes, alternative farming requires 'more information, trained labour, time and management skills per unit [of] production'.[50] In short, organic farming means all-round gains: the farmer increases his profits, waste nitrates no longer find their way into drinking water, and one will actually be able to buy a tomato that tastes like a tomato; but the report remains unclear on whether farmers, conditioned by 50 years of what have now become conventional methods, have the skills, patience or inclination to change their ways, to undertake what, in fact, would be a real green revolution.

Notes

1. *New Scientist* 22 October 1988
2. *Green Magazine* November 1989 p. 11
3. *New Scientist* 17 November 1990
4. Ibid. 26 November 1988
5. Hecht 1990
6. Charles 1989
7. O'Neill, Graeme 1990
8. *Green Magazine* August 1990 p. 11
9. Charles 1989
10. *New Scientist* 18 August 1988
11. *Guardian* 20 September 1988
12. Milgrom 1988
13. Anderson 1990
14. Tucker 1988a
15. *Green Magazine* August 1990 p. 15; see also Gourlay 1988 p. 85
16. *New Scientist* 10 March 1990
17. Ibid. 16 September 1989
18. Beard 1989
19. *Green Magazine* March 1990 p. 11
20. *New Scientist* 2 September 1989
21. Quoted Porritt 1990 p. 463
22. Ibid. p. 454
23. MacKenzie 1990b; *Guardian* 23 June 1990
24. *Guardian* 29 November 1990
25. Walker 1990
26. Bergman 1990
27. See Gourlay 1988 p. 245
28. Postel 1988 p. 131 Table 7.4
29. Goldsmith and Hildyard 1988 p. 259
30. Postel 1988 pp. 131−2
31. Ibid.
32. Quoted Goldsmith and Hildyard 1988 p. 204
33. *Observer* 22 October 1989; *Guardian* 20 July 1989; *Newsweek* 27 June 1987
34. *WR 1988−89* p. 46
35. *Guardian* 20 July 1989; *Observer* 24 September 1989, 22 October 1989
36. Hadsley 1990
37. *WR 1988−89* p. 46; *Guardian* 20 July 1989; *Observer* 22 October 1989
38. Goldsmith and Hildyard 1988 p. 204; *Guardian* 8 September 1989; *Observer* 24 September 1989; *New Scientist* 16 September 1989
39. *Guardian* 20 July 1989
40. Scobie 1989
41. MacKenzie 1989c
42. *Guardian* 3 December 1989
43. *New Scientist* 5 May 1990
44. Postel 1988 p. 132
45. *HoC* 1989 para. 64
46. Richards 1989
47. *WR 1988−89* p. 46
48. *Guardian* 28 February 1989
49. All data on IPM from Postel 1988 pp. 124−9
50. *Guardian* 9 September 1989; *New Scientist* 16 September 1989

9. Policies, politicians and palavers

While scientists carried out research and industrialists applied the results, the world's politicians contributed their speciality — talk. The end of the 1980s and the beginning of the 1990s were marked by a series of meetings, some of them new ventures, others the continuation of previous global or regional gatherings, usually under the auspices of the United Nations, in attempts to discover answers to environmental problems. Few of the meetings dealt with waste specifically by name: UNEP's attempt to conclude a treaty on the trade in hazardous waste and the London Dumping Convention parties' deliberations on nuclear waste were exceptions. Nevertheless, waste remained the hidden agenda. Whether the subject was acid rain, the hole in the ozone layer or climatic change, the basic cause was still waste; the problem, how to reduce it. Other waste problems, such as the identification and cleaning up of hazardous landfills, the elimination of nitrates from drinking water or the prevention of poisoning by pesticide residues, were more appropriately considered by national governments or regional groupings.

For the first time since the 1972 Stockholm UN Conference on the Human Environment, itself the result of an upsurge of public awareness of environmental concerns, governments thoughout the world were forced to pay more than lip-service to issues in which they had shown little previous interest. In Western Europe, where public opinion polls placed environmental issues at the top of the agenda, and the emergence of Green political parties, particularly in West Germany, could not be ignored, even the most *laissez-faire* governments could no longer escape the challenge to their concepts of growth posed by calls for 'sustainable development' or 'alternative' modes of living. The ideologues of unfettered growth, opposed on principle to regulation in the confidence that, through some undiscoverable mystique, the market would make all things well, were faced with calls for positive action that could no longer be ignored.

The toxic waste trade

In March 1989, at the invitation of the UNEP, delegates from 111 countries met in Basel, Switzerland, to approve the Convention on the Control of

Transboundary Movements of Hazardous Wastes and their Disposal. Countries signing the treaty undertook to produce as little hazardous waste as possible, to ensure that their own disposal facilities were 'adequate', and to cut imports and exports to the 'minimum consistent with environmentally sound and efficient management'. They agreed further not to export wastes to countries that had banned them, or when they had 'reason to believe that the wastes will not be handled in an environmentally sound manner'. Importing countries had to receive full details of the waste, which could be exported only on written consent of acceptance to receive it.[1]

Before they left Basel the representatives of 34 countries and the EC had signed the treaty, followed by individual EC members, namely France, Spain, Italy, the Netherlands and the Nordic countries, but not by West Germany or the United Kingdom. Among other non-signatories were the USA, the USSR and five African states, whose welfare the treaty was allegedly designed to protect but whose attitude to it was symbolized by their vacant seats at the final session — Nigeria, Togo, Gabon, the Congo Republic and the Comoros Islands.[2]

Two years of negotiations through the UNEP before the parties met at Basel had revealed irreconcilable differences in attitude, and consequently in policy, which affected not merely trade in toxic waste but also the extent to which governments were prepared to implement waste policies within their own boundaries. On the question of drawing up a procedure for notifying countries in advance of shipments of waste so that the authorities could then decide whether or not to accept them, there was argument over whether lack of a reply should be construed as 'tacit acceptance'. When the parties had met in Geneva in November 1988, the US and Britain supported the interpretation that it did. Similarly with the right to cross territories other than the importing country. US delegates invoked the 'right of innocent passage' as applied in the 1982 UN Law of the Sea Convention to allow waste to cross land, sea lanes or airspaces without notification, but the only support for this view came from Britain. A further controversial issue was the definition of hazardous waste itself. The draft treaty used two lists from guidelines prepared by the OECD, the first of wastes that included substances 'whose effects ... are not known', the second defining hazardous characteristics such as 'explosive', 'toxic' or 'ecotoxic'. Substances fitting either list were to be notified, yet nowhere did the treaty specify either the concentrations or conditions necessary for inclusion, or even define precisely such terms as 'ecotoxic'.[3]

Meetings between European and African countries in Caracas and Dakar early in 1989, at which the Africans had demanded an international ban on toxic waste exports, produced a counter-proposal to intensify 'international control and monitoring' of such exports. When delegates eventually reached Basel, the US was still objecting to the policy that waste should not be exported unless the importer's means of handling it were as environmentally sound as those of the exporting country. Claiming that no country was as stringent in its controls as itself, the US considered that the clause would prohibit exports. (It was later dropped.) Both the US and Japan objected to a provision banning exports to countries not signing the treaty — a revealing insight into potential future plans. Moreover, as incinerator ash and household wastes, although covered by the draft, were not defined as hazardous in the USA, it would be impossible to enforce this provision. They also objected to a rule by which a government was held responsible if a company in its jurisdiction failed to honour a permit.[4] Third World countries countered with a last-minute demand for a clause permitting ships to be inspected on the high seas, but the UK and others objected, again on the grounds that it would interfere with the rights of innocent passage.

In retrospect, it appears a miracle that a treaty was eventually signed. Even the British, while taking the convention home for examination by international lawyers, signed a non-binding declaration, sponsored by the Netherlands, which confirmed their strong intention to dispose of waste at home and to ban any waste trade with countries lacking the legal, administrative and technical capacity to handle the waste. By February 1991, when the convention still required 13 more ratifications to become law, environment ministers from 20 African countries had adopted their own convention, which banned the import of all hazardous waste into Africa, while, the same week, OECD environment ministers initiated a new regional agreement to lift restrictions on the trade in recyclable waste, hazardous or not, in Europe.[5] Thus the movement to restrict the trade in hazardous waste resulted in its simultaneous banning and legalization!

Dumping the nuclear dumpers

The Convention for the Prevention of Marine Pollution by Dumping of Wastes and Other Matter 1972, better known from its place of origin as the London Dumping Convention (LDC), has operated since 1975 on a global scale. Contracting states must apply a licensing system to any waste dumped at sea from ships or aircraft and, before giving authorization, consider carefully the environmental effects. The Convention prohibits the dumping of certain toxic substances, except in 'trace quantities'.

From 1983 discussions on the dumping of radioactive waste have dominated annual consultative meetings. In 1983 the parties agreed to a two-year moratorium on the dumping of low-level radioactive waste while scientists reviewed the potential harm to the environment and to human health. The dumping of high-level waste was already banned, but new techniques for 'shooting' it into the seabed or using tunnels underneath the sea aroused opposition between those who were concerned only to find a feasible technique and others who considered the seabed part of the sea and thus a forbidden zone for disposal. By 1985 the scientific studies were not yet complete and, with world opinion moving against the dumping of radioactive waste at sea, the meeting adopted by 25 votes to 6 a resolution calling for an indefinite suspension pending the completion not only of scientific studies but of 'other aspects'. These included wider political, legal, economic and social aspects of dumping and transferred the onus of proof to prospective dumpers who had to show that any proposed action was not harmful to the environment or human health — a condition considered by some to be so impossible of fulfilment as to be in effect a permanent ban on dumping. Among the six voting against were France, the USA and the UK. Immediately after the meeting, the British delegate claimed that, although the decision was not legally binding, the UK would comply with it until its own research into the Best Practicable Environmental Option (BPEO) was completed.[6]

Five years later the ban became permanent. The 1990 consultative meeting carried a Spanish proposal to ban sub-seabed disposal of nuclear waste by 29 countries against 4 (the UK, USA, USSR and France). All 4 had nuclear submarines to dispose of, as well as reactors at older nuclear power stations shortly to need decommissioning. Non-nuclear nations, however, were adamant that countries producing the waste should dispose of it within their own borders.[7]

The LDC had meanwhile agreed to the phasing out of the incineration of toxic wastes at sea. At the 1988 meeting, after two days of wrangling over a Danish attempt to introduce a ban by the end of the year, the 65 nations represented agreed on a five-year postponement to 1994. Foremost in exerting pressure for the delay were the USA and the UK. The resolution did, however, introduce an immediate halt to the export of noxious liquid wastes for burning by countries not party to the convention. This closed the loophole by which sea incineration plants could have been set up in the territorial waters of some Third World countries.[8]

The 1990 meeting also approved a ban on the disposal of industrial waste at sea after 1995. Surprisingly, this was agreed by all 43 nations present. Success must have turned their heads for delegates went on to propose an extension of their activities, at present limited to dumping from ships or aircraft, to cover pollution reaching the sea from sources on land. Precisely how one dumps waste at sea from a land-based source, except by using a missile, escapes this non-specialist but doubtless the delegates had other, less esoteric means in mind.

All this is highly desirable, but where does it get us? The seas of the world may no longer be a global dustbin, but the waste remains. The nuclear powers still have their outworn submarines to dispose of and their obsolete reactors to dismantle. In practice, these will have to be broken up into smaller, more manageable parts and disposed of on land, that is, buried. The problem of nuclear waste has not been solved, merely transferred elsewhere.

Local difficulties: the North Sea and acid rain in Europe

Two meetings of environment ministers of states bordering the North Sea, one in London in November 1987, the other at the Hague in March 1990, revealed important differences between Britain and her European partners in their attitude towards, and assessment of, the problems, for which geography is in part to blame. While British coastal waters are deeper and have stronger currents that take away pollution, the waters of the German, Dutch and Belgian coasts are shallower and more susceptible to risk, especially in view of the toxic waste entering the water through the Rhine and other European rivers. Not surprisingly, while German and Dutch scientists produced evidence of highly contaminated waters, threatening marine life, their British counterparts failed to corroborate their results. And while, at the London conference, the Germans attacked Britain as the only country to dump sewage sludge in the North Sea, they forestalled a counter-attack on incineration by announcing that they proposed to end use of this method by 1995.

The major difference, however, was over the question of precautionary measures. While the British Government preferred to wait until an international scientific task force had established the 'facts', others urged early action before it became too late. Against UK Environment Secretary, Nicholas Ridley's warning of striving for 'unattainable perfection' and the need for all measures to be 'cost effective', they found an unexpected ally in Prince Charles, who, in opening the conference, took a personal stand at variance with that of HM Government: 'Some argue that we do not have enough proof of danger to justify stricter controls on dumping, or to warrant the extra expenditure involved. They say that we must wait for science to provide the proof'. If science had taught us anything, it was that the environment was full of uncertainty. 'It makes no sense to test it to destruction. While we wait for the doctor's diagnosis, the patient may die.'[9]

What the popular press seized on in terms of individuals remains important as a clash of attitudes. Whether it is a question of the North Sea, acid rain, the ozone hole or global warming, there have been those who have argued against action, especially if spending money is involved, until we have 'scientific proof'. Against them are those who say simply that, by the time we have proof, it may be too late, the 'patient' is already dying and nothing we do will prevent it. When the world of waste threatens to bury us, and the future of the planet is at stake, the demand that we wait for proof is tantamount to global suicide.

The 1990 conference was more positive in its practical achievements. Britain's eve of conference announcements that it would end the dumping of sewage sludge by 1998 and of industrial waste by 1992 or shortly afterwards (see earlier) were viewed as rather obvious attempts to deflect criticism of a stonewalling record. Yet, despite lack of firm data, all nine governments agreed to reduce waterborne and airborne waste emissions of cadmium, mercury, lead and dioxins by 70 per cent (from a 1985 baseline) by 1995 and decided on a detailed list of 36 toxic and persistent substances, emissions of which were to be halved within the same period. Detailed plans, including the highly expensive technical task of analysis and monitoring, were left to civil servants to work out. The new British Environment

Secretary, Chris Patten, initiated a successful proposal to destroy all PCBs by 1998, with each country developing its own destructive facilities — and the incinerator-manufacturing industry doubtless anticipating new orders. In general, despite at times acrimonious discussions, Conference marked a step forward in the tidying-up process, even if it ended on a sour note with Britain isolated as the only country refusing to accept a ban on the disposal of radioactive waste under the seabed.[10] Not that the UK planned to dump waste there; it merely proposed to keep its options open, and did so — until the LDC decided otherwise.

Conferences on how to deal with emissions of NO_x and SO_x waste gases causing acid rain have become a regular feature of recent European history with Britain again in the role of odd man (perhaps, more accurately, odd woman) out. At first denying any connection between waste gases from British power stations, industry and cars and the acid blight descending on Europe (the 'lack of scientific evidence' gambit), then using special pleas based on the high sulphur content of British coal compared with that of Western Europe, and finally pushing its own preference (and that of British car manufacturers) for lean-burn, that is, fuel-economic car engines as opposed to the preference of continental governments (and car manufacturers) for catalytic converters, the British Government has eventually been driven to abandon one position after another and finally to accept, as a member of the EC, regulations, albeit suitably tailored, devised in Brussels.

The full story is too long and complex to be given here and, for present purposes, it is more important to assess the attitudes underlying government policies than to baffle the reader with statistical targets. The situation at the end of 1990 may be summed up as follows: Under the 1983 Convention on Long-Range Transboundary Air Pollution, promulgated by the UN Economic Commission for Europe and thus covering both West and East Europe, a 1985 protocol stipulates mandatory reductions at source of sulphur dioxide by 30 per cent by 1993 (using 1980 as the base year), and a second protocol the freezing of nitrogen oxide emissions. The 21 countries quickly accepting this became known as the '30 per cent club'[11], of which the UK, querying the selection of 1980 as a base line, was not a member.

After numerous meetings and much wrangling, particularly between the British and West German governments, the EC has gone even further. Large fossil fuel-burning plants must cut emissions of sulphur dioxide by about 40 per cent by 1998 and 60 per cent by 2003; nitrogen oxides are to be cut by 30 per cent by 1998, and by 1993 all new cars sold in EC countries must be fitted with catalytic converters to reduce nitrogen oxides and other waste pollutants.[12] Originally the EC had wanted a 60 per cent sulphur dioxide cut by 1995, and the resulting compromise at a meeting in Luxembourg in 1988 was, in effect, a victory for the British Government, which had throughout voiced concern about the high cost, estimated as in the region of $2b, of fitting power stations with the necessary equipment. Behind the British Government's attitude lay its plans to privatize the electricity industry, which would become considerably less attractive to investors if saddled with a new financial burden. Three months previously the government had thwarted all attempts at agreement, bringing the much-vaunted European Year of the Environment to a close by taking what European governments called a 'totally unreasonable position' and the European Commissioner for the Environment referred to as 'a big step backwards'.[13]

The question remains: will these reductions be enough? In March 1990, speaking to scientists of the joint British–Scandinavian team mentioned earlier, British Prime Minister Margaret Thatcher promised a 60 per cent cut within 13 years. A summary of the scientists' findings, agreed the following morning, concluded that, for Welsh streams, 'even a 60 per cent reduction in [Acid] deposition would give only a modest improvement at most acid sites', while studies in southern Norway led scientists to conclude that 'even a 90 per cent reduction would not guarantee successful restocking with trout'. And in Scotland so much sulphur from acid rain had accumulated in soils where there was as yet no acidification of lakes and streams that, 'if present levels of emissions continue, some areas might tip over the edge'. [14] In view of scientists' invariable caution, politicians would appear to have much still to learn.

Local difficulties: pollution and people in the USA

Faced with a challenge from the World of Waste, how far are individuals prepared to pay more for a cleaner world and, more importantly, change their accustomed lifestyles? One cannot generalize from a single example but recent events in California[15] provide much to think about.

California is unique in combining three features:

- it has an unusual law-making system in which, after collecting 500,000 signatures in favour of a proposition, citizens then vote on it, and, if more than half the votes are in favour, the initiative becomes law;
- Los Angeles is the city of the car: for 12 million people there are 8 million vehicles, 120,000 new cars are made daily and the inhabitants drive 100 million miles each day with 83 per cent of all journeys by single drivers;
- its climate: a lid of hot air hangs over the city, concentrating the waste gases beneath it, while the glorious sunshine triggers complex chemical reactions and sea breezes waft the notorious brew of waste emissions inland, where they are trapped by the semi-circle of high mountains separating the city from the desert. Everyday products such as paint, deodorants and barbecue lighter fluid expel more noxious waste gases over southern California than oil refineries. At the height of summer, barbecues release five tons of toxic organic substances into the air during the course of a day.

In the concluding years of the 1980s Californians introduced a number of laws to deal with the problems. After 100 people had fallen ill from aldicarb pesticide poisoning in 1985 and the entire watermelon crop had to be destroyed, Proposition 65 to curb the use of any carcinogenic or teratagenic chemical that might get into the water supply in 'significant' amounts was passed by a two-to-one majority and took effect in February 1988. The first part of the act listed 29 chemicals, including lead, asbestos, benzene, arsenic, chromium and vinyl chloride; the second, taking effect the following October, added a further 149. Companies employing more than ten people which knowingly discharged these substances into drinking water faced fines of thousands of dollars a day, part of which went to any member of the public initiating an action!

After the water, the air. The state government took the initiative with a monster 45-volume, 5,500 page Air Quality Management Plan, covering every conceivable source of the 9,000 tons of waste poison released daily into the air. They had little option. In 1988 southern Californians breathed air that failed to meet national standards on 232 days a year, and on 75 of which the smog was so bad that schoolchildren and people with respiratory and heart problems were advised to stay indoors. The plan viewed the car as the chief culprit. Under its regulations companies with 25 or more employees were to draw up plans for reducing the number of car journeys to work by such methods as car-sharing, four-day weeks and more working at home, or face the prospect of fines up to $25,000 a day. Car pool lanes were to enable cars with two or more passengers to speed past traffic jams, cleaner fuels were planned (see Chapter 8) and the state proposed to ban the construction of new drive-in establishments because people left their engines running while they were served. In 1990 came the re-birth of non-polluting public transport in Los Angeles in the form of a new tram service, the first since General Motors, Firestone and Standard Oil bought up the old tramways and closed them down. Plans exist for a new network of subways and light railways with tunnels, but, unlike Zürich, where trams have priority over cars at traffic lights and can thus offer a better system, the Los Angeles trams face a competitive market.

In October 1989 came Proposition 128, known to its supporters as 'Big Green' from its comprehensive attack on various waste-producing activities, such as banning up to 20 pesticides in five to eight years, eliminating emissions of CFCs by 1997, and reducing those of carbon dioxide by 40 per cent by the year 2010, and its attempt to curb other environmentally harmful activities. It proposed a moratorium on logging to protect the unique redwood trees, the world's largest and oldest, and a ban on oil-prospecting inside the three-mile coastal line. Despite opposition from the Californian Farm Bureau and several chemical companies, which attempted to remove the provisions on agriculture, and hostility from the White House, which had already seen car manufacturers forced to adopt tougher Californian standards rather than federal ones, polls continued to show that, when Californians voted in November 1990, Big Green would win.

The result was unexpected; Big Green lost by a margin of almost two to one. The same week, in New York State, voters vetoed local government plans to borrow $2 billion that would have been used to protect water supplies, close waste dumps, subsidize recycling projects and buy land for parks. The question is why? The Californian initiative did not ask people to make personal sacrifices, as did previous action against air pollution; yet it was rejected. Its sheer size, the inclusion of such a variety of proposals, may have united disparate groups against it; there was also a possible backlash against the plebiscite method of creating laws by direct vote. Finally, the deepening economic recession and the prospect of job losses may have caused environmental issues to appear of less immediate concern. Underlying all this are deeper and more disturbing trends that affect not only California but the USA and the West as a whole. Two sessions of Reaganism at the White House, like a decade of Thatcherism in Britain, have left their mark on the electorate so that opposition to 'regulatory mechanisms' (apart from those of the market) has now become firmly rooted in the minds of many people. This is the real legacy of those reactionary years, a legacy that successor administrations have done little to dispel and which we must examine in more detail later.

Ironically, while California was voting out Big Green, the US Congress was introducing tough new laws to clean up the air. Although George Bush was elected as a green president, when his Clean Air Bill eventually reached Congress, it was supported by Congressmen from car industry constituencies! The bill's measures to combat toxic emissions and acid rain were valid enough but its provisions on smog prevention were much weaker than those adopted in California. Prospects of a clash increased when, in September 1989, governors of eight north-eastern states announced that they would impose stricter measures in line with Californian standards.[16] The act that emerged towards the end of 1990, the first for 13 years, was thus considerably stronger than it would otherwise have been. On acid rain it resolved to clear the air by forcing coal-fired power stations to reduce emissions of sulphur dioxide by 10m tonnes a year from 1980 levels by the year 2000, and to reduce emissions of nitrogen oxide by 2m tonnes a year by 1995. To ease costs for the dirtiest power plants, cleaner companies were able to sell them 'emission credits' that would allow them to emit pollutants beyond permitted levels. The act also aimed at encouraging new technology by allowing such plants four years to meet the required standard if they planned to use clean technology, for which the Federal Energy Regulatory Commission was to create an incentive programme.

On air pollutants, Congress identified 189 toxic chemicals to be regulated and the maximum available control technology (MACT) to be used to reduce emissions of carcinogenic pollutants. If the EPA considered such controls inadequate, the act allowed for their further tightening. In this case, industries would be given up to 25 years to develop new strategies and the steel industry 30 years to do so for coke ovens. Combating smog would also involve technological change, with the EPA developing rules for the manufacture of cleaner petrol that would not contain more than 1 per cent of benzene, 25 per cent of aromatic hydrocarbons, or heavy metals such as manganese. Already the petroleum industry has foreseen difficulties in meeting both the required reductions in volatile organic compounds and the lower emissions of carbon dioxide and nitrous oxides demanded by 1995.[17]

Inevitably passage of the act raised questions of costs, with those most affected pushing up the estimated price. While large industries, such as coal, oil, chemicals, electricity and steel, gave estimates of $50b a year in 1995 and $90b by 2005, the National Resources Defense Council, Washington, maintained that more accurate figures would be $10–12bn in 1995 and $20–25b in 2005. Those who fail to keep within the law face even bigger expenses of up to $25,000 a day for failure to meet standards, or fines of up to $1m (and up to 15 years in prison) for those who knowingly release hazardous air pollutants.[18]

So much for the legal framework. One waits to see how rigorously it will be enforced.

Talking out the ozone hole

It took half a dozen meetings at a global level before the world's politicians agreed to action to curb waste gases destroying the protective ozone layer above our heads. Now that everyone is aware of the damaging effects of CFCs, one wonders why the UNEP needed ten years to secure a first agreement, the 1985 Vienna Convention for the Protection of the Ozone Layer; even then, this was directed mainly towards research and exchange of information.[19] Discovery of the hole over Antarctica in 1985 was followed by the inevitable clash between those demanding no action without proof that CFCs were the cause and those in favour of taking precautions, in short, the same conflict of attitudes that hampered action on the North Sea and acid rain.

When discussions started, the EPA proposed a freeze on the production of CFCs at current levels, leading to an eventual ban. The USSR, the Scandinavian countries and West Germany favoured a phasing out, even if, until May 1987, official EC policy was for a freeze, the main opposition to action coming from Spain and the UK, whose attitude was described as barely distinguishable from that of its largest industrial producer, ICI. New data in March suggesting that the ozone shield over Western Europe was disappearing four times faster than computer predictions caused a rethink, and Britain agreed to a single 20 per cent cut in CFC production by 1990, followed by a scientific review, while continuing to oppose UNEP plans for further 20 per cent cuts every four years and a complete ban by the year 2000.[20]

When the politicians started talking in Montreal in September 1987, with the USA and environmental groups pressing for an 85 per cent cut, agreement on a 50 per cent reduction seemed a formality. In the early stages delegates even toughened the provisions by including three types of halons. Then the snags appeared. On what was reportedly the personal initiative of President Reagan, the USA demanded that the treaty should not take effect until ratified by countries producing 90 per cent of the chemicals concerned. In short, any of the main producers, that is, the USA, EC, Japan and the USSR, could block it by failing to ratify it. The USSR then insisted on changes in deadlines to fit in with its current five-year plan, and Third World delegates, led by Brazil and Argentina, sensing a threat to development plans for more refrigerators, demanded exemptions and temporary expansion of production.

The compromise treaty that eventually emerged was greeted both as a triumph for UNEP, which it was, and an 'ozone pact full of holes', which was also true. Under its terms, developed countries would cut their consumption of CFCs by 50 per cent in two stages by the year 2000. At the same time they would cut production by only 35 per cent to increase exports to Third World countries; output in fact could be *increased* by 10 per cent until 1990. The agreement would take effect when ratified by 67 per cent of the participating countries; the USSR was allowed to complete the two CFC plants already planned; and the EC acquired the right to apportion cutbacks within the community.

After all the horsetrading, was the Montreal Protocol stringent enough to 'save the ozone layer'? Scientists had little doubt. In their assessment the damage would continue unless there was a worldwide cut of 85 per cent.[21] The British public supported them. Armed with lists provided by environmental organizations of environment-friendly, that is, non-CFC-using aerosols, they shopped around for safer products. (The USA had banned CFCs in aerosols in the mid-1970s, as did Norway and Sweden.) In opposition, the British Manufacturers Association campaigned against proposals to label cans to show whether or not they used CFCs, a procedure described by the government as 'otiose'. Even the fast-food chains were affected: McDonalds announced an end to their use in fast-food cartons, and Wimpy said that they were looking for alternatives.[22]

In June 1988 all 12 EC countries agreed to ratify the Montreal Protocol before the end of the year, to freeze production by July 1989, and to make further cuts of 20 per cent from 1992 and 30 per cent from 1996, each country retaining the right to take stricter measures if it so wished.[23] Two months later the EPA stated that the USA must halve both production and consumption of CFCs by 1990.

When the protocol came into force in November 1988, many countries were already seeking means of strengthening its provisions. Against this, Japan called for relaxation, arguing that it could meet tougher targets only if limits were changed to emission of CFCs rather than production. While European and American scientists described alternative methods to using CFC-113 for cleaning electronic circuits, the Japanese insisted that they had no available substitutes. Meanwhile Canada went ahead with the announcement, in February 1989, that it hoped to eliminate all emissions by 1999.[24]

New divisions emerged. As the EC agreed to a total ban by 2000 (provided substitutes were available) and President Bush quickly followed suit, at an international conference in London in March 1989 prior to discussing a global target of an 85 per cent cut, China and India, which had still to sign the treaty, voiced Third World objections to the unfair financial burden inflicted on those least able to bear it. As the head of the Chinese delegation said:

> The developed countries have produced global problems of great magnitude. They took advantage of cheap energy in the past to accumulate wealth, which they can now use to manage the environment. The developing countries face expensive energy [costs — for CFC replacement] and so cannot accumulate wealth to protect the environment.

While China produces less than a tenth of the USA's waste CFCs, its plan to put a refrigerator in every house would make it, if CFCs were used, the world's largest user. China, therefore, called for the establishment of an International Ozone Layer Protection Fund, to be paid for by rich nations, which would pass on the expensive know-how of CFC substitutes to those signing the Montreal Protocol.

India supported the proposal, arguing that the fund could be used to compensate chemical companies and manufacturers of equipment for the free transfer of their knowledge to poor nations, which would otherwise have to increase production of CFCs greatly in the decade before they joined the rich in making cuts.

A third voice, that of the scientists, stressed the need for urgency. Bob Watson from NASA maintained that:

> for every year that fully halogenated CFCs are emitted into the atmosphere it will take an additional decade or more for the abundance of atmospheric chlorine to be reduced below two parts per billion [the level below which the Antarctic ozone layer would repair itself].

As it stood, the treaty was not tough enough: 'Even if the Montreal Protocol was ratified by all nations, the Antarctic ozone hole would remain for ever'.[25]

Two issues dominated international meetings, even those not specifically about the ozone layer: the need for tougher measures; and the setting up of a fund to assist Third World countries. Scientists had already set the pace with evidence to a meeting in Helsinki in the spring of 1989 that the cuts agreed at Montreal were inadequate. A preliminary meeting in Geneva in March 1990 agreed a new timetable for ten CFCs not listed in the original protocol and added other chemicals.[26] The conference on sustainable development at Bergen in May brought the question of financial aid to the fore with the USA, which refused to support a key clause pledging 'new and additional money', being accused by the European Environment Commissioner, Carlo Ripa di Meana, of 'desertion' and 'causing undesirable and unhelpful divisions in the leading group'. Even the British Environment Minister, David Trippier, rounded on the United States, which, unless it provided more funds to help the Third World, could wreck attempts to cure the hole in the ozone layer.[27]

When delegates assembled in London in June 1990 for a full review of the protocol, a report by the UK Stratospheric Ozone Review Group not only showed that the hole in the ozone layer was getting worse but that there was a possible catastrophic speeding up of the process. Despite this, the USA still refused to provide funds so that Third World countries could acquire new technology and proposed the diversion of existing funds from the World Bank.[28] Behind the US attitude lay the fear that contributing to a fund would act as a precedent for forthcoming discussions on measures to combat the Greenhouse Effect. The impasse was formidable. As long as the USA refused to approve the setting up of a fund, neither India nor China would sign the protocol and the future of the ozone layer would remain in doubt. After much argument the USA agreed to a fund, while India and China undertook to sign the protocol in 1992. The USA was also unsuccessful in arguing that the establishment of the fund should not be regarded as a precedent for future global initiatives.

The cuts agreed were a marked improvement on the original protocol. CFCs would be phased out by the year 2000, with cuts of 50 per cent by 1995 and 85 per cent by 1997; halons (except for certain essential uses) would also be phased out by 2000, with a 50 per cent cut by 1995. Thirteen countries, led by Finland and New Zealand and including three CFC-producers — Canada, the Netherlands and West Germany — argued strongly for a 1997 deadline for CFCs rather than 2000, but were even more strongly opposed by the USA, USSR and Japan. For the first time two other ozone-depleting chemicals were included: carbon tetrachloride, to be phased out by 2000 with a cut of 85 per cent by 1995; and the widely used solvent, methyl chloroform, to be phased out by 2005 with a 70 per cent cut on present levels by 2000. While the British DTI wanted cuts in the latter restricted to between 60 and 65 per cent by 2000 and no date fixed for phasing out, the Conference presented British Prime Minister Margaret Thatcher with the UN Global 500 award for 'outstanding environmental achievement'. British environmentalists, more familiar with her record, were not amused.

Still not covered by the protocol are the CFC substitutes, the HCFCs developed as 'transitional substances', though delegates approved a resolution phasing them out by 2020 if possible and by 2040 at the latest. This time, ICI and Du Pont (as seen earlier) were not happy.[29]

But would the cuts be effective? When the Stratospheric Ozone Review Group reported in July 1991, it now claimed that the concentration of ozone in a band across the northern hemisphere had declined by 8 per cent between 1979 and 1990, that is, the loss was *twice as fast* as earlier studies had suggested. Dr Joe Farman estimated that by 1997 20 per cent of the ozone over Britain and Europe would have disappeared and ultraviolet radiation risen by 40 per cent. It was no longer a question of stabilizing waste emissions but of reducing them to pre-1970s levels. A year after the London agreement only two of the 69 countries represented had ratified it, while the proposed fund of US $240 million to help developing countries buy ozone-friendly technology had received a mere US $9.4 million. (But see Chapter 10.) Once again the politicians had failed to follow the scientists' lead.[30]

Greenhouse gas

The responses of politicians to the problem of waste gases causing the Greenhouse Effect were predictable: an opening denial that the problem existed, followed by calls for further research and a fall-back position that action should be delayed until there was a general consensus. Meanwhile, there was the question of costs and the demand that environmental measures should not interfere with economic growth.

Between November 1988, when delegates of 33 nations agreed in Geneva to set up three review committees of the Intergovernmental Panel on Climatic Change (IPCC) to prepare assessments for a conference on global warming, and October 1990, when governments from 130 countries, also meeting in Geneva, considered their reports and agreed only on minimal action, there were a dozen or so meetings at which scientists, politicians, or both, argued the pros and cons of climatic change. As with parallel discussions on CFCs, this 'gassing about gases' was more important for what it revealed of the participants than for decisions on practical action.

With hindsight, the outcome of the IPCC was largely determined through allocation of the review committees. Britain undertook to lead the scientific review group, with Dr John Houghton, head of the Meteorological Office and at the time a known sceptic of global warming, in charge. The Soviet Union led the second committee, whose task was to assess the impact of climatic change, and the USA led the third, on political options for meeting the challenge.[31] In Britain, Prime Minister Margaret Thatcher, determined to substantiate her newly green credentials following a speech to the Royal Society in September 1988, called cabinet ministers and senior officials to a special meeting at Downing Street on how to fight the Greenhouse Effect.[32] She was not overtly assisted by the Energy Secretary Cecil Parkinson's cutting funds for research into energy and conservation and voicing his opposition to a more interventionist programme to promote energy conservation as a means of combating greenhouse gases[33], or by the Environment Secretary, Nicholas Ridley's 'kite-flying' proposal for a 'carbon tax' on fires in both the home and in industry as a means of reducing emissions of carbon dioxide.[34] Though he withdrew the suggestion when opposition spokesmen claimed that he was merely paving the way for increases in nuclear power, this did not prevent inclusion in the bill for privatization of the electricity industry, then before Parliament, of a clause imposing on it a statutory duty of producing at least 20 per cent of their power from nuclear and other non-fossil fuels.[35] When the House of Lords inserted an amendment that would force the industry to promote energy conservation, Parkinson used the large Tory majority in the Commons to overturn it, as well as to vote down 30 amendments proposed by the Association for the Conservation of Energy that would have introduced conservation measures.[36] In short, while Mrs Thatcher herself was strong on rhetorical support for action, her government contradicted her words almost as soon as they were uttered. It is difficult to imagine this happening without her consent.

Opportunity for a display of environmental leadership came in July 1989 when leaders of the world's seven major industrial nations (G7) — Japan, Britain, Canada, France, Italy, West Germany and the USA — met in Paris. Almost a third of the final communiqué focused on global environmental issues, rejected 'persisting uncertainties' as an excuse for delaying action, and called for a concerted response and the early adoption worldwide of policies based on 'sustainable development'. Mrs Thatcher stressed the role that nuclear power could play in limiting output of greenhouse gases and President Bush said that the environment was now on the 'front burner',[37] a not entirely appropriate metaphor in view of the amount of tropical rain forest going up in smoke.

Four months later, the British Government showed a different face, when, on the eve of a 65-country UN conference at Nordeweich, near the Hague, to agree on measures to combat the Greenhouse Effect, it refused to sign the agreement unless specific target figures were deleted (that is, that carbon dioxide emissions in industrailized countries should be 'stabilized' at present levels by the year 2000 and the 'feasibility' investigated of reducing them by 20 per cent by the year 2005). While France, West Germany, Italy, the Netherlands, Norway, Sweden, Belgium and Greece were prepared to sign, Britain considered the figures 'arbitrary and vague' and instead proposed waiting for the results of the special IPCC committee. As UN officials stressed the need for urgency and Mrs Thatcher prepared to address the UN General Assembly that same week, many wondered what had become of her claim to the 1988 Conservative Party Conference that 'Britain has taken the lead internationally and we shall continue to do so'. Fortunately, and significantly, Britain was not alone at Nordeweich; the USA and Japan also objected to setting precise targets.[38] How one could achieve even the minimum necessary without a target to aim at remained a mystery.

Within the EC the struggle continued over an attempt to formulate the community's negotiating position for future discussions with the IPCC. When environment ministers met in March 1990, commission officials were expecting the British to attempt to tone down a directive calling for stabilization of carbon dioxide emissions at existing levels by 2000, largely through energy efficiency.[39] The following month, George Bush belied his image of 'environment president' by telling representatives of 17 countries invited to Washington that evidence for global warming was still uncertain and rejecting immediate responses that would put the economy at risk. The White House even banned use of the phrase 'global warming', while pledging that it would spend more than $1,000 million on research into 'global climate change'. 'Environmental policies that ignore the economic factor — the human factor — are destined to fail .... All of us must make certain that we preserve our environmental well-being and our economic welfare.' Not surprisingly, 68 per cent of people in a poll published by the *New York Times* said that he had 'mainly just talked about the environment'. Unfortunately, in the great American drought of 1988, half the grain-producing counties lost half of the nation's grain crop, and 2,000 cargo-carrying barges on the Mississippi were grounded when the river level dropped ten metres. Dr James Hansen, a scientist from the National Aeronautics and Space Administration (NASA) told Congress, 'It is time to stop waffling so much and to say that the evidence is pretty strong that the greenhouse effect is here.'[40]

In Washington the US administration's efforts did not stop with presidential speeches. Before the meeting US delegates received a set of confidential 'talking points', in which it was stated, under the heading 'debates to avoid', that it was 'not beneficial to discuss whether there is or is not warming or how much or how little warming .... A better approach is to raise the many uncertainties that need to be better understood on this issue'. Against this the West German delegation argued, equally predictably, that 'existing gaps in our present knowledge must in no way be used as an excuse for global inertia'. The Dutch request for a change in agenda to include discussion of action to freeze or reduce carbon dioxide emissions from fossil fuels received no reply from the White House. Two days' discussions resulted only in separate concluding statements from opposing factions. The Europeans called for immediate cuts in CO_2 emissions and a response to global warming 'without further delay', and while Bush's concluding speech went so far as to agree that 'research is no substitute for action', the conference closed with a reminder from an American spokesman that 'so many scientific questions remain yet to be answered'.[41]

The circus continued the following month (May) with the Bergen Conference to discuss the Brundtland Report, 'Action for a Common Future'. This conference was remarkable in a number of respects. For the first time it included representatives from Eastern Europe; the meeting of political delegates was preceded by a conference of non-governmental organizations, Third World groups and representatives of industry, which produced its own 'Agenda for Action', and Britain and the USA, anticipating opposition, sent their 'second teams'. British Environment Secretary Chris Patten declined to attend on grounds of pressure of work, and the director of the EPA, William Reilly, stayed away because he did not back the Bush position. The conference's decisions on CFCs have already been noted (see pp. 204–5) and it was probably the need to produce a consensus before the forthcoming London Conference (see p. 205) that led to compromise. The proposed communiqué was a forthright declaration that both Britain and the USA would have opposed: 'Policies must be based on the precautionary principle. Environmental measures must therefore anticipate, prevent and attack the cause of environmental degradation, even if scientific proof is lacking'. Britain surprised the conference by distancing itself from the US position, acknowledging for the first time that global warming was a reality and that efforts to reverse it would have considerable effect on domestic policy, including transport. It joined the US, however, in maintaining that the conference was not the right place for setting targets for emissions. By toning down the wording all 34 countries eventually signed the final declaration — the USA even accepted the precautionary principle — but the result was such a fudge that many delegates denounced it even before the ink was dry.[42]

Everything now depended on the reports of the three IPCC review groups. The first, the scientists' assessment, appeared in draft before its official publication at the beginning of June, thus enabling Mrs Thatcher to re-establish her green credentials in a speech the previous week when opening the Hadley Centre for Climate Prediction and Research at the Meteorological Office, Bracknell, Berkshire. On 17 March she had attacked 'airy fairy greens' and declared: 'We are not going to do away with the great car economy'. In her Bracknell speech on 25 May she promised to stabilize carbon dioxide emissions at 1990 levels by 2005, by which time, without action, emissions would have risen by 30 per cent. This would mean 'significant adjustments to our economies — more efficient power stations, cars which use less fuel, better insulated houses and better management of energy in general'. Lower than those of all other Western European countries, and far short of the cut of more than 60 per cent which the scientists considered necessary, the target was immediately criticized as inadequate. Dr Houghton, who chaired the committee and now supported its conclusions, maintained that, if everyone took the same steps as Britain, it would not stop global warming.[43] But with electricity privatization in the offing and the votes of British motorists an electoral issue, could one really expect otherwise?

Optimists had still to contend with political manoeuvring at the IPCC. While the first working group of scientists was almost unanimous in its confirmation of global warming, thereby effectively isolating the USA which could no longer plead 'scientific uncertainty' with any credibility, and the second group outlined the potential effects already sketched in Chapter 7, the third group, entrusted with making recommendations for action, was dominated by the USA and Japan. Unlike the other groups, its conclusions were based less on how to prevent or minimize global warming than on how to live with it. Hence such proposed steps as building sea walls. More important was the emphasis on a large increase in nuclear power as the cheapest and best way to cut emissions. In short, with no solution in sight for coping with the world's nuclear waste, they were prepared to add to it. Opponents quickly pointed out that there were better ways than the nuclear. They claimed that, in Britain, every £1 invested in nuclear power saved six kilograms of carbon dioxide from reaching the atmosphere, but every £1 spent in replacing electric light bulbs with fluorescent lighting saved 27 kilograms. Moreover, according to the UKAEA, in 1989 fossil fuels in power stations produced only 11 per cent of global carbon dioxide emissions. To change them to nuclear would thus have no effect on nearly 90 per cent of emissions.[44]

Inevitably, events were reflected in the meeting of the 'big seven' (G7) in Houston, Texas, in July. President Bush had been reputedly convinced by White House Chief of Staff John Sununu that computer predictions of global warming were vague and unreliable. (Sununu had publicly stated that he was unconvinced by the 170 international scientists of group one and was himself under pressure from industry over possible punitive costs of 'panic legislation'.) He now ensured that environmental issues remained on the back burner, and, despite efforts by Mrs Thatcher and Chancellor Kohl, the final communiqué contained only three pages on the subject.[45]

In September the three IPCC task groups met in Sundsvall, Sweden, to produce a joint report, an impossible task and one not made easier by US attempts to amend the scientific evidence to stress its uncertainty. In the end, the science emerged intact but the remainder, including targets for the reduction of emissions, was reduced to vague generalizations. New Zealand announced that it would cut emissions of greenhouse gases by 20 per cent by 2005, Japan promised plans to stabilize emissions at around 10 per cent above current levels by 2000, and Canada intimated that it would announce targets shortly. The USA and Saudi Arabia opposed all target-setting; the latter feared that any reduction in energy consumption in the West would affect Saudi exports of oil.[46] Meanwhile, Third World countries were lobbying for their own interests. Brazil and Indonesia refused to accept any action that would limit their use of forests unless the developed world did something about emissions from power stations and cars. Mexico wanted preferential terms for the transfer of technology to the Third World written into any agreement, while scientists pointed out that, if China and India followed the Western example in their attempts to boost prosperity, as they threatened to do, they would be inviting disaster on themselves and on the rest of the world.[47]

When governments from 130 countries met in Geneva in November 1990 for the Second World Climate Conference, with the aim of agreeing a policy that could form the basis for a World Climate Convention to be signed in Brazil in 1992, positions had, if anything, hardened. The USA was still opposed to including any targets for reducing emissions and had reverted to its previous scepticism. Delegates from Pacific islands threatened with inundation reported that, when shown a quotation from the IPCC report on climatic change, President Bush had dismissed it with 'That's not what my scientists are telling me'. The US further stressed the 'crippling costs' to the economy of reducing its output of greenhouse gases, thereby ignoring four new studies it had commissioned which showed that, through using natural gas, improving energy efficiency and running cars on ethanol, emissions could be stabilized or even reduced, at little or no cost. The British, determined to avoid the possibility of increased costs affecting privatization of electricity insisted on 2005 as the target date for stabilizing emissions of CO_2 at 1990 levels, while the EC wanted the year 2000. Diplomacy found a neat way round the impasse by allowing the UK exemption, providing the 2000 target date was met by the community as a whole. In short, other countries would have to make up for British deficiency. Japan arrived at the conference with two targets: one to produce no more carbon dioxide by 2000 than it does now; the second, supported by the Ministry of International Trade and Industry, arguing that the freeze should apply by head of population, that is, there would actually be an increase of 5 per cent over the next ten years. The Soviet Union, like the USA, refused to accept any target for cuts but the likelihood was that, with industry in a state of paralysis, emissions would actually decrease. Conversely, 600 scientists presented the politicians with a demand for cuts of up to 50 per cent if the world was to be saved from disastrous climatic change, adding that many industrialized countries could cut their emissions by 20 per cent over the next 15 years simply by using technologies that were already available and cost-effective.

Despite this, no figures appeared in the final communiqué, which stated simply:

> We urge all developed countries to establish targets and/or feasible national programmes or strategies which will have significant effects on limiting emissions of greenhouse gases not controlled by the Montreal Protocol [on CFCs].

Fearful of driving the USA into isolation and so boycotting the 1992 conference, delegates accepted the inevitable, though not without protest. At the last minute Trinidad and Tobago objected to the statement's lack of any call for specific action and was joined by some 15 developing countries and Austria. The objection was withdrawn only so that delegates could 'go home', but a promise from the USA for extra financial aid and the transfer of technology to developing countries 'on a most favoured basis' doubtless acted as a sweetener.[48]

Meanwhile, a study by the Centre for Energy and Environment at the University of Gröningen in the Netherlands queried the targets which the EC had set itself. It concluded that the objective of reducing emissions of CO_2 within the next 20 years would not be realized if present levels of economic growth persist. A strict regime for imposing energy efficiencies would lead to short-term stabilization for a few months or years, but the community's growth potential was so vast that expanded demand for energy would rapidly swamp any reductions; emissions of CO_2 would rise above existing levels by 40 per cent by as early as 2010. The team based its findings on a programme that included strict measures to promote energy efficiency, a doubling of investment in nuclear power (itself a highly dubious proposition) and the replacement of decommissioned coal-powered stations with renewable sources of energy. Any reduction in emissions achieved through using renewable sources would soon be negated by expansion in demand.[49]

The greatest danger may not, however, come from Europe but from the developing world. In August 1989 scientists at a Pugwash workshop heard Professor Zhu Jiaheng outline China's energy needs and its plans to meet them. By the year 2000 energy demand would double that of 1980 and by 2030 be six times as great. With its policy of self-reliance China depends on coal, of which it has over 700,000 million tonnes of proved recoverable reserves, the largest of any country in the world,[50] to satisfy primary energy consumption at the rate of two-and-a-half times the world average. While world scientists proposed a 50 per cent reduction in CO_2 emissions, bringing global emissions down to three billion tonnes per year by 2030, the Chinese plan involved the production of nearly three billion tonnes in China alone by that time. The result was 'an energy plan which spells death-by-climate for millions and disaster for all.'[51]

At this point the problem of waste emissions becomes inseparable from the problem of development. Western scientists present listened to this Chinese scenario with increasing consternation and awkwardness, consternation because it was an invitation to global suicide, awkwardness because, as members of the human race who had enjoyed the material benefits of industrialization for two centuries, including the development of their own field of science, they were in no position to lecture the Chinese. When the president of the most powerful nation on earth is insistent that 'growth' must continue and afraid he will lose electoral votes if he tells American families they must forego one of their cars, how can one say to the Chinese 'You must not!'

Notes

1. Lean, Hinrichsen and Markham 1990 p. 104
2. BRRI 1989 pp. 108–9
3. *New Scientist* 19 November 1988
4. Ibid. 18 March 1989
5. *Guardian* 23 March 1989, 15 February 1991
6. Based on an account by the author in ACOPS 1985–86 pp. 24–6
7. *Guardian* 2 November 1990
8. Ibid. 7 October 1988
9. Ibid. 25 November 1987
10. Ibid. 9 March 1990; *New Scientist* 17 March 1990
11. Lean *et al.* 1990 p. 88
12. Ibid.
13. *Guardian* 22 March 1988
14. *New Scientist* 31 March 1990
15. Data taken from reports in the *Guardian* 15 November 1986, 25 February 1988, 12 October 1989; *New Scientist* 3, 10 November 1990; Lean 1989; BBC Horizon programme 'California Dream' 11 February 1991
16. *Guardian* 16 September 1989
17. Melamed 1990

18. Ibid.
19. Lean *et al.* 1990 p. 100
20. Gourlay 1988 pp. 211–12
21. *Observer* 6, 13, 20 September 1987; *Guardian* 17 September 1987
22. *Observer* 20 September 1987
23. *Guardian* 17 June 1988
24. *New Scientist* 11 August 1988, 19 November 1988; *Guardian* 22 February 1989
25. *New Scientist* 11 March 1989
26. Ibid. 24 March 1990
27. *Guardian* 15 May 1990
28. Ibid. 21 June 1990
29. Milne 1990b
30. *New Scientist* 22 June 1991, 27 July 1991; *Observer* 21 July 1991
31. *New Scientist* 19 November 1988
32. *Observer* 8 January 1989
33. *Guardian* 24 April 1989
34. Ibid. 9 June 1989
35. Ibid. 10 June 1989
36. *Observer* 11 June 1989
37. *Guardian* 17 July 1989
38. *Observer* 5 November 1989; *Guardian* 12 March 1990
39. *Guardian* 12 March 1990
40. Ibid. 18 April 1990
41. Ibid,; Joyce 1990
42. Brown, P. 1990c; *Guardian* 12, 14, 16, 17 May 1990; *New Scientist* 12, 19 May 1990
43. *Guardian* 24, 26 May 1990
44. Ibid. 2 July 1990
45. Ibid. 10 July 1990
46. Ibid. 5 October 1990; *New Scientist* 8 September 1990
47. *Guardian* 24 August 1990
48. Ibid. 29, 30 October 1990; *Observer* 4 November 1990; *New Scientist* 27 October 1990, 10, 17 November 1990
49. *New Scientist* 19 May 1990
50. *WR 1990–91* Table 21.3
51. Leggett 1989

10. Dilemmas of development

Talking to save the planet

When leaders of the seven major industrial nations met in London in July
1991, the publicity surrounding a specially invited guest, the president of a
rapidly disintegrating Soviet Union, Mikhail Gorbachev, pushed
environmental issues into the background and overshadowed a parallel,
alternative meeting of environmentalists from across the world, The Other
Economic Summit (TOES). Accusing the G7 leaders of 'failing the test of
leadership, the planet and future generations on major environmental issues'
for not addressing such crucial issues as the atmosphere, energy and waste,
delegates damned their respective governments for inaction. Germany was
the only G7 country with no motorway speed limit, and the new transport
policy for East Germany relied on roads; Italy continued to export toxic
waste to the Third World; and of the USA it was claimed that, if all
countries used an equivalent amount of energy and relied on the same means
of producing it, there would be a five-fold increase in greenhouse emissions
and a five degree temperature rise in ten years.[1]

All talk, however, was directed with one eye on the future and the
forthcoming UN Conference on Environment and Development (UNCED),
already dubbed the Earth Summit, scheduled for June 1992 in Rio de
Janeiro. While Western leaders in London gave verbal support to UNCED,
a meeting of Third World ministers in Beijing issued a declaration
disclaiming responsibility for the environmental crisis and demanding large
amounts of aid as a condition for their co-operation. China used the
opportunity to announce its ratification of the Montreal Protocol, thereby
increasing the fund set up to help Third World CFC-producers to US $200m
(from which the Chinese would also benefit).

What, then, were the prospects for the Earth Summit? Would it really
save the planet? Or would it degenerate into the North–South confrontation
that had already appeared at preparatory meetings? Much depended on one
man, Maurice Strong, organizer of the 1972 Stockholm Conference, now
entrusted with the more difficult task of persuading the hundred presidents
and prime ministers proposing to attend that, as he saw it, if we don't stop

destroying irreplaceable resources, changing the climate faster than we can cope with the change, and keeping most human beings in desperate poverty leading to environmental and human degradation, then the world economy, and the civilization it supports, will collapse. Strong's plan was to persuade world leaders to sign two documents: an Earth Charter of environmental and economic principles, and Agenda 21, a list of targets and schedules for solving particular problems. The leaders would also be asked to approve resolutions on monitoring their activities, on building scientific and technological capabilities, especially in developing countries, and on setting up financial processes for the transfer of clean technologies to poor countries. Above all, the task would be to change perceptions and make world leaders see the need for economic change. In Strong's view, the real barriers to a sustainable world economy 'are not to do with technology, or even with money. They are to do with attitude and political will.'[2]

Perceptions and attitudes

What are these perceptions and attitudes that need to be changed?

Margaret Thatcher's address to the UN General Assembly on 8 November 1989 on 'the threat to our global environment'[3], delivered with her inevitable penchant for simplistic expression and use of 'the bluntest form', typifies the approach of many Western politicians. Before any action is taken, she claimed, 'we need the best possible scientific assessment; otherwise we risk making matters worse', a statement with which no one would disagree, were it not that the quest for scientific certainty too often becomes the politician's excuse for delay. Next, 'we need to get the economics right'. This means that 'first we must have continued growth in order to generate the wealth required to pay for the protection of the environment'. Second, 'it is industry which will develop safe alternative chemicals for refrigerators and air-conditioning ... devise biodegradable plastics ... [and] find the means to treat pollutants and make nuclear waste safe'. As for targets to reduce greenhouse gases, 'we think it important that this should be done in a way which enables all our economies to grow and develop.'

Here we reach the heart of the matter. Thatcher's vision of the future is a continuing consumerist society of refrigerators, air-conditioning, biodegradable plastics and nuclear waste, to ensure which the environment must be 'protected'; to protect it we need 'wealth', and in order to achieve wealth there must be 'growth', that is, economic growth. Yet it is unrestricted growth that has brought the environment to its present state of degradation. How then can this provide a solution? Is there not a contradiction, a global dilemma, between taking action to avert the threat of environmental disaster and at the same time insisting on economic growth?

It is important to try to understand the Thatcherite attitude to the environment, which, at numerous points in her speech, she refers to as 'our environment'. Does this indicate ownership, as in 'our house', or merely relationship, as in 'our country', or is it an extension of Mrs Thatcher's penchant for the royal plural? And who are the 'us' to which the 'our' refers? The human race as a whole ('our environment is threatened by the sheer numbers of people')? Or is the application more restricted so that it excludes those who are not 'one of us', a large group for whom Mrs Thatcher's antipathy is on record. Among these ambiguities the only certainty is the distinction between 'our global environment', which includes 'nature itself' and which we must now 'protect', and the amorphous 'us', who are not part of that environment. In short, if we interpret 'us' at its widest, there is a dichotomy between the human race and the rest of the planet, which exists primarily for its benefit, that is, to ensure growth. Ultimately this derives from the Old Testament God giving man (sic), 'dominion over the fish of the sea, and over the fowl of the air, and over the cattle, and over all the earth and over every creeping thing that creepeth upon the earth'.[4] The idea that humanity itself may be merely one among many inhabitants of this planet and thus as much a part of the natural world as the creatures allegedly assigned to its domination, though based on more valid science than Hebraic myth, would appear to have no place in Thatcherite conceptualization.

Not surprisingly, the Thatcherite approach is endorsed by President Bush. 'The environment has no better allies than strong economies, that generate new technologies that allow us to make vital investments in our common future.' We have already seen how Bush deployed the gambit of scientific uncertainty to defer action on global warming by arguing that economic growth should not be sacrificed to combat a warming of the Earth that might never happen.[5] Ironically, the same attitude to the desirability of growth occurs in the Third World; in discussions of the Montreal Protocol, the Chinese complaint (quoted earlier) was not against growth but against the unfairness of their situation, in particular the expensive energy costs, compared with the West's advantage of cheap energy, which they now faced in accumulating wealth to protect the environment. Even more ironical are the subsequent subterfuges adopted by both North and South in preliminary discussions of the UNCED documents at Geneva in August 1991. While Third World countries, resentful of the lopsided relationship of dependency created by 20 years of so-called 'development assistance', criticized the West for attempting to impose a new 'environmental imperialism' on less developed countries — Malaysia even threatened to boycott the Earth Summit in protest against the 'assault' on the country's timber trade by the world's environmentalists[6] and used the gambit of interference with national sovereignty to oppose an inter national agreement on tropical rainforest destruction — the USA adopted the same tactic and argued against accepting a target for carbon dioxide emissions on the grounds that this would be interfering with *its* national sovereignty![7]

The attitude revealed in Margaret Thatcher's UN address, whereby the environment exists for the benefit of humanity whose task of 'protecting' it can be accomplished only through continued economic growth, is thus not limited to Western leaders but has infected those of Third World countries. Yet it is this attitude that Maurice Strong must change if the Earth Summit is to be meaningful.

Is there, then, an alternative?

Less than two months before Mrs Thatcher's speech, another scientist, the British Astronomer Royal, Sir Francis Graham-Smith, wrote a short account of lessons learned from the Voyager II space probe: 'The motive for Voyager was the search for knowledge, but the first gain has been acceptance of the view long held by experts that the Solar System holds no place other than Earth where life can exist.' This quiet statement has momentous implications for human responsibility. Should we, through carelessness, stupidity or greed, bring about the destruction of life on Earth, we destroy a phenomenon that exists nowhere else in the solar system. But are we anywhere near this cataclysm? Sir Francis continued:

> The more that is seen of the planets, their moons and their atmospheres, the more it is realized that conditions on Earth are special and precarious. We live within a thin skin on the surface of one of the smaller planets, balanced between the searing heat of Mercury and Venus and the freezing cold of the outer planets. Only Earth has an atmosphere which can sustain life.
>
> Voyager II will have been worthwhile if it does nothing more than make people realize that *there is a limit to the mess that can be made of this planet before life becomes impossible* [my stress].[8]

In the making of that mess the production of waste, especially waste gases, must rank among primary causes.

The contrast between Thatcherite optimism with its call for 'continued economic growth' and the astronomer royal's quiet warning, could not be greater. But it is politicians who have power and make news headlines, while the wider views and wisdom of astonomers are ignored.

Concepts of growth

What do Western politicians mean by 'growth'? Is it synonymous with 'development'?

In World Bank terminology growth is indicated by an increase in a country's Gross National Product (GNP) which, in turn, is calculated by adding its Gross Domestic Product GDP (that is, 'the final output of goods and services produced by the domestic economy, including net export of goods and services') to the net income factor from abroad, that is, 'income in the form of overseas workers' remittances, interest on loans, profits and other factor payments that residents receive from abroad less payments made for factor services'. In estimating the GDP most countries use the production method of combining the final outputs of the various sections of the economy (such as agriculture, manufacturing, services) 'from which the value of the inputs to production has been subtracted',[9] that is to say, the cost of initial raw materials is deducted but the resultant waste is not. For purposes of comparison GNP is usually expressed in dollars, 'growth' as an annual percentage increase.

Today the usefulness of this concept as it stands is questioned by environmentalists, feminists and Third World thinkers. Vandana Shiva, for example, argues that:

> The problem with the GNP is that it measures some costs as benefits (e.g. pollution control) and fails to measure other costs completely. Among these hidden costs is the new burden created by ecological devastation .... It is hardly surprising, therefore, that as GNP rises, it does not necessarily mean that either wealth or welfare increases proportionately.[10]

Lester R. Brown of the Worldwatch Institute points out that, while 'GNP includes depreciation of plant and equipment ... it does not take into account the depreciation of natural capital, including nonrenewable resources such as oil or renewable resources such as forests'. He concludes that, 'if all the environmental consequences of economic activity — from resource depletion to the numerous forms of environmental damage — were included, real economic progress would be much less than conventional economic measures indicate'.[11]

One can only speculate as to whether such considerations enter the thoughts of a Thatcher or a Bush, whose use of terms such as 'growth', or 'development' is more for emotive, or electoral, value than as scientific indicators of the human condition. In practice, 'continued economic growth' means little more than, as a minimum, there will be no decline in the material living standards of a large number of people in the world's richest countries whose support is necessary to keep present leaders, or like-minded successors, in power.

With all its defects the GNP of a country is still useful to highlight the problems, and defects, of the world today. We may query the accuracy, or even meaningfulness, of the figures, but there can be no disputing that 'this century has witnessed a phenomenal economic boom. By 1990 the world was producing 20 times as much in goods and services as in 1900, while industrial production had grown fiftyfold.'[12] Whatever 'the world' produced, it is also indisputable that rich countries have got richer, the majority of the poor poorer, and that, during the Reagan–Thatcher era of the 1980s, the gap between rich and poor widened in all countries.

By 1990 more than half the world's economic output was produced by three countries — the USA, West Germany and Japan, a truly remarkable situation when one recalls that two of these were defeated militarily in World

War II. Six countries top the league of the world's richest — Switzerland, Luxembourg, Bermuda, Japan, Iceland and Norway — with incomes per head of GNP of over US$20,000, while the USA has $19,780. In contrast, 47 countries, mainly in Africa and Asia, with a population of three billion people, have corresponding per capita incomes of US$500 or less. On a worldwide basis average incomes may have doubled since 1950, but, while citizens of rich countries got three times richer, those of the poorest have remained the same or declined.[13]

Until the 1970s it was possible to speak of 'development' in Third World countries. After the 1973 oil crisis, 'stagnation' was more appropriate; in the 1980s 'growth' has given way to 'retrogression'. During that decade three-quarters of all Latin American countries suffered a 10 per cent drop in per capita income, three-quarters of all African countries one of at least 15 per cent. On this basis 13 African countries, with a third of the continent's population, are now poorer than they were at the time of independence. Not only have poor countries become poorer but within them the poorest people have become even worse off in relation to the rich:

> In most countries between 60 and 70 per cent of the people earn less than the average. In countries as diverse as Malawi and Mexico, Côte d'Ivoire and Costa Rica, Malaysia and Kenya, the poorest two fifths of the people earn a quarter to a third of the average. In Peru, they earn less than a sixth.[14]

Inequality has increased. In 'communist' China the incomes of the richest fifth of the population are three times as great as those of the poorest fifth, in Bangladesh seven times, in India and the Philippines ten times, in Côte d'Ivoire 25 times and in Brazil 28 times as great.[15] Even in Britain the government eventually conceded that the rate of growth for the poorest 10 per cent was not twice the average, as they had at first maintained, but less than half, that is, 2.6 per cent, compared with 5.4 per cent.[16] In short, the poor had got poorer, the rich richer, a phenomenon which increased homelessness, the rise of cardboard cities and the appearance of young people begging on London streets might have caused any caring government to look twice at its statistics. When Mrs Thatcher spoke of the 'continued growth' necessary to produce wealth, she would have been both more accurate, and more honest, to speak of 'growth for *some*'.

The reasons underlying the failure of many Third World countries to follow their chosen path of development are too well known to require more than a brief summary. Development was conceived by the Western-educated élites who took over government on independence as achieving wealth through the same means as the West, namely industrialization. In this they had two disadvantages: lack of technological knowledge and absence of energy-producing resources. Multinational corporations provided the first — on their own terms, which included avoidance of regulations governing health and safety standards and protection of the environment. The results were seen *in extremis* in Bhopal. Importing oil provided the source of energy; but imports had to be paid for. Here the Green Revolution came to the rescue as cash crops for export replaced produce for home consumption, marginalizing the peasant population who were driven from poor land to worse, or off the land completely. Multinationals ran plantation economies using the landless peasantry as a new form of slave labour. Meanwhile, the oil-producing countries deposited their vast profits in the world's leading banks, which, unwilling to see the money lying idle, offered loans to Third World countries to invest in projects which, it was claimed, would be for their benefit. Hence the spate of mega-dam building, with its disastrous effects on the ecology and its displacement of indigenous peoples and wildlife. When the bubble burst with the oil crisis and resulting cutbacks in Western economies, Third World countries were left with external debts which it was impossible to pay and even the servicing of which kept them in perpetual bondage. At the same time decreased demand in the West caused a fall in prices for such commodities as formed the Third World's natural reserves but which, far too often, were their only reserves, for example, copper in Zambia, cocoa in Ghana, sisal in Tanzania.

Today the future of the 'peripheral' Third World is indissolubly bound to the 'centre' of the West through a perpetuation of the old imperial system in which local ruling élites play the role of former colonial servants and receive their rewards in the shape of large cars, large houses and hordes of servants. They cannot, however, escape the impending catastrophe by which industrialization means waste; and waste, in the form of greenhouse gases, now spells environmental cataclysm.

Ideologies of development

So much for growth, and its excesses. But what lies behind the assumption that 'growth' is a 'good thing'? The material advantages of a consumerist society are obvious, but is this *real* development? And where does the continued production of waste fit into our global future?

It may seem outrageous to suggest that previous theories of development were constructed in a vacuum, yet orthodox economics and all projects to raise Third World living standards to those of the world's richer countries were based on the assumption that the environment did not exist, that wealth could go on being created indefinitely. Development theorists were so busy keeping their eyes down to earth that they failed to notice what was going on over their heads and disregarded the fact that 'conditions on Earth are special and precarious'. For a contemporary theory of development to have validity, the starting points must be that 'there is no place other than Earth where life can exist' and that 'there is a limit to the mess that can be made of this planet before life becomes impossible'. The key word is 'limit'.

The first breach in the assumption that things could go on getting better and better came with the publication in 1972 of two seminal books. In *The*

Limits to Growth the Club of Rome shocked the Western world by pointing out what should have been obvious, that the resources on which modern civilization depended for its energy, mainly fossil fuels (oil, coal and gas) were finite and that at some future date they would be exhausted. *A Blueprint for Survival* by a team from *The Ecologist*, led by Edward Goldsmith, published the same year, caused less of a stir but showed greater ecological awareness and is still relevant. It begins bluntly:

> The principal defect of the industrial way of life with its ethos of expansion is that it is not sustainable. Its termination within the lifetime of someone born today is inevitable — unless it continues to be sustained for a while longer by an entrenched minority at the cost of imposing great suffering on the rest of mankind.[17]

Against this 'ethos of expansion' (or 'continued economic growth') *The Ecologist* group sets the goal of a 'stable society' on the scientific grounds that 'all ecosystems tend towards stability' and that 'the more diverse and complex the ecosystem the more stable it is'.[18] Stability is not stagnation, but 'a system's ability to ... survive in the face of environmental change', that is, 'change will be minimized and will occur only as is necessary to ensure adaptation to a changing environment'. The ecosphere, the sum total of inter-related systems that include all living creatures and the air, water or soil which is their habitat, is characterized by organization:

> The opposite of organization is randomness or, what is often referred to as entropy. In fact, it can be said that the ecosphere differs from the surface of the moon and probably from that of all the other planets in our solar system. [The Astronomer Royal would now make the probability a certainty], in that randomness, or entropy, have been progressively reduced, and organization, or negative entropy, have been correspondingly increased. According to the second law of thermodynamics, there is a tendency in all systems towards increasing randomness, or entropy. This must be so, since to move in this direction is to take the line of least resistance and also because whenever energy is converted (and this must occur during all behavioural processes) waste, or random parts must be generated.[19]

Though written 20 years ago, this passage is even more relevant today and, for present purposes, is important in showing where waste fits into the scheme of things.

The goal of stability had little appeal for governments, whether of the industrialized West or the Third World. At the same time, they could not ignore the fact that resources were finite and would one day run out. Hence the current emphasis on 'sustainable development', as popularized and given respectability in the UN World Commission on Environment and Development (WCED)'s report, *Our Common Future* (Brundtland Report, published in 1987). Unlike *The Limits to Growth*, the report is optimistic, predicting not 'ever-increasing environmental decay, poverty and hardship' but 'the possibility for a new era of economic growth ... based on policies that sustain and expand the environmental resource base'[20] 'Sustainable development' is defined broadly as 'development that meets the needs of the present without compromising the ability of future generations to meet their own needs'.[21]

Brundtland is wide-ranging in scope, from population problems and the use of pesticides to urbanization and the use of nuclear energy. Inevitably it suffers from the blandness and compromise of a committee production. Space, and relevance, permit consideration of three aspects only: its conclusions on energy, industrialization and waste.

On energy the Report recognizes the basic dilemma of development:

> To bring developing countries' energy up to industrialized country levels by the year 2025 would require increasing present global energy use by a factor of five. The planetary ecosystem could not stand this, especially if the increases were based on non-renewable fossil fuels. Threats of global warming and acidification of the environment most probably rule out even a doubling of energy based on present mixes of primary sources.[22]

The central argument of this book could not be put more concisely. Yet the commission remained optimistic. Unable to agree on the use of nuclear power, but equally aware of the Greenhouse Effect, its members fell back on energy conservation and the use of alternative sources as offering potential ways forward. How this is to be achieved so that 'given expected population growth, a five to tenfold increase in world industrial output can be anticipated by the time world population stabilizes sometime in the next century',[23] without meanwhile endangering 'the planetary ecosystem', remains one of those mysteries for which Brundtland supplies no clear answer.

On waste, the commission mentions the thousands of waste disposal sites in industrialized countries that need to be cleaned up and, sensibly but vaguely, argues that it is more important

> to reduce the amount of waste generated. This will reduce the volume that otherwise must be treated or disposed of. This is first and foremost a problem of industrialized countries. But it is also a problem in NICs [newly industrializing countries] and developing countries, where the same severe problems are expected.[24]

Waste is thus restricted in scope as the commission fails to recognize that the full implications of this 'end-product' are no less important than those of the sources of energy.

The fundamental flaw of the Brundtland Report, is that, despite the committee's international membership, in advocating more rapid economic growth in both industrial and developing countries it is permeated by a Western world view, the dominant ideological pattern of which, as seen by Vandana Shiva and Jayanta Bandyopadhyay,

> derives its driving force from a linear vision of progress, from a vision of historical evolution created in eighteenth and nineteenth century Western Europe and universalized throughout the world, especially in the post-war development decades. The linearity of history, pre-supposed in this theory of progress, created an ideology of development that equated development with economic growth, economic growth with expansion of the market economy, modernity with consumerism, and non-market economics with backwardness. The diverse traditions of the world, with their distinctive technological, ecological, economic, political and cultural structures, were driven by this new ideology to converge into a homogeneous monolithic order modelled on the particular evolution of the West.[25]

Shiva and Bandyopadhyay are right to site the origin of this 'linear vision of progress' in eighteenth- and nineteenth-century Western Europe, that is, arising from, and justifying, the growth of an expanding and buoyant industrial capitalism. In itself, however, the linear vision is neutral; there is no reason why humanity should not be guided by a linear vision of regression, rather than one of progress, as the British historian, J. B. Bury, in a book long out of print, *The Idea of Progress*, ably demonstrated. At its beginning with the Greeks, the Western world view was the antithesis of nineteenth-century amelioration. The Age of Gold, when all things lived and worked in harmony, was succeeded by the less perfect Age of Silver, which in turn gave way to the warlike Age of Bronze, and so to the undesirable present Age of Iron. The historical accuracy of this scheme was unimportant. What mattered was its acceptance as a guiding principle for perception and action, just as the 'linear vision of progress' is not merely accepted today but so thoroughly determines the thinking of politicians that it is impossible for them to conceive otherwise. Where the Greeks looked backwards, contrasting the obvious imperfections of the present with the mythical Age of Gold, our leaders are still imbued with the concept which Ramsay Macdonald expressed bathetically in the 1930s: 'We shall go on, and on, and on, and up, and up and up'!

Between Greek linear regression and modern linear progress, the medieval world looked neither back nor forward but, under the twin peaks of Pope and Emperor attempted to establish a stable society founded on reciprocal obligations. The rich man in his castle received tribute from the peasant at his gate and in return offered protection and security. There was a place for everyone, and everyone had his or her place. With Augustine's *City of God* as an ideal, lesser schoolmen-philosophers were free to calculate the number of angels accommodatable on the head of a pin.

The Golden Age, however, refused to die, reappearing in millennial form as Christian myth or revolutionary vision. When the successful twentieth-century stockbroker sings at Christmas:

> For lo! the days are hastening on
> By prophet-bards foretold,
> When with the ever-circling years
> Comes round the Age of Gold,
> When peace shall over all the Earth
> Its ancient splendours fling . . .

does he really believe in the Golden Age or subscribe, not to a linear, but to a cyclical world view of 'ever-circling years' destined to bring it round again? Whatever his vision, it is hardly likely to be that of the revolutionary poet Shelley:

> The world's great age begins anew,
> The golden years return,
> The Earth doth like a snake renew
> Her winter weeds outworn . . .

The poet's reptilian image is both a clue and a question. The progress of the seasons and of the natural world is basically cyclical. Is modern Western humanity's linear vision the mark of superior beings or merely an aberration from the natural order?

This is no academic or literary question, since it lies at the root of contemporary theories of development. Anthropological research reveals the continued existence of peoples whose universe is non-linear. In north-eastern Uganda the 'backward' and 'primitive' semi-pastoral Karimojong, like many other 'egalitarian' societies, follow an age-set system by which one generation succeeds another as elders. Each has its emblem, which members of the group praise in song or imitate in dance. In turn the Lions, the Mountains, the Gazelles and the Zebra become the leading generation, to be superceded by a further cycle of Lions, Mountains, Gazelles and Zebra. This is how it has always been and, so far as they are concerned, always will be. The women, too, belong either to the Tree generation or the Anthill, each succeeding the other *ad infinitum*. There is no progress, only repetition, as one hot, dry season repeats the pattern of its predecessor, and the rains, when they come (if they come) follow the cycle of previous years, the women prepare to plant sorghum and the young men to drive their huge herds of cattle to watering-places on the periphery of their land.[26]

This different world view implies different modes of perception. During the course of a song in praise of his favourite ox, a song which he, like his fellows, has composed, a young Karimojong man may sing of himself as the ox's owner (and thus distinct from it), as the 'father of the ox' (and thus related to it) and as the ox itself (and thus identified with it). In terms of Aristotleian logic — a thing is either A or not-A — this is an impossible contradiction; yet, in the Karimojong 'paralogic', it happens.[27] And it can happen only because there are other, equally valid ways of viewing the world than the current Western linear vision.

Were the Western world view limited to those industrialized countries that produced it, there would be some justification for adopting it. The tragedy is that, as Shiva and Bandyopadhyay point out, this 'homogeneous monolithic order modelled on the particular evolution of the West' has become universalized irrespective of appropriateness. Sachs traces the beginnings of this trend to President Truman's inauguration speech to Congress on 20 January 1949, when he defined the greater part of the world as 'underdeveloped areas' for which 'the key to prosperity and peace' lay in 'greater production'. Hence his plan for a programme of technical assistance to 'relieve the suffering of these peoples' through 'industrial activities' and so give them 'a higher standard of living'.[28] Hence also division of the world into developed and underdeveloped countries, a division that could be overcome only through 'economic growth' and adoption of the Western idea of progress. The path of world history was thus determined by Western economic and cultural hegemony, with the vast majority of humanity, despite the diversity of their traditions, lumped together as backward, in contrast to those who were 'ahead'.

In this attempted transformation the leaders of the West were at first supported by the idealism of their peoples, who genuinely believed in the desirability of a New World Order after World War II, and by the leaders of newly independent Third World states, whose mainly Western education gave them the same view of progress, by which planning and economic growth were to supercede traditional backwardness and the mental habits of generations.

The 'trickle-down' theory of development failed to work as the poor in Third World countries became visibly poorer and development itself dissolved in debt; industrialization produced not benefits but pollution and waste; and peasants were marginalized by mining operations or the excessive demands for land of the Green Revolution. Only then did a new generation of thinkers arise to query the assumptions of the old, a generation not limited to the Third World but burgeoning also in the West.

Ironically, the view of development as industrialization, particularly the creation of heavy industry as typified by the Soviet Union and Eastern Europe, with their high production of waste and pollution of the environment, has already been superceded in more technologically advanced countries by yet a further stage of linear progression. With the coming of the microchip, computerization and robotization have replaced traditional forms of labour, but the Brave New World of 1930s scientific visionaries like H. G. Wells, in which machines would do the dirty work and human beings, freed from working more than three days a week, have opportunities to become 'fully human', has not been realized. The supposition that labour, under capitalist modes of production, offered no individual satisfaction to the worker and was inevitably degrading led Harold Laski to proclaim that

'Man is what he is in his leisure time'; thus increased leisure was necessary for human fulfilment. In practice, today's leisure is the 'leisure' of the permanently unemployed, the job seekers and the homeless. The radical transformation of society in Thatcherite Britain has been the replacement of traditional classes by new groupings of: a permanently secure technological élite; a vast and less secure mass employed in unproductive industries, including finance, designed to 'service' them; and non-workers. The end result, in André Gorz's words, is the creation of a new 'servile class':

> The unequal distribution of work in the economic sphere coupled with the unequal distribution of free time created by technical innovations thus leads to a situation in which one section of the population is able to buy extra time from the other and the latter is reduced to serving the former .... A 'servile' class, which had been abolished by the industrialization of the post-war period, is again emerging.[29]

The existence of this class is less obvious than in the days when people of affluence employed huge armies of servants but only because 'their personal services are to a large extent socialized or industrialized: the majority of servants are employed by service enterprises which hire out labour'. The result is

> a social system which is unable to distribute, manage or employ this new-found free time; a system fearful of the expansion of this time, yet which does its utmost to increase it, and which, in the end, can find no purpose for it other than seeking all possible means of turning it into money.[30]

In Gorz's view this system has now reached a state of crisis. It marks the collapse of the 'utopia', that is, 'the vision of the future on which a civilization bases its projects, establishes its ideal goals and builds its hopes', in short, its values. Nothing remains of the 'industrialist utopia' which

> promised us that the development of the forces of production and the expansion of the economic sphere would liberate humanity from scarcity, injustice and misery; that these developments would bestow on humanity the sovereign power to dominate Nature, and with this the sovereign power of self-determination.[31]

Perhaps it is this desire to 'dominate Nature' that contains within it the seeds of suicide. Yet it is this model which the 'advanced' world has thrust upon underdeveloped countries and seen accepted by their leaders.

Even if one does not accept it fully, Gorz's analysis is valuable for the light it throws on what happened to the UK during the Thatcher decade. Howard Brenton's diagnosis of the assault on cultural values offers a useful counterpoint. Like many writers Brenton felt that 'during the decade we were overtaken by something malevolent ... as if some kind of evil was abroad in our society, a palpable degradation of the spirit'. To him

> Thatcherism, like all authoritarian dogmas, was brightly coloured. Writers were trying to get at the darkness, the social cruelty and suffering behind the numbingly, neon-bright phrase — 'the right to choose', 'freedom under the law', 'rolling back the state'. It was as if a hyperactive demon was flitting about amongst us, seeking with its touch to turn everything into a banal conformity, a single-value culture with one creed — 'by their sales returns shall ye know them'.[32]

When the crash came in 1987, and in 1988 the beggars appeared on London streets, 'a curious peeling away from reality set in. What people in public life said on television about the country seemed finally to lose any relation at all to what it was like to live in it or to walk down any street'.[33]

Thatcherite values extolled a parochial vulgarity. Outside the UK nothing really existed, whether it was the Commonwealth or the European Community. Her notorious 'Rejoice!' over the Falklands came from a grocer's daughter, not a Conservative prime minister. Her greatest victory was not over General Galtieri but over Arthur Scargill and the miners, the last representatives of the old industrial order that robotization was destined to supplant. Throughout their years of struggle the miners had retained a sense of community which even the decimation of the industry could not destroy. They, and their womenfolk, stood for an older tradition of caring and co-operation, the antithesis of Thatcher's infamous dictum, 'There's no such thing as society, only individuals and their families'. Miners were able to be both highly individualistic and members of their families because they belonged to their own society. Left undefined, Thatcherite individualism appeared for what it was — the selfish domination of the have-nots by the haves, the rise of the Yuppy order, the subservience of everything to a market that, far from producing efficiency through competition, was loaded, like the tax system, medical care and company perks, in favour of the rich.

The system survived because Thatcher was able to put across her beliefs in the black-and-white simplistic vision of a populist politician and because the British people were offered a boom in consumer spending. While Thatcher herself extolled the virtues of 'thrift' and 'good housekeeping', the banks and building societies offered unlimited credit and the property market soared as houses were bought, not to be lived in, but for selling at a quick profit. In the enterprise culture there were easy pickings for those with money and a minimum of enterprise, while those who showed enterprise by starting small businesses were the first to suffer when the bubble burst.

Even with Thatcher gone, the legacy of consumerist values remains. No home in Britain today is 'complete' without its washing machine, its video and, above all, its car. That these are considered necessities for newly-weds shows the extent to which this insidious corruption has spread. Among the British, ownership of a Porsche or a Volvo is a symbol of status; among the 'backward' Karimojong the ability to compose a song or to dance well is the criterion for respect by one's peers. If the replacement of creative ability by ownership of a mass of metal marks the end of the development road, are we more — or less — *human* than contemporary primitives? When the Berlin wall came down and thousands of East Germans drove their dilapidated cars into the West, was it freedom that spurred them on, or thoughts of a new fridge?

Meanwhile, the three-day working week that robotization promised had mysteriously disappeared. Somehow the privileged members of Gorz's élite found themselves not only working harder than ever and for even longer hours but subject to new and greater forms of stress. For those working in London, the daily strain of travelling on an uncertain, underfunded and rapidly deteriorating rail network with increased possibilities of delays from snow or IRA bombs, showed itself in the rise in heart diseases. When the rich take to valium, the rejected to cocaine and the 'servile class' resort to television, Gorz's collapse of utopia is only too evident.

Personal conclusion

I find it impossible to write a satisfactory ending to this book. There are too many unknowns, too few certainties. Much depends on the type of world we wish to achieve and this in turn depends both on the values we hold, our ideals, and on the possibilities of achieving them, the practical politics.

The basic dilemmas of our present situation are how to reconcile continued economic growth with the dangers now threatening the fragile ecosystem of planet Earth, and whether the Western scheme of things, now set as a goal, offers the best chance for the peoples of the world to develop as human beings.

At the heart of everything lies the question of waste. If there is one lesson to be drawn from what I have written, it is that any theory of development must look not only at the beginning of the process — the limits imposed by availability of resources, but also at the end — the limits determined by the amount of waste produced. When waste takes the form of greenhouse gases and there is scientific certainty that continuation at the present emission rate will bring about global warming, even if doubts remain about the precise effects on different regions of the Earth, we have no option but to take notice. Logically, there would appear to be a choice between three routes:

- we do nothing to prevent a hotter planet beyond preparing for such changes as may be most probable, for example, constructing defensive sea walls to protect the worlds' most vulnerable places against inundation;

- at the opposite end, we alter our lifestyles completely, forgoing all use of fossil fuels, consigning our cars to the scrap heap in favour of horse-drawn transport, and using alternative sources of energy, such as solar or wind power, that do not have the same disastrous effects;
- we aim at a compromise, sustainable development, which, through conservation of energy, use of alternative power supplies, recycling of waste, clean technology and minimal use of hazardous fuels, may be possible.

How feasible is 'sustainable development' as a practicable proposition? At the Pugwash workshop mentioned in Chapter 9, where the Chinese spelt out their energy requirements, Professor José Goldemberg, former energy minister of Brazil, outlined a plan for a 'low-energy' future. He and his colleagues have calculated that an average world consumption of just over 1kW of energy per person, used with maximum efficiency, would be sufficient to supply adequate lighting, space heating, space cooling, food preservation, cooking, hot water and leisure at a level similar to that enjoyed by European countries in the 1970s. At present the world average is double this figure; in the USA it is ten times as great, but in China it is only 0.8kW per person. The Chinese plan, however, to increase their energy consumption to 2.5kW by 2030. Obviously, if Goldemberg's target is to be achieved, there must be considerable reduction in the USA (and other Western countries), while the Chinese will have to amend their proposals. In Goldemberg's low-energy world there will be no increase in overall production. Energy efficiency will, however, be the first requirement, renewable forms of energy become of primary importance, and coal burning will be cut dramatically.[34]

I am in no position to query the theoretical basis of the Goldemberg plan and, at this level, sustainable development would appear a possibility. Similarly, technology may provide the answer for coping with other forms of waste, though the long-term disposal of nuclear waste is less clear. It is when one reaches the practical aspects that doubts arise. In Chapter 9 we saw how difficult it was for politicians to reach agreement on the necessary steps to be taken, even when scientists demonstrated the necessity. In this chapter I have taken the argument a stage further to show why this happens. The crux of the matter is that the world's present leaders, from all quarters, are so imbued with the ideology of growth that they cannot conceive of an alternative, at least not for their part of the world. I exempt from this stricture one leader who takes the prospect of global warming only too seriously — the Hon. Bikenibeu Paeniu, Prime Minister of Tuvalu, whose life is dominated by the fear that the atolls for which he is responsible will disappear beneath the waters.

But can one convince a George Bush of the need for action any more than one could convince a Margaret Thatcher? And, even if one could, would he have the courage to tell the American people not merely to give up that second car but to tighten their belts? For what? So that a little island in the

Pacific could survive a few years longer? Possibly not. So that the US wheat belt could avoid the prospect of future aridity? Possibly (but remember what happened to Big Green and what Bush's scientists are telling him). And would people believe him? Until a disaster happens, humanity in general prefers to believe that it cannot happen, and to the hypothetical man-in-the-street the prospect of global disaster appears even less likely than a major earthquake in the UK.

Perhaps a concerted push from environmentalists, scientists and enlightened politicians may yet wake up the world before it is too late. My personal inclination is to doubt it. As one looks around the world, the effects of greed, short-sightedness and stupidity — from the desecration of the polar regions to the massacre of tropical forests, from the *Exxon Valdez* to Chernobyl and the deliberate incineration of Kuwaiti oil wells, from the effects of all forms of waste examined in this book: human, domestic, chemical, nuclear, mining, pesticides, fertilizers and obnoxious gases — there is little to suggest that, apart from a few rainforest Indians, humanity cares very much for the fragile planet on which we live. Perhaps it is the fate of humanity to go the way of the dinosaurs and be succeeded by a more caring species. If so, will it be any great loss, except to those immediately concerned? The great achievements of the human race are in music, art, philosophy, literature, medicine, not in the high-technology of destruction in which that ultimate in hypocriscy and double standards, the Gulf War, demonstrated our proficiency. It will be a pity to lose the products of human creativity; but, for the suffering our actions have caused to other inhabitants of this planet, there should be no mercy.

Poets have always been far-seeing. Symbolic of our age is the aerosol can with its CFCs, which, in Tony Harrison's poem, 'V', is fittingly celebrated as the means for inscribing obscene four-letter words on tombstones in a Leeds churchyard. Does this mark the final breakdown of the 'human' with its counterpart of 'nice' individuals who, shocked by Harrison's repeated declamation of the words on television, demanded, not action against the sprayers, but the banning of the poem so that they could continue to bury their heads in the sand?

When the Earth finally warms up and the worst happens, we shall not be able to say we were not warned. Over 50 years ago Louis MacNiece concluded his 'Bagpipe Music' with a prognostication of disaster. At the time it was the imminence of war that threatened. Twenty years later his words were used to predict nuclear catastrophe. Today, for the first time, there is the possiblity that, as the prospect of a nuclear winter decreases, to be replaced by the threat of an over-torrid summer, what was written as metaphor may become reality:

> The glass is falling hour by hour.
> The glass may fall for ever,
> But if you break the bloody glass,
> You won't hold up the weather.

Shall we be third time lucky, or unlucky?

Notes

1. *New Scientist* 20 July 1991
2. MacKenzie 1991
3. As reported in the *Guardian* 9 November 1989
4. Genesis 1:26
5. *Guardian* 18 April 1990; *New Scientist* 28 April 1990
6. *New Scientist* 24 August 1991
7. *Guardian* 5 August 1991
8. Ibid. 26 August 1989
9. *WR 1990−91* p. 251
10. Shiva 1989 p. 7
11. Brown, L. R. 1990 p. 8−9
12. Lean, Hinrichsen and Markham 1990 pp. 41
13. Ibid.
14. Ibid.
15. Ibid.
16. *Observer* 8 April 1990
17. Goldsmith *et al* 1972 p. 14
18. Ibid. p. 19
19. Ibid. pp. 88−90
20. Quoted in De la Court 1990 p. 12
21. Ibid. p. 19
22. Quoted Ibid. p. 58
23. Ibid. pp. 61, 68
24. Ibid. pp. 70−71
25. *The Ecologist* 19:3. 1989. Quoted De la Court 1990 pp. 128−9
26. See Gourlay 1970, 1971
27. Gourlay 1972
28. Quoted Sachs 1990
29. Gorz 1989 p. 6
30. Ibid. p. 7
31. Ibid. p. 8
32. Brenton 1990
33. Ibid.
34. Leggett 1989

Acronyms and abbreviations

ACP	(UK) Advisory Committee on Pesticides
AFRC	(British) Agriculture and Food Research Council
AGR	Advanced Gas-cooled Reactor
ARE	Asian Rare Earths Sdn Bhd
ATSDR	(US) Agency for Toxic Substances and Disease Registry
BCL	Bougainville Copper Ltd.
BHP	Broken Hills Propriety
BMA	British Medical Association
bn	billion
BNF	British Nuclear Fuels
BRGM	(French) Bureau of Geological and Mining Research
BRRI	Bureau de Reportage et de Recherche d'informations
BWR	Boiling water reactor
CEA	(French) Commissariat for Atomic Energy
CEGB	Central Electricity Generating Board
CERES	Coalition of Environmentally Responsible Economies
CERLA	(US) Comprehensive Environmental Response, Compensation and Liability Act
CFCs	chlorofluorocarbons
COPA	(UK) Control of Pollution Act 1974
CRA	Conzinc Riotinto of Australia
CRDI	Congolaise de Récupération de Déchets Industriels
CSCE	Conference on Security and Cooperation in Europe
CSIRO	Australian Government research organization
DDT	dichloro-diphenyl-trichloro-ethane
DENR	(Philippine) Department of Environment and Natural Resources
DEP	(US) Department of Environmental Protection
DNR	(US) Department of Natural Resources
DOE	(US) Department of Energy
DoE	(UK) Department of the Environment

DTI   (UK) Department of Trade and Industry

EC   European Community
ECA   (SA) Environmental Conservation Act
EDF   Electricité de France
EEB   European Environmental Bureau
EEC   European Economic Community
ENDS   Environmental Data Services
EPA   (US) Environmental Protection Agency
EQI   Environmental Quality International
EURATOM European Atomic Energy Community Treaty 1957

FBI   (US) Federal Bureau of Investigation
FGD   flue gas desulphurization
FoE   Friends of the Earth

G7   Group of seven advanced industrial nations
GDP   Gross domestic product
GEMS   Global Environmental Monitoring System
GESAMP   (UN) Group of Experts on the Scientific Aspects of Marine Pollution
GNP   Gross national product

HCB   hexachlorobenzene
HCFCs   hydrochlorofluorocarbons
HCH   hexachlorocyclohexane
HFCs   hydrofluorocarbons
HGV   heavy goods vehicle
HLW   high level (radioactive) waste
HMIP   Her Majesty's Inspectorate of Pollution

IAEA   International Atomic Energy Authority
ICI   Imperial Chemicals Industry
ILW   Intermediate level (radioactive) waste
IMO   International Maritime Organization
INFORM   New York environmental research group
IPCC   (UN) Intergovernmental Panel on Climatic Change
IPM   Integrated Pest Management
IRRI   International Rice Research Institute

KPC   Kaltim Prime Coal

LDC   London Dumping Convention / International Convention for the Prevention of Marine Pollution by Dumping of Wastes and Other Matter 1972

LLW	Low level (radioactive) waste
m	million
MAC	maximum acceptable concentration
MACT	maximum available control technology
MAFF	(UK) Ministry of Agriculture, Fisheries and Food
MARPOL	International Convention for the Prevention of Pollution from Ships 1973
MEP	Member of the European Parliament
MERC	Maine Energy Recovery Company
mg/l	milligrams per litre
MoD	(UK) Ministry of Defence
MPCA	Minnesota Pollution Control Agency
MSW	Municipal solid waste
NASA	(US) National Aeronautics and Space Agency
NERC	(UK) National Environmental Research Council
NIMBY	Not-in-my-backyard
NIREX	Nuclear Industry Radioactive Waste Executive
NRA	(UK) National Rivers Authority
NRPB	(UK) National Radiological Protection Board
OAU	Organization of African Unity
OECD	Organization for Economic Co-operation and Development
OED	Oxford English Dictionary
OTA	(US) Office of Technology Assessment
PAH	polycyclic aromatic hydrocarbon
PCBs	polychlorinated biphenyls
PCDF	polychlorinated dibenzo-furans
PDV	phocine distemper virus
PFA	pulverized fuel ash
PIC	products of incomplete combustion
PNG	Papua New Guinea
ppb	parts per billion
ppm	parts per million
PVC	polyvinyl chloride
PWR	Pressurized Water Reactor
RCEP	Royal Commission on Environmental Pollution
RCRA	(US) Resource Conservation and Recovery Act
RORSAT	Radar Ocean Reconnaissance Satellite
RTG	Radioisotope Themonuclear Generator
RTZ	**Rio Tinto-Zinc**
SDI	(US) Strategic Defense Initiative

SERI	Solar Energy Research Institute
SRI	Socially Responsible Investment
SWAPO	South-West Africa People's Organization
TCDD	tetrachlorodibenzo-paradioxin
THORP	Thermal Oxide Reprocessing Plant
TOES	The Other Economic Summit
3M	Minnesota Mining and Manufacturing Company
TWN	Third World Network
UKAEA	United Kingdom Atomic Energy Authority
UNCED	United Nations Conference on Environment and Development
UNEP	United Nations Environment Programme
UNITA	National Union for the Total Independence of Angola
USAID	US Agency for International Development
WCED	World Conference on Environment and Development
WDA	Waste Disposal Authority
WHO	(UN) World Health Organization
WIPP	Waste Isolation Pilot Plant
WWF	World Wildlife Fund

Bibliography

In alphabetical order of author or acronym used in Notes

Ackefors, Hans A. and Enell, Magnus E. (1990) 'Discharge of nutrients from Swedish fish farming to adjacent sea areas'. *Ambio* xix, 1. February 1990 pp. 28–35

ACOPS Advisory Committee on Pollution of the Sea (1985–86) *1985–86 Yearbook*. London. ACOPS

Agarwal, A., Chopra, R. and Sharma, K. (eds) (1982) *The State of India's Environment 1982. A Citizens' Report*. Centre for Science and Environment, New Delhi

Agarwal, A. and Narain, S. (eds) (1985) *The State of India's Environment 1984–85. The Second Citizens' Report*. Centre for Science and Environment, New Delhi

Anderson, Ian (1990) 'An end to chemical fertilizers?' *New Scientist* 8 December 1990

Anon. (1989a) 'Sud's Lore'. *Green Magazine* October 1989 pp. 54–58

——(1990a) 'Fuming Mad'. *Green Magazine* June 1990 pp. 22–4

——(1990b) 'Fuming Mad'. *Green Magazine* Summertime 1990 p.26

Ardill, John (1988) '98 water sources contaminated'. *Guardian* 19 November 1988

Beard, Jonathan (1989) 'Gravity puts the squeeze on sewage'. *New Scientist* 3 June 1989

Bedding, James (1989) 'Money down the drain'. *New Scientist* 15 April 1989

Beder, Sharon (1990) 'Sun, surf and sewage'. *New Scientist* 14 July 1990

Bennetto, Jason (1990) 'Radioactive waste leaking into London's tap-water supplies'. *Observer* 8 July 1990

Bergman, David (1990) 'Bhopal polluters accused of hypocrisy'. *New Scientist* 24 November 1990

Booth, Nicholas (1989) 'Space junk'. *Green Magazine* November 1989 pp. 44–7

Borgese, Elizabeth Mann and Ginsburg, Nathan (eds) (1985) *Ocean Yearbook 5*. Chicago and London. University of Chicago Press.

Bowcott, Owen (1989) 'Winds lift gloom over seaside slime'. *Guardian* 9 August 1989

Bown, William (1990) 'Europe's forests fall to acid rain'. *New Scientist* 11 August 1990

Brenton, Howard (1990) 'The art of survival'. *Guardian* 29 November 1990

Briggs, Shirley A. (1990) '"Silent Spring": the view from 1990'. *The Ecologist* 20:2. March/April 1990 pp. 54–60

Brown, Lester R. (1990) 'The Illusion of progress' in Worldwatch Institute *State of the World 1990* pp. 3–16 London, Sydney, Wellington. Unwin Paperbacks

——and Young, John E. (1990) 'Feeding the world in the nineties' in Worldwatch Institute *State of the World 1990* pp. 59–78. London, Sydney, Wellington. Unwin Paperbacks

Brown, Paul (1988) 'Britain the dump of Europe'. *Guardian* 31 August 1988

——(1989a) 'The dump at the bottom of the world'. *Guardian* 20 February 1989

——(1989b) 'Protesters warn US on pollution in the Antarctic'. *Guardian* 24 February 1989

——(1989c) 'PCB threat to ocean mammals'. *Guardian* 31 August 1989

——(1990a) 'Drinking water is unsafe'. *Guardian* 21 July 1990

——(1990b) 'Shell could not find pipe corrosion'. *Guardian* 5 December 1990

——(1990c) 'The heat is on'. *Guardian* 4 May 1990

Brown, Tim (1990) 'The ozone paradox'. *Guardian* 4 May 1990
BRRI Bureau de Reportage et de Recherche d'Informations (1989) *Nos déchets toxiques. L'Afrique a faim: v'la nos poubelles*. Geneva. Edition du CETIM (Centre Europe — Tiers Monde)
Buerk, Michael (1989) 'Poland's lethal legacy'. *Observer* 12 November 1989
Charles, Dan (1989) 'Will these lands ne'er be clean?' *New Scientist* 24 June 1989
Charlesworth, Kate (1989) 'Life, the Universe and almost everything: Down below'. *New Scientist* 11 March 1989
Clouston, Erland (1990) 'Those sweet dying waters'. *Guardian* 16 March 1990
Cook, Stephen and Halsall, Martyn (1989) 'The nets draw tighter'. *Guardian* 15 December 1989
Cross, Michael (1990a) 'Nuclear power goes to the polls.' *New Scientist* 17 February 1990
——(1990b) 'Public opposition slows down Japan's nuclear plans'. *New Scientist* 2 June 1990
De la Court, Thijs (1990) *Beyond Brundtland: Green Development in the 1990s*. London. Zed Books
Denison, Richard (1989) 'Ash utilization: an idea before its time?' Extracts in *Waste Not* No. 48, 28 March 1989
DoE Department of the Environment (1989a) *Digest of Environmental Protection and Water Statistics* No. 12. London HMSO
——(1989b) *Dioxins in the Environment*. London HMSO
Dudley, Nigel (1988) 'Acid rain and wildlife'. *Environment Now* No. 7 August 1988
ECA *Environmental Conservation Act* (1982) South African Government publication
EEB European Environmental Bureau (nd1) 'Locating and assessing soil contamination' in TWN 1989 pp. 111–14
——(nd2) 'The crisis of old waste dumps' in TWN 1989 pp. 89–93
Erlichman, James (1989a) 'On the chemical treadmill'. *Guardian* 15 December 1989
——(1989b) 'Crop spray tests for cancer risk'. *Guardian* 17 July 1989
——(1989c) 'How alar was praised — and then condemned'. *Guardian* 20 October 1989
——(1990) 'The deadly cocktails'. *Guardian* 2 March 1990
Ewins, Peter J. and Bazely, Dawn R. (1989) 'Jungle law in Thailand's forests'. *New Scientist* 18 November 1989
Fannin, Robert (1990) 'Eternal voyage across a sea of plastic'. *Guardian* 28 September 1990
Flavin, Christopher (1990) 'Slowing global warming' in Worldwatch Institute *State of the World 1990* pp. 17–38. London, Sydney, Wellington. Unwin Paperbacks
French, Hilary F. (1990) 'Clearing the air' in Worldwatch Institute *State of the World 1990* pp. 98–118
Gabb, Annabella (1989) 'March of the waste merchants'. *Management Today*. October 1989 pp. 58–64
Goldsmith, Edward; Allen, Robert; Allaby, Michael; Davull, John; Lawrence, Sam (1972) *A Blueprint for Survival*. London. Tom Stacey
Goldsmith, Edward and Hildyard, Nicholas (eds) (1988) *The Earth Report: Monitoring the Battle for our Environment*. London. Mitchell Beazley
——(1990) *The Earth Report 2: Monitoring the Battle for our Environment* London. Mitchell Beazley
Gooding, Kenneth (1989) 'Preparing for the green decade'. *Financial Times* 2 October 1989
Gorz, André (1989) *Critique of Economic Reason*. London, New York. Verso
Gourlay, K. A. (1970) 'Trees and anthills: songs of Karimojong women's groups'. *African Music* 4:4 pp. 114–21
——(1971) 'The making of Karimojong cattle songs'. *Mila* II:I pp. 34–8. University of Nairobi. Institute of African Studies
——(1972) 'The ox and identification'. *Man* (NS) 7:2 pp. 244–54
——(1988) *Poisoners of the Seas*. London. Zed Books
Green, Patrick and Young, Shelagh (1990) 'Radioactive omissions'. *Green Magazine* May 1990 pp. 22–5

Greenpeace International (1988) 'International trade in toxic wastes: policy and data analysis' in TWN 1989 pp. 39–52

Gribbin, John (1988) 'The Greenhouse Effect'. *New Scientist* 22 October 1988

——(1989) 'How to swamp the world'. *Guardian* 7 March 1989

Hadsley, Neville (1990) 'The bottle to turn back the clock'. *Guardian* 28 September 1990

Hammond, Ian (1989) 'CRA — the Australian connection. *Engineering and Mining Journal* August 1989

Harrison, Olivia (1990) 'Spray drift'. *Green Magazine* February 1990

Harwood, John and Reijnders, Peter (1988) 'Seals, sense and sensibility'. *New Scientist* 15 October 1988

Hecht, Jeff (1988) 'Waste burial blamed for earthquakes'. *New Scientist* 1 September 1988

——(1990) 'Sunlight gives toxic waste a tanning'. *New Scientist* 14 April 1990

Hinrichsen, Don (1988) 'Acid rain and forest decline' in Goldsmith, E. and Hildyard, N. (1988) pp. 65–78

HoC House of Commons Environment Committee (1986) *First Report: Radioactive Waste*. London. HMSO

——(1989) *Second Report: Toxic Waste*. London. HMSO

Holliday, F.G.T. (Chairman) (1984) *Report of the Independent Review of Disposal of Radioactive Waste in the North-east Atlantic*. London. HMSO

Holliman, Jonathan (1989) 'Nuclear dump provokes protest in Japan' in TWN 1989 pp. 94–5

Hughes, Sylvia (1990) 'Secret report attacks French nuclear programme'. *New Scientist* 17 March 1990

Jacobson, Jodi (1990) 'Holding back the sea' in Worldwatch Institute *State of the World 1990* pp. 79–97

Joyce, Christopher (1990) 'US fails in bid to play down global warming threat'. *New Scientist* 28 April 1990

Laidler, Keith (1989) 'A whole lot of mining going on'. *New Scientist* 26 August 1989

Lake, Anthony (1990) 'Talks sink plans to clean up Mediterranean'. *New Scientist* 3 November 1990

Lean, Geoffrey (1987a) 'Poison spray incidents ignored by inspectors'. *Observer* 26 April 1987

——(1987b) 'Pollution by farmers rising fast'. *Observer* 23 August 1987

——(1988) 'Waste tip gas puts thousands at risk'. *Observer* 26 June 1988

——(1989) 'Sunshine State plans a green future'. *Observer* 3 September 1989

——(1990a) 'Broads becoming a wildlife desert, says secret report'. *Observer* 2 September 1990

——(1990b) 'Ministers weaken nitrate pollution control'. *Observer* 21 January 1990

Lean, Geoffrey and Ghazi, Polly (1990) 'Britain's buried poison'. *Observer*/FoE investigation. *Observer* 4 February 1990

Lean, Geoffrey; Hinrichsen, Don and Markham, Adam (1990) *Atlas of the Environment*. London. Arrow Books

Lean, Geoffrey and Pearce, Fred (1989) 'Your tap water pure or poisoned'. *Observer* 6 August 1989

Lean, Geoffrey and Schneider, Mycle (1990) 'France admits nuclear plans threaten Britain'. *Observer* 18 March 1990

Leggett, Jeremy (1989) 'The coals of calamity'. *Guardian* 15 August 1989

Long, Simon (1990) 'More than a panda'. *Guardian* 9 March 1990

Lowe, Marcia D. (1990) 'Cycling into the future' in Worldwatch Institute *State of the World 1990* pp. 119–34. London, Sydney, Wellington. Unwin Paperbacks

Lowry, David (1988) 'Corrupt to the core'. *Environment Now* 7 August 1988

MacKenzie, Debora (1989a) 'If you can't treat it, ship it'. *New Scientist* 1 April 1989

——(1989b) 'Spanish eyes turn to poison dump'. *New Scientist* 1 April 1989

——(1989c) 'Italian firm first with "truly biodegradable" plastic'. *New Scientist* 25 November 1989

——(1989d) 'Half-burnt toxins turn up as dioxins in milk'. *New Scientist* 12 August 1989

——(1990a) 'Europe's agriculture policy "destroys the environment"'. *New Scientist* 28 April 1990

——(1990b) 'Cheaper alternatives for CFCs'. *New Scientist* 30 June 1990

——(1991) 'Strong words to save the planet'. *New Scientist* 10 August 1991

MacQuitty, Miranda (1988) 'Pollution beneath the Golden Gate'. *New Scientist* 30 June 1988

Magnusen, Ed. (1985) 'A problem that cannot be buried'. *Time*. 14 October 1985

Malm, Olaf; Pfeiffer, Wolfgang C.; Souza, Cristina M. M. and Reuther, Rudolf (1990) 'Mercury pollution due to gold mining in the Madeira River Basin, Brazil'. *Ambio* xix, 1. February 1990 pp. 11–15

Manz, George Martin (1989) 'Canadian joint venture dumps copper tailings into Calancan Bay' in TWN 1989 pp. 60–61

Marquez, Gabriel Garcia (1989) *Love in the Time of Cholera*. London. Penguin Books.

Maywald, Armin; Zeschmar-Lahl, Barbara, and Lahl, Uwe (1988) 'Water fit to drink' in Goldsmith and Hildyard 1988 pp. 79–88

Medvedev, Zhores A. (1990) 'The environmental destruction of the Soviet Union'. *The Ecologist* 20:1 pp. 24–9

Melamed, Dennis (1990) 'Congress gets tough on heavy polluters'. *New Scientist* 3 November 1990

Milgrom, Lionel (1988) 'Chemical crowns for pollution-free waste'. *New Scientist* 29 September 1988

Mills, Stephen (1989) 'Salmon farming's unsavoury side'. *New Scientist* 29 April 1989

Milne, Roger (1989a) 'The waste trail leads south'. *New Scientist* 1 April 1989

——(1989b) 'Nirex to agree on short list for national waste dump'. *New Scientist* 14 January 1989

——(1989c) 'Parasite in farm waste threatens water supplies'. *New Scientist* 29 July 1989

——(1990a) 'Burial mounds planned for over-the-hill reactors'. *New Scientist* 7 July 1990

——(1990b) 'CFC clampdown eases pressure on the ozone layer'. *New Scientist* 7 July 1990

Moody, Roger (1991) *Plunder!* Partizans/CAFCA. London, New Zealand

Nicholson, Sally (1990) 'Gold mining threat to Amazonia'. *WWF News* April 1990

O'Neill, Bill (1989) 'Nuclear safety after Chernobyl' *New Scientist* 24 June 1989

——(1990) 'Venice turns the tide on its polluted lagoon'. *New Scientist* 3 February 1990

O'Neill, Graeme (1990) 'Destroy-it-yourself treatment for toxic waste'. *New Scientist* 30 June 1990

Pain, Stephanie (1988) 'How the heat trap will wreak ecological havoc'. *New Scientist* 15 October 1988

——(1990a) 'On the edge of disaster'. *New Scientist* 28 April 1990

——(1990b) 'Dolphin virus threatens last remaining monk seals'. *New Scientist* 3 November 1990

Parker, Dave (1989) 'PCBs: the poison catch'. *Green Magazine* October 1989 pp. 18–21

——(1990) 'Death of the dolphins'. *Green Magazine* January 1990 pp. 23–5

Pathmarajah, Meera and Meith, Nikki (1985) 'A regional approach to marine environmental problems in East Africa and the Indian Ocean' in Borgese and Ginsburg 1985. Chicago and London. University of Chicago Press

Patterson, Walt (1989) 'Energy issues another challenge'. *New Scientist* 28 January 1989

Pearce, Fred (1989) 'Methane: the hidden greenhouse gas'. *New Scientist* 6 May 1989

——(1990) 'Whatever happened to acid rain?' *New Scientist* 15 September 1990

Peckham, Alexander (1989) 'Testing the water'. *Green Magazine*, December 1989 pp. 45–6

Perera, Judith (1988) 'Where glasnost meets the greens'. *New Scientist* 8 October 1988

Pollock, Cynthia (1986) *Decommissioning: Nuclear Power's Missing Link*. Worldwatch Paper No. 69

Porritt, Jonathon (1990) 'Where on earth are we going?' *BBC Wildlife 8*, 7 July 1990 pp. 455–69

Postel, Sandra (1988) 'Controlling toxic chemicals' in Worldwatch Institute *State of the World 1988* pp. 118–36. New York, London. W. W. Norton

Powell, J. H. (1982) 'Mining impacts on the aquatic environment with special reference to the Bougainville copper project' in *Report of the Mine Rehabilitation Workshop, Bougainville, 10–13 May 1982.* Bougainville Copper Limited, North Solomons Province, Papua New Guinea

Powledge, Fred (1982) *Water: the Nature, Uses and Future of our most Precious and Abused Resource.* New York. Farrer Straus Giroux

Radford, Tim (1988a) '7,000 reasons to watch this space'. *Guardian* 1 October 1988

——(1988b) 'Water nitrate cut will take decades'. *Guardian* 17 November 1988

RCEP 10 Royal Commission on Environmental Pollution (1984) *10th Report: Tackling Pollution — Experience and Prospects.* London. HMSO

Reader's Digest (1990) *How is it done?* London, New York. Reader's Digest

Reed, Cathy (1989) 'Even low levels of ozone in smog harm the lungs'. *New Scientist* 9 September 1989

Richards, Keith (1989) 'All gas and garbage'. *New Scientist* 3 June 1989

Routledge, Lewis (1990) 'The acid tests'. *Guardian* 16 March 1990

RSRS United Nations Environment Programme Regional Seas Reports and Studies — 8. *Marine Pollution in the East African Region* 1982

——13. Pathmarajah, Meera. *Pollution and the Marine Environment in the Indian Ocean.* 1982

Sachs, Wolfgang (1990) 'On the archaeology of the development idea'. *The Ecologist* 20:2 March/April 1990 pp. 42–3

Sattaur, Omar (1989) 'The threat of the well-bred salmon'. *New Scientist* 29 April 1989

Schoon, Nicholas and Bridge, Adrian (1990) 'Complex route of hazardous chemical shipments to Essex'. *Independent* 19 September 1990

Scobie, William (1989) 'Italy goes to war on shopping bags'. *Guardian* 24 September 1989

Sheridan, Michael (1989) 'Life of rubbish for Filipino locusts'. *Independent* 10 July 1989

Shiva, Vandana (1989) *Staying Alive.* London. Zed Books

Silvertown, Jonathan (1989) 'A silent spring in China'. *New Scientist* 1 July 1989

Sinclair, Jan (1990) 'Ozone loss will hit health and food, says UN study'. *New Scientist* 3 February 1990

Singh, Gurmit (1985) 'Papan — more than just a dump'. *Inside Asia* Nos 3–4, June–August 1985 pp. 37–8

Smil, Vaclav (1984) *The Bad Earth.* London. Zed Press

Smith, Malcolm (1989) 'Curtains for some'. *Guardian* 27 October 1989

Stansell, John (1990) 'A Mediterranean holiday from pollution'. *New Scientist* 5 May 1990

Stewart, John Massey (1990) 'The great lake is in peril'. *New Scientist* 30 June 1990

Subrahmanyam, P.V. R and Swaminathan, T. (1989) 'R and D needs in hazardous waste management in India'. Paper presented at the Seminar on Hazardous Waste Management and Planning, Bombay, 9 November 1989, organized by the Centre for Environmental and Management Studies, New Delhi

Suttill, Keith R. (1989) 'Excellence and style'. *Engineering and Mining Journal* August 1989

TAO Couper, A. (ed) (1983) *The Times Atlas of the Oceans.* London. Times Books

Thorpe, Nick (1990a) 'The land is sick — and so are the people'. *Guardian* 21 January 1990

——(1990b) 'East pays deadly price for ice that fuelled the Cold War'. *Guardian* 24 June 1990

——(1990c) 'After the revolution, Dresden turns its fire against the filthy Elbe'. *Guardian* 4 February 1990

Traynor, Ian (1990) 'On the frontline of filth'. *Guardian* 9 January 1990

Tucker, Anthony (1988a) 'Threats of toxic hazards that speak volumes'. *Guardian* 13 December 1988

——(1988b) 'Nutrient ways to restore acid lakes'. *Guardian* 17 May 1988

Turner, Francesca (1989) 'Mere or mire'. *Guardian* 31 August 1989

TWN. Third World Network (1989) *Toxic Terror: Dumping of Hazardous Wastes in the Third World.* Penang, Malaysia. Third World Network

Walker, Martin (1990) 'Wealthy US victims of greenmail pay high ransom to eco-lobby'. *Guardian* 18 April 1990

Weir, David and Porterfield, Andrew (1987) 'US exports of hazardous wastes to the Third World' in TWN 1989 pp. 26–35

Wells, Sue and Edwards, Alasdair (1989) 'Gone with the waves'. *New Scientist* 11 November 1989

Whitelegg, John (1989) 'Transport in turmoil'. *Guardian* 24 November 1989

WHO UN World Health Organization (1983) 'Examples of toxic waste' in TWN 1989 pp. 102–10.

Woodin, Sarah and Skiba, Ute (1990) 'Liming fails the acid test'. *New Scientist* 10 March 1990

WR 1988–89 (1988) World Resources Institute, International Institute for Environment and Development in collaboration with United Nations Environment Programme *World Resources 1988–89*. New York. Basic Books

WR 1990–91 (1990) World Resources Institute with United Nations Environment Programme and United Nations Development Programme *World Resources 1990–91*. New York, Oxford. OUP

Wright, Martin (1989) 'All credit to Cairo's tip dwellers'. *Panoscope* No. 11. March 1989

Zhu, J. L. and Chan, C. Y. (1989) 'Radioactive waste management: world overview'. *International Atomic Energy Authority Bulletin* 4/1989 pp. 5–13

Index

Note: Major entries (indicated by capitals, e.g. ACID RAIN) are divided into two sections, the first according to topic, e.g. Factors affecting, the second according to location (usually the name of a country) e.g. Brazil. Both sections should be consulted.